Informational Picture Books for Children

Patricia J. Cianciolo

2000

Project editor: Louise D. Howe

Cover design by Lesiak Design

Text design by Dianne M. Rooney

Printed on 50-pound white offset, a pH-neutral stock, and bound in 10-point coated cover stock by Data Reproductions.

The paper used in this publication meets the minimum requirements of American National Standard for Information Sciences—Permanence of Paper for Printed Library Materials, ANSI Z39.48-1992. ⊗

Library of Congress Cataloging-in-Publication Data

Cianciolo, Patricia J.
   Informational picture books for children / by Patricia J.
Cianciolo.
     p. cm.
   Includes bibliographical references and index.
   ISBN 0-8389-0774-1
   1. Children's literature, English Book reviews.   2. Picture books
for children—United States Book reviews.   I. Title.
   Z1037.A1C54   1999
   028.1'62—dc21   99-39597

04 03 02 01 00   5 4 3 2 1

To the memory of my parents who valued education and who were convinced that education could lead one to knowledge, wisdom, and morality and to the best of their ability provided the example, encouragement, and means so that their children would realize that end; and to my teachers (especially Dr. Martha L. King) who modeled and dedicated their lives to helping their students appreciate the merits and importance of being lifelong learners and independent thinkers.

To furnish the means of acquiring knowledge is . . . the greatest benefit that can be conferred upon mankind. It prolongs life itself and enlarges the sphere of existence.

—John Quincy Adams in the
Report on the Establishment of the
Smithsonian Institute (1846)

Contents

List of Illustrations

Preface

I nformational Picture Books for Children is intended to serve as a timely resource for any persons who are working (or are preparing to work) with children in the elementary and middle school age range and who are responsible for selecting quality trade books for use in school and public libraries, classrooms, or the home. This includes school and public library personnel, curriculum developers, teachers, and parents. It is also hoped that this publication will serve as a source through which these professional and nonprofessional book selectors and curriculum leaders can acquire background knowledge about evaluating and using informational picture books.

Over two hundred fifty informational picture books are described in this publication. They reflect the kinds of topics children ages six months through fourteen years are interested in having read aloud to them or reading independently in their free time. They also reflect the kinds of topics teachers and librarians tend to focus on in their work with students in the nursery school and kindergarten through grade nine. A small number of informational picture books are available for infants and toddlers and also for young adults. The small sampling for those at these extremes of the age range is not by choice; it just happens there are relatively few informational picture books addressed to children in these age ranges. The informational picture books represented in this publication include factual books, concept books, and biographies and autobiographies. The eight major subject matter areas under which these informational picture books are classified are The Natural World, Numbers and Arithmetic, The Physical World, Finding New Worlds, Children and Families, Peoples and Cultures, Language, and Arts and Crafts.

Most of the informational picture books discussed here were published from 1994 through 1999, although there are a few from the late 1980s and early 1990s. Although I did include a few informational picture books that were discussed in *Picture Books for Children*, fourth edition (American Library Association, 1997), I tried for the most part to avoid repetition. It was not an easy decision, for those books are still timely and very worthwhile. The reader is therefore advised to refer to the current edition of *Picture Books for Children* to supplement the recommendations in this new publication.

I would like to take this occasion to say I am grateful to several people who encouraged and helped me in various ways to accomplish my goal of writing a book that will assist teachers, librarians, and parents to introduce children to many of the excellent contemporary informational picture books. To my editor, Patrick J. Hogan, Editorial Director of ALA Editions, I would like to offer a hearty thank you for his encouraging me to write *Informational Picture Books for Children* and even for his occasional telephone calls to check on my progress and to nudge me (actually, quite gently!) to finish this book sooner rather than later. I appreciate the help my sister Polly, a former librarian and editor, gave me with the initial organization of the hundreds of books included in this publication, thereby making what I thought at that point was a daunting task seem possible. I am particularly indebted to Louise D. Howe, project editor, for her careful reading of the text and her helpful suggestions to make this a more polished publication.

Informational Picture Books
Definitions, Selection Criteria, and Trends

DEFINITIONS

What Is an Informational Book?

Perusal of the professional literature about informational books will reveal that some of the noted authors and critical reviewers differ considerably in how they define this kind of literature. There also is significant disparity in expectations of its effects on readers' mental capabilities. For example, David Macaulay, award-winning author of informational books, went to great length in his 1989 Zena Sutherland lecture to take issue with the nomenclature commonly used to define and describe informational books. He describes the process that led him to prefer the term "informational book" rather than "nonfiction" for the kind of books he writes and explains that an informational book is one that is designed to impart information, to communicate knowledge.[1] Margery Fisher, internationally known and respected critic of children's literature, is a bit more precise about what the function of informational books should be. She emphasizes that authors of this kind of literature for children in the elementary school through the middle school age range should strive to communicate facts and ideas as a teacher in the broadest sense would: they should lead young readers in a way that fosters in them both the will and the mental ability to assess facts and ideas and moves them toward a carefully planned and prudent independence of thought and action. She says that to accomplish this authors are obliged to expose

1

their readers to exceptions, doubts, and complexities. In addition, she urges authors of informational books for young readers not to give in to the temptation of vocabulary control and oversimplification—practices all too frequently used by contemporary writers of informational books, practices that will ultimately curb children's growth and development in higher-order thinking.[2]

What role, if any, should fiction play in informational books? In her 1990 Zena Sutherland lecture, Jean Fritz addressed the issue of making use of incidental fiction in her award-winning picture book biographies *Make Way for Sam Houston* (Putnam, 1987) and *Bully for You, Teddy Roosevelt* (Putnam, 1991) and in other popular and well-written historically oriented biographical books for children. She claims that this brings to her books a sense of story that in no way distracts from their authenticity or their essential facts.[3] Both Macaulay and Fisher also discuss the contribution that incidental fiction and imagination can make to informational literature. Their stance on this issue is quite compatible with the position expressed by Fritz in her talk and reflected in her writing of picture-book biographies and full-length biographies for children.

Considering what these experts tell us about the role that fiction may play in creating an informational book, it appears that the distinction lies in the *intent* of the literary work. In a piece of fiction, be it a novel or a short story, the story comes first and has priority. Facts, concepts, or theories of whatever kind—be they scientific, historical, biographical, sociological—exist primarily to support the elements of story. The writer of an informational book, however, sets out to help the reader acquire knowledge, and the techniques he or she uses, which may well include the narrative or storytelling form, are subordinate to that end. The writer of an informational book sets out to inform or to teach. The primary goal of a writer of quality fiction should not be to teach or to inform, despite the fact one can indeed learn something from it. In most cases, the writer of quality fiction sets out to depict and to comment about particular aspects of the human experience, hoping that the book will both entertain readers and elicit affective responses about the aspects of the human experience addressed in the story.

Personally, I have some reservations about stories that primarily present information or concepts. This does not mean to imply that I consider using the technique of story as a vehicle to transmit information to be totally unacceptable. It does mean that I think information books should more often than not be presented in an expository style. Indeed, there seems to be considerable justification for providing children with informational books that are written in a straightforward factual or expository style. First and foremost, one has to learn eventually that one reads a story in an entirely different manner than one reads an informational selection. Why not learn that lesson early in one's childhood? A well-written and attractively illustrated informational book tells its own "story." In fact, even young children will find that if it is written well and it helps them to understand themselves, significant others, and their world better, and offers them insights about things with which they are familiar or unfamiliar, an informational book (especially an informational picture book) will prove as interesting and totally absorbing, and sometimes as exciting, as any good work of fiction or narrative poem.

What Is a Picture Book?

Because of its unique blending of text and illustrations, the picture book is considered a genre apart from any other kind of literature and can be expected to exemplify high-quality writing and illustration. Thus, it is expected that both the author and the artist will make conscious use of their skills, special talents, and creative imagination, contributing about equally to the creation of quality literature. Picture books, like any other literature, can enrich, extend, and expand young readers' background of experiences, their literary and aesthetic interests, tastes, and preferences by providing a variety of sensory images and vicarious experiences, settings, and themes. A picture book is a kind of literature that communicates to children as young as six months of age and mature as adolescents and young adults of eighteen or nineteen. No longer are teachers and librarians justified in classifying picture books as "Easy Books." If one needs to be convinced that picture books are more properly classified as "Everybody's Books," they need only read the informational picture books that are discussed throughout *Informational Picture Books for Children,* for in it they will find concept picture books for the very youngest, one example of which is *1 2 3 Yippie,* a humorous and cumulative number concept book for children ages one to three, written and illustrated by Lisa Jahn-Clough (Walter Lorraine/Houghton Mifflin, 1998). Many informational picture books are intended for children five to ten years of age: one such book is *Yikes—Lice!*, a zany but thoroughly enlightening account of how one gets lice, how they multiply and how they can be exterminated, written by Donna Caffey and illustrated by Patrick Girouard (Whitman, 1998). A highly sophisticated and esoteric information picture book for adolescents and young adults is the 1999 Caldecott Honor Award book *Tibet: Through the Red Box,* written and illustrated by Peter Sis (Frances Foster/Farrar, Straus & Giroux, 1998). This book is set in the time when the Chinese were preparing to take over Tibet.

By far the majority of the books included in this publication are informational picture books, but a few books that are more appropriately considered profusely illustrated informational books are also included.

3

While books of this kind do indeed contain numerous illustrations, the amount of information presented in the form of text clearly exceeds the amount of information presented in the illustrations. Perhaps an example of an informational picture book and a profusely illustrated informational book might clarify their differences. *Shadows in the Dawn: The Lemurs of Madagascar,* written by Kathryn Lasky and illustrated with photographs by Christopher G. Knight (Gulliver/Harcourt Brace, 1998), serves as an example of an excellent informational picture book. In this book one sees a superb balance between Lasky's carefully written text and Knight's action-filled full-page color photographs; they blend their special contributions to introduce their readers to the complex society of ring-tailed lemurs that live in the canopy of the rain forests on the tropical island of Madagascar. Each uses his and her unique talents to enable readers to envision the instinctive behavior of the baby lemurs: leaping through the tamarind trees, playing with their age-mates, clinging to their mothers when they are still dependent on them for food or when they are threatened in some way. Author and illustrator blend their specialized skills and talents to help the readers realize the implications of some of the emotionally gripping and threatening competitive social situations with which the lemurs are often confronted. Such equalization of efforts and talents does not happen by chance; they obviously have planned very carefully (but not self-consciously or awkwardly) to provide an artful balance between text and illustrations, so that the resulting picture book radiates excellence.

An example of a profusely illustrated informational book is *Talking with Tebé: Clementine Hunter, Memory Artist* (Houghton Mifflin, 1998). In the process of writing this fascinating biography, Mary Lyons included many full-color illustrations of quilt tops and paintings this famous African American created, depicting herself and her fellow plantation workers picking cotton, gathering figs, cutting sugar cane, harvesting pecans, and cooking and doing laundry for the family that owned the plantation. Lyons also included some black-and-white photographs of Tebé and the rent-free wooden shack behind the "big house" of the Melrose Plantation, where she lived and worked over seventy-five years as a manual laborer. These illustrations highlight most effectively some very important and interesting perspectives about Tebé's lifestyle and her amazing accomplishments, but they barely begin to depict and embellish the rest of the great wealth of biographical information Lyons includes in her text.

Books Included in This Publication

The books I have selected to discuss and recommend for use with students of school age are for the most part informational picture books.

Each has been carefully evaluated and deemed to aptly and artistically impart information—facts, concepts, issues, and theories—about accomplishments of people who lived in the past or are living and functioning in today's world, about aspects of nature, the physical world, and so much more. They are books in which text and illustrations are skillfully and originally created and combined, so that they truly constitute literary works of art. In other words, books that have the potential to inform, and when I could find them (for they were few and far between) informational books that teach readers of school age about aspects of the human condition, their world, and the worlds of others in a manner that is artistic. Experience and careful research in response to literature demonstrates clearly that readers of informational picture books respond aesthetically (cognitively and affectively) to the written content of the books *and* to the way in which the visual images of that content are presented.

There is a general, though often unexpressed, feeling among professors, critics, and reviewers of literature for children and adolescents that informational books are neither "creative" nor "artistic" literary accomplishments. Thus most often they are reviewed strictly on the basis of their content rather than for their total literary merit (of which the content is only one aspect). My experience as both teacher and researcher convinces me that one has to evaluate literature of all types on its overall literary merit. The same holds true for informational picture books: Only when the images presented in both text and illustrations are of the highest quality are readers likely to have an authentic literary experience *and* be able to assimilate meaningful information.

Those who are responsible for selecting informational books for use in public or school libraries or in elementary and middle school/junior high school classrooms will attest to the fact that there are good informational books and inferior informational books. Actually, in the process of selecting the books for inclusion in this publication, I found there were by far many more inferior informational picture books than those of notable quality! The challenge with which I was confronted (and with which all book selectors are often confronted, especially if they do not use reliable book-selection resources) was to separate the good informational literature from the inferior informational literature.

CRITERIA FOR EVALUATING INFORMATIONAL PICTURE BOOKS

There is no question that one must establish criteria or standards for identifying informational books written in prose (or, for that matter, in verse) in which the information is comprehendible, accurate, and exciting, and that are typified by creativity, inspiration, and imaginativeness as opposed to those that are obscure, incompetent, boring, or written in a manner that is perfunctory and lacking in uniqueness. To select the informational picture books recommended in this publication I identified and used a number of specific and pertinent criteria or standards, including some affective factors, that children and early adolescents as well as professional book selectors (public and school librarians and teachers) could also use to evaluate informational picture books. These criteria and standards pertain to both the content and the effectiveness with which information is presented in the words and illustrations (pictures, graphs, diagrams, charts, tables, etc.). Each of these specific criteria and standards is identified and discussed briefly below.

1. *The facts or concepts included should be explained accurately and should be current and complete.*

Very rarely in contemporary books for children are the facts or concepts explained inaccurately; I am most pleased to find that writers and illustrators and editorial personnel are not only too professional to let that happen, but, in the main, most creators and publishers take too much pride in their work and seem to have too much respect for their audiences to present content that is lacking in authenticity. The major problem in connection with this criterion is that the information included is not always as up-to-date and complete as it should be. Obviously one must always check the publication date to determine whether the author can be faulted for not meeting this criterion. Purchasing a publication containing information that is no longer timely can be justified when nothing else with more current or more complete information is available, or when that older publication offers a different perspective on the topic that is still valid and is not included in the newer, more up-to-date one.

I was tempted to include one informational picture book about Arctic explorations that was published in 1998 because it was the only one I was able to locate that described the explorations in language most children in grades three and above could read independently and understand. Furthermore, it was illustrated with full-page reproductions of stunning full-color acrylic paintings. Why did I choose not to include that book? First and foremost, the author covered only explorations attempted between 330 B.C. and 1911. She said that later explorations were "great achievements," but she chose not to include them in her book because they were achievements of technology (that is, the explorers had not limited their travel to dogsled and were resupplied by plane or airlifted out). I included instead *Pioneering Frozen Worlds,* written by Sandra Markle (Atheneum, 1998) and *Over the Top of the World: Explorer Will Steger's Trek Across the Arctic,* written by Will Steger and Jon Bowermaster (Scholastic, 1997). Both of these well-written and child-oriented books are impressive for their currentness and comprehensiveness. Despite the use of technology (i.e., planes, computers, and radios), the achievements of these explorers were not only phenomenal, but heroic as well, and added immeasurably to our knowledge about the Arctic region's climate, animal and plant life, ecosystem, and much more. There seems little justification in cases like this for recommending the use or purchase of informational books whose coverage is outdated or incomplete.

2. *The writer should assume that the book will be a starter rather than a stopper.*

A "starter" gives a clear and vivid outline or overview of a subject so that the reader wants to pursue it further. In contrast, a "stopper" gives the reader the impression that the book is self-contained and there is no need to read further about the subject. Expanded depth and breadth of thinking and reading should always be encouraged. It seems apparent that Andrea Davis Pinkney viewed her picture book biography *Duke Ellington: The Piano Prince and His Orchestra* (Hyperion, 1998) as a starter! First and foremost, her respect and high regard for Duke Ellington's talents and accomplishments as a symphonic master, celebrated classical jazz composer, and pianist and her recognition of the past and present impact of his music are certain to be readily apparent to her readers. This attitude about her subject, in-and-of itself, should encourage a good share of her readers to make a concerted effort to listen to Ellington's recordings and to search for other books about him, his music, and his impact on the history of music. Furthermore, seeing the bibliography of sources in the back matter in which books and discographies are listed would serve as a motivator to read more books by and about "The Duke" and to learn more about the members of his original orchestra, about classical jazz, and about other well-known jazz musicians, both Ellington's contemporaries and those of our own times. Two picture-book biographies of one of Ellington's contemporaries one might suggest in conjunction with Pinkney's book are *If I Only Had a Horn: Young Louis Armstrong,* written by Roxanne Orgill and illustrated by Leonard Jenkins (Houghton Mifflin, 1997) or *Satchmo's Blues,* written by Alan Schroeder and illustrated by Floyd Cooper (Doubleday, 1996). One might also encourage children to read *Jazz: My Music, My People,* written and illustrated by Morgan Monceaux and accompanied by a brief, insightful foreword by the celebrated jazz trumpeter Wynton Marsalis (Knopf, 1994).

3. *The scope of the coverage and the perspective of the content should appeal to a wide age range.*

One never knows how much depth of detail or breadth of scope will be needed to spark that new interest in a topic. Suffice it to say, the breadth and depth of coverage should be appropriate for the age, ability, and background knowledge of the intended audience. It is well to keep in mind that in most cases a child's "reading achievement level" (determined by reading achievement scores or grade placement) or even the "readability level" of a specific book (determined by a readability formula or recommendation by the publisher, a curriculum specialist, or a book reviewer) has little or no bearing on whether or not a particular book will be interesting or appealing to children. Furthermore, it is well to keep in mind that children are quite capable of comprehending expository and narrative and poetic writing at a higher level when they listen to it read aloud to them than when they read it independently. Thus, one is often justified in using certain books with students even when the readability level appears to be somewhat higher than that of the books they are able to read on their own.

Although an *age range* (spanning about three or four years) is likely to be a better indicator than is a specific age or grade level, no one can say that all children within a given age range will be interested in a specific book. A far better indicator of a child's interest in a book will be his or her present interest in the topic and background of experiences (whether actual or vicarious). Occasionally children like to read something that merely confirms what they know already, but perhaps offers a different interpretation of that knowledge. Most often, however, they enjoy reading something that stretches and challenges them, that not only enables them to build upon what they already know, but enriches and extends that knowledge. Two books about Galileo—Leonard Everett Fisher's *Galileo* (Macmillan, 1992) and Peter Sis's *Starry Messenger: Galileo Galilei* (Farrar, Straus & Giroux, 1996)—demonstrate how this criterion has been satisfied in different ways. Fisher's book gives a general overview of Galileo's accomplishments and very briefly discusses Galileo's conflict with the Church over the nature of the universe and the consequences of that conflict. Fisher presents his information in a precise and linear fashion. His illustrations are dramatic and powerful; they are easily interpreted and although they embellish and extend the very polished text, one can readily see how soundly they support it. Fisher's book would serve most effectively as an introduction to this man and his amazing accomplishments. The students could then read other books that would provide more information about Galileo's personal history or his scientific accomplishments. Just the knowledge that Sis delves more deeply than Fisher into the consequences of Galileo's conflict with the Church might be motivation enough to read Sis's *Galileo Galilei.* A reader unfamiliar with such a sophisticated and complicated style of presenting information might need some tips on how to deal with it. Obviously, prospective readers should be made aware that this book should not (and probably cannot) be read quickly. They may have to be alerted to the fact that Fisher and Sis write in different styles; furthermore, they organize their content in very different ways—Fisher in a linear manner and Sis in a style that is psychological if not idiosyncratic—so their books should be approached with very different attitudes. The reader who can integrate and combine what these books have to offer will have a richer picture of Galileo and his times. The books by these two celebrated author-illustrators bring different treasures to their readers. If individual reading needs and interests are to be met, both books have their place in a school or public library collection or in a permanent classroom library collection.

4. *Books on topics of special interest to a small percentage of the student population as well as those of interest to a large percentage of the students should be included in the collection.*

It is well to keep in mind that by the time children are likely to choose informational books for recreational reading, or to satisfy individual reading interests or special reading needs, their reading interests and habits are beginning to be quite firm and frequently specialized, and in some respect idiosyncratic. They tend to be quite individualistic in the literary genre(s) they favor, the authors and illustrators they prefer, and certainly the subject matter they want to read about. This is not to say these individual preferences remain constant. Indeed, they are quite vulnerable to change. A recommendation by a special friend, teacher, or librarian can cause young readers to move on to a new "favorite" topic, genre, author, or illustrator. We all know how a new commercial movie, a popular television program, a significant news event, or even a film presented in the classroom or library can influence a person to move on to new interests and rush to the library to get the original story of that film or a book about that subject. This is not to say that children never choose a book solely because its title or cover illustration caught their eye. Perhaps a child was "reading the shelves" and noticed a book or two about an unfamiliar subject and decided to read them. Furthermore, it is not unusual for children to feel that, for whatever reason, they have had their fill of a subject and simply stop reading books about it.

Most teachers and librarians could provide examples of books that are read to satisfy special interests of individual students and those popular with a large percentage of their student population. I will cite an example of what happened when one title caught the attention of a fourth-grade boy as he perused the latest acquisitions displayed in the library at the beginning of the school year. The boy picked up *Boss of the Plains: The Hat That Won the West,* written by Laurie Carlson and illustrated by Holly Meade (DK Publishing, 1998), flipped through it, walked over to one of the tables and spent a good portion of the rest of the library period reading it. He seemed thoroughly enthralled by it. When he finished reading it, he asked the librarian to reserve it for him, so he would be the first one to check it out when she was ready to take the display down and circulate the books. (Wisely, she had them all processed before she displayed them, so his wait would not be very long!) When he told her how much he liked the book, she told him that she had two other books about western and cowboy attire, both of which devote quite a bit of space to western hats. The two of them walked over to look at the books she mentioned: *Ranch Dressing: The Story of Western Wear,* written and illustrated with photographs by M. Jean Greenlaw (Lodestar/Dutton, 1993) and *Hats Are for Watering Horses: Why Cowboys Dressed That Way,* written by Mary Blount Christian and illustrated by Lyle Miller (Hendrick-Long, 1993). He examined the two books quite carefully and checked both of them out for the week. You may be sure he read what each author had to say about the cowboy hats (and probably compared that with what he had learned from the Carlson book he had chanced upon). I would not be one bit surprised if he also read most or all of what Christian and Greenlaw had to say in these books about everything else cowboys wear. Perhaps it was an interest in cowboys rather than in the "ten-gallon" cowboy hat pictured on the cover that attracted him to Carlson's book in the first place—one can only conjecture. But it would probably not be too far-fetched to think he would also have enjoyed reading such books as *Cowboys: Roundup on an American Ranch,* written by Joan Anderson and illustrated with full-color photographs by George Ancona (Scholastic, 1996) or *Black Cowboy, Wild Horses: A True Story,* written by Julius Lester and illustrated by Jerry Pinkney (Dial, 1998).

5. *Stereotypes must not be presented. The writer should alert the reader to what in the book is fact and what is theory, to what is conjecture, opinion, or an educated guess, and to which of each is held by a majority or a minority.*

These aspects are often at the heart of expository writing, and informational books constitute one kind of expository writing. Also, selecting and using informational literature that contains aspects such as these are often at the heart of censorship pressures. Frequently reviewers do not alert their readers to these aspects of their subjects. Instead they make assumptions or deliberately avoid pointing these issues out to their readers. Dealing with this criterion requires thoughtful and critical reading by the professional book selector and by the child reader. Teaching children to be critical readers of all kinds of literature, especially expository literature, is far too complicated to discuss at length here.[4] Suffice it to say that it is the responsibility of teachers and librarians to teach children, *even in the early elementary grades,* how to engage in critical reading of informational books in which these aspects are of concern.

It goes without saying that stereotypes should be avoided, and I am pleased to say that stereotyping (*re* race, religion, gender, age, size, mental capacity, physical or emotional disabilities) is seldom found in contemporary books for children and adolescents. Nonetheless, children should be taught how to recognize and deal with stereotypes. Children can learn how to determine what in a book is based on facts and to verify whether the facts presented are accurate and authentic, to determine what in the book is based on conjecture and how much of this is generally accepted.

Although it is desirable that an author present varying points of view, it is neither unusual nor necessarily improper for an author to put forth only one point of view. However, educated readers must learn at some point that it is their responsibility to determine the author's qualifications to write about the topic discussed. There are several sources of evidence for making such determinations. It is not at all uncommon for contemporary authors of informational books to list some of the sources they referred to when writing them or to recommend titles for further reading by the students; one should always examine some of the titles listed in these bibliographies. Learning about the author's background might provide some degree of information about his or her credibility and background on a given issue. The biographical sketch included in the back matter of the book or on the cover jacket will provide this kind of information, as will such sources as the volumes of *Something About the Author* (Gale Research).

At times it is wise to help readers determine for themselves whether the information presented in a book is authentic and accurate (especially when a book focuses on some controversial issue). Children should be taught how to identify the persuasive and propaganda techniques used by writers. They should also be helped to acquire the habit of reading more than one book on a specific topic or issue. Only then can they compare and contrast (1) the facts each author does or does not present, (2) the breadth and depth of each author's discussion of the facts, and finally (3) the evidence each author presents regarding the accuracy and authenticity of these facts.

Here are examples of how two authors developed theoretical bases when they did not have precise evidence from primary sources (interviews, actual observations, or other documentation) to confirm the facts on aspects of their specific topic. Leonard Everett Fisher told his readers that in order to write and illustrate *Anasazi* (Atheneum, 1997), he had to develop a theory to explain what happened to a once-thriving civilization of the Anasazi, Native Americans who lived in our nation's Southwest two thousand years ago but vanished from the area before the Europeans arrived. To develop his theory and learn about the Anasazi, he relied on archeological clues. Much of his text and illustrations are based on the information he gathered from such sources as their stone dwellings, their stone and bone tools, remnants of their clothing, human and animal skeletons, woven blankets, woven and clay pots, and the petroglyphs—carved images of human figures, rabbits, bighorn sheep and other wildlife they carved on building walls, boulders, and cliffs— as well as their flat decorative murals.

J. Lynett Gillette, the author of *Dinosaur Ghosts: The Mystery of Coelophysis* (Dial, 1997), demonstrated effectively the scientific method of inquiry typically used by paleontologists to determine what sudden catastrophe killed the hundreds of Coelophysis dinosaurs whose remains were found at Ghost Ranch in New Mexico in 1947. The author identifies some of the hypotheses tested by professor Edwin Colbert from the American Museum of Natural History in New York City and other paleontologists. They examined the condition of the bones and positions of the skeletons of these dinosaurs and other animals found in the burial grounds to explain why and how they died. The hypotheses they tested put forth several possible causes that might explain the Coelophysis burial grounds at Ghost Ranch: mud? volcanoes? asteroids? poisonous water? a flood? a drought? some combination of these? To test each hypothesis the paleontologists had to match the evidence that would indicate the specific event occurred or condition existed with the evidence they actually found. The only explanation (hypothesis) that the scientists have so far discovered enough clues (evidence) to support is that of a drought followed by a sudden rainstorm.

The full-color, full-page illustrations depicting these hypothetical scenes enable the readers to see quite clearly why all except the one tested negative. But the readers are reminded that this solution is not conclusive. "Could more information turn up that might point us toward a whole new scene?" asks the author. Her response to her own question is, "Of course, since the site is still being studied. Scientists are always ready to change their ideas to fit what they learn. New discoveries about the fossils and rocks at Ghost Ranch can still be made by anyone with the patience to study them" (p. 31).

It is obvious that the focus in *Our Journey from Tibet,* written by Laurie Dolphin and illustrated with photographs by Nancy Jo Johnson (Dutton, 1997) is on the hardships, injustices, and human rights violations the Tibetans experienced for more than forty years under the

Chinese Communist colonization. This true story, based on interviews with the real Sonam, is told from her point of view when at age nine, she with her two sisters, Payamg and Dekyi, and a group of other children made a dangerous and illegal journey from their village in Tibet to India and finally settled in at the Tibetan Children's Village, where they were enrolled in a Tibetan "school in exile" to study the Tibetan language, the history of their people, and the religion of Buddhism. The photographic illustrations clearly highlight the essence of aspects of Sonam's traditional Tibetan family life in the small village of Sog Dzong and the lifestyle she and the other children experienced in their new home and school in the Children's Village in Dharamsala. The author has included a letter from His Highness the Dalai Lama. The important point here is that children need to be taught how to recognize the persuasive techniques used throughout this book to convince them of the mistreatment the Tibetans have experienced and to alert them to the measures currently being taken in India, under the leadership of the Dalai Lama, to preserve the Tibetan heritage, language, and culture so that someday these exiles can return to their village in Tibet to share with those who had to stay behind, the culture they have learned in Dharamsala. It would be helpful to compare the perspective put forth by Dolphin and Johnson with that advanced by Peter Sis in his 1999 Caledcott Honor Award book *Tibet: Through the Red Box* (Frances Foster/Farrar, Straus & Giroux, 1998).

6. *The information should be presented and explained clearly in the text and illustrations; both of these aspects should be unique and imaginative, interesting, and stimulating.*

Alone and together each of these aspects of an informational picture book should reveal the author's and illustrator's respect for their audience as well as an enthusiasm for the subject; they should encourage the reader's curiosity and wonder. The information about the subject should be presented verbally and visually in a manner that is interesting and timely. The writer's conviction affects the reader; it invigorates the reader and stimulates his or her interest in the subject and it communicates a point of view. A writer's attitude toward both his or her subject *and* intended audience is often revealed in his or her vocabulary and use of language. The language should consist of appropriate terminology and should model expository writing and research skills. It goes without saying that *all* the characteristics of good writing should be major criteria for selecting books for use by children. The illustrations should reflect *all* the characteristics of quality visual art. One would be amazed at how many books were rejected for inclusion in this publication because either the writing or the visual art was inadequate. In some, the writing was flat and perfunctory. In others, the illustrations amounted to little more than slapdash sketches or paintings, or else the subjects of the photographs appeared awkward and self-conscious or the photographs were devoid of vitality and sparkle, emotion and passion. Fortunately there are any number of titles one could highlight here that more than meet this criterion. The three books discussed below reflect positively the aspects of this important criterion. Two books are written and illustrated by Virginia Wright-Frierson, namely, *A Desert Scrapbook: Dawn to Dusk in the Sonoran Desert* (Simon & Schuster, 1996) and *An Island Scrapbook: Dawn to Dusk on a Barrier Island* (Simon & Schuster, 1998) and one entitled *The Most Beautiful Roof in the World: Exploring the Rainforest Canopy,* written by Kathryn Lasky and illustrated with photographs by her husband, Christopher G. Knight (Gulliver/Harcourt Brace, 1997). In her "Dawn to Dusk" scrapbooks, Wright-Frierson reveals that she has obviously spent many thoughtful and enraptured hours observing and studying flora and fauna of the desert and saltwater plants and animals and has managed to capture the aura and reality of the unique beauty in each kind of terrain. She also alerts her readers to aspects of the ecosystem in both "scrapbooks." These books are not for a "fast read"; nor are they books to be read in bits and pieces. I hope readers (both children and adults) will take the time to read and reread and to think about the implications of what the author's poetic prose is saying and will look carefully at the pictures and savor the wealth of information and images of the barrier island and the desert depicted in them.

The creators of *The Most Beautiful Roof in the World: Exploring the Rainforest Canopy* use and combine their talents effectively. Lasky's use of language is succinct and information-laden, but easily understood, and Knight's full-color photographs are characterized by artistic sensibility in evoking content, theme, or mood. Readers are certain to recognize and appreciate the special ability this husband-and-wife book team has to express, so sincerely and uninhibitedly through their expert use of words and pictures, their awe and enthusiasm for the virtually unknown ecosystem at the very top of the rain forest at Blue Creek, Belize. I am certain that neither Lasky and Knight nor their readers will soon forget that the rainforest canopy is inhabited by thousands of creatures—bats, monkeys, vipers, tree salamanders, poison-dart frogs, spiders, butterflies, stinging ants, cockroaches, leaf- and plant-eating insects, and birds as well as different species of plants ranging from orchids to cacti, bromeliads, and trees. Fortunately, many more books have been recently published about these and other aspects of the rain forest. Readers of *The Most Beautiful Roof in the World: Exploring the Rainforest Canopy* should be inspired to seek out what other authors have to say on this vast and relatively unexplored topic.

7. *Whether it is logically or psychologically developed, the organization of the information should be clear, interrelationships should be indicated, and patterns should be provided. It should be clear from the outset what aspects of a topic the book covers and the depth in which they will be examined.*

It is not unusual to find that the concept books and factually oriented informational picture books for infants and nursery school and kindergarten aged children (six months through age four or five) tend to be more psychological (child-centered) in their development. Three concept books demonstrate this approach quite aptly: *The Best Thing about a Puppy,* written by Judy Hindley and illustrated by Patricia Casey (Candlewick, 1998), introduces preschoolers to the "good" and "bad" things about an energetic puppy; in *Watch Us Play,* written and illustrated by Miela Ford (Greenwillow, 1998) preschoolers will find great fun in seeing and hearing about the antics of lion cubs; and *Pots and Pans,* written by Patricia Hubbell and illustrated by Diane de Groat (HarperCollins, 1998), helps infants and toddlers to notice objects in their immediate environment (pots and pans and their covers) and to enjoy making noises with them in time to the rhythm of simple verses. Nor is it unusual for the informational aspects of the books addressed to kindergarten through the lower primary grades (ages four to five through age seven) to couch the information in a skeletal story or slight narrative verse. Example of this approach in providing information is evidenced in *The Beekeepers,* written by Linda Oatman High and illustrated by Doug Chayka (Boyds Mills, 1998). In this story we see how a little girl's grandfather teachers her how to dislodge swarming bees from a tree and lead them to an empty hive.

In child-oriented books written in a straightforward, factual style and apparently intended for readers slightly older (i.e., ages five through nine or ten), the authors frequently encourage their readers to participate in activities that demonstrate certain facts or theories about a subject, and thereby help them to understand their significance and implications better. Melvin Berger, author of *Chirping Crickets,* illustrated by Megan Lloyd (HarperCollins, 1998), encourages his readers to make the sound of a cricket by using a nail file and a stiff paper; he also gives them directions for catching, caring for, and observing a pet cricket.

Another example of a book that contains numerous mind-stretching activities, all of which are easy and safe to implement, is *Pioneering Frozen Worlds,* written by Sandra Markle and illustrated with photographs (Atheneum, 1998). A fascinating variety of experiments enables the readers to engage in the process of scientific inquiry by gathering information about the earth's frozen polar regions. All of the experiments are easy for children to carry out and require containers and equipment found in most homes (i.e., pots, pans, plastic bags, and a flashlight) and clothing regularly worn by children (i.e., trousers or slacks, sweaters). Usually the readers are asked one or more questions about the cause or consequence of a particular problem or situation; several possible explanations are suggested. Easy-to-follow directions for an activity that simulates a condition related to the climate or geography of these polar regions are presented. Completion of the activity enables the readers to arrive at a "correct" explanation to the question or problem that has been posed.

Most of the informational picture books for older readers (ages nine through fourteen and older) provide a table of contents or use dramatic section and topic headings throughout the book; if nothing else, a carefully developed index is usually provided in the back matter so the reader can determine if and where specific aspects on a topic are located. Usually a glossary is appended in books that are written at an introductory level or deal with a particularly technical topic. The second edition of *Dougal Dixon's Dinosaurs,* written by Dougal Dixon (Boyds Mills, 1993, 1998), satisfies this criterion most effectively. It contains a detailed table of contents: not only is each of the five chapters named in the table of contents, but the specific dinosaurs or topics discussed in each chapter and the pages on which they can be found are identified. All of the captions that accompany the illustrations provide significant information. The extensive back matter is invaluable; it provides additional facts and figures about dinosaurs not covered in this book and encourages the readers to follow up and do further reading on related topics. The glossary, which is illustrated, provides definitions and explanations of scientific and technical terms used in the book and often compares the creature, process, or function with something in today's world. The index is comprehensive and detailed.

8. *The format of the book should be attractive and readable.*

Illustrations play an important role in helping children to better understand and appreciate the information offered in the current informational picture books. For this reason, it is important that the illustrative material should be placed as close as possible to the relevant portion of the text. The illustrations should complement and supplement the text, and their style and tone should be compatible with and complementary to the overall format (to the kind and size of the type and to the size and shape of the book). I read more than 2,500 informational books in order to select those that I felt justified in including in this publication, and by far the majority of the books I read were illustrated with full-color photographs and cartoon-style drawings rendered in simple line and four-color wash or full-color wash. There is no one style of illustration or one art medium more suitable than another for use in informational picture books, and I have made a conscious effort to include books whose illustrations reflect a variety of art styles and were rendered with a wide variety of media. For the most part illustrative materials seem to be quite compatible with and complementary to the subjects focused on in the books and the traditional principles of good book design. All of this perhaps reflects not only the talents and professionalism of the book illustrators but also their effective working relationships with those responsible for art editorial decisions. Two informational picture books among the many that might be offered as examples of expert formatting are *Fire into Ice: Adventures in Glass Making,* written and illustrated by James Houston (Tundra, 1998) and *Bestiary: An Illuminated Alphabet of Medieval Beasts,* written and illustrated by Jonathan Hunt (Simon & Schuster, 1998). Everything about *Fire into Ice: Adventures in Glass Making* is sophisticated and elegant. Each glass sculpture is photographed against a plain background—usually black, but deep green, blue, and magenta backgrounds are also used. A bright light seems to be placed above the objects to highlight every graceful line that shapes the hand-blown or carved containers and the sculptured arctic wildlife creatures or book characters embedded in them. In addition, the combination of the dark background and the intensified lighting seems to enhance Houston's goal of having his glass sculptures exude the aura of ice, so that the arctic animals, other wild creatures, and even legendary figures such as Rip Van Winkle, Excalibur, and the Unicorn, embedded in the glass appear to be moving, sitting, or lying in the great depths of the ocean. Houston's preliminary sketches, done in pen and ink, serve to enhance the reader's understanding of how this talented artist, writer, and explorer works and how he expresses his affinity for the environment and the people of the Far North that ultimately inspired so many of his sculptures. Every aspect of the making of this book is compatible and highlights the ambiance of Houston's glass sculptures and study sketches: the crisp, fine type printed on smooth, white paper stock, full-page pictures of his dramatic glass sculptures counterbalanced with small black-and-white pen-and-ink line and crosshatch drawings and a few hand-colored pencil sketches with a lot of white space. Even the endpapers are filled with pen-and-ink sketches of arctic water and land animals, mythological and legendary characters, and Inuits involved in native games and work activities printed on an ice-blue background. One seldom sees formatting that is as carefully and artistically thought through and implemented as in this book.

Jonathan Hunt's *Bestiary: An Illuminated Alphabet of Medieval Beasts* (Simon & Schuster, 1998) is another example in which all aspects of the format play an especially artful and important role in helping children to better understand and appreciate the information offered in this oversized book. The dramatic pictures, which depict creatures from facts, myths, and medieval stories, are placed as close as possible to the related text. The bright, clean watercolor and acrylics used in the double-page and smaller line and wash paintings and the ornamented letters and decorative borders on the pages throughout the book are strongly suggestive of medieval illuminations. They are thoroughly in keeping with the content and the medieval theme and setting of the book. The style and tone of the illustrations are compatible with and complementary to the style and size of the type (15-point Weideman) and to the size and shape of the book. Even the map on the endpapers looks like an illuminated manuscript, and the mythical animals discussed and depicted in the book are shown in the part of the world where they were purported to have lived. If the readers have not discovered or understood the stories about these mythical medieval animals before reading this book, one can be quite certain they will be thoroughly sold on them by the time they have read it and have examined the wonderfully detailed and exhilarating illustrations and decorations many times over.

TRENDS

Literature is a beautifully dynamic field and, as in any genre, the writing of informational literature reflects the impact of the attitudes, preoccupations, issues, and concerns that are fast emerging or already prevail in an era in which it is written. Even a casual examination of the newer informational books, especially those published within the last five years, indicates not only the splendid diversity of topics focused on in the informational picture books now available to children, but the innovative and artful ways the content relating to these topics is presented. We can also celebrate not only the overall artistic talent evidenced in the illustrations in these books currently being published, but the array of art styles and approaches to illustrating the artists are using. In addition, the illustrations are truly beautiful and sophisticated paintings and drawings and evidence thoughtful, careful, and skillful work on the part of artists.

■ *There is widespread use of sidebars in all kinds of informational picture books.*

The use of sidebars is a "magazine-style" technique frequently used to provide additional pictures and extensive commentary alongside what appears in the body of the text or in the captions that accompany the illustrations. This practice is obviously intended to elaborate upon and further inform the readers about factual matter that was not covered in the text *per se*. It is a practice that has mixed blessings: it provides more information for the reader who wants more information than most others (although those others may also enjoy having it made available to them). On the other hand, it is a practice that tends to inhibit comprehension because it interrupts the flow of one's reading. Interesting and informative sidebars appear throughout *One More Border: The True Story of One Family's Escape from War Torn Europe,* written by William Kaplan with Shelley Tanaka and illustrated by Stephen Taylor and with photographs (Groundwood Books/Douglas & McIntyre/Distributed by Publishers Group West, 1998). These supplement the main text by providing more information about the family and their life in Memel, Lithuania, before the Germans invaded the city and about the tense relationship between Russia, Japan, and Germany (reluctant allies at best!) through which the Kaplan family had to travel in order to reach Canada and freedom from persecution. These sidebars give readers a greater appreciation for the events that were occurring at the time and the dangers the Kaplans were exposed to; they also help the readers understand why the Kaplans were so willing to put up with the hardships and dangers they experienced and so appreciative of the freedom they ultimately found.

There are numerous excellent sidebars in *Over the Top of the World: Explorer Will Steger's Trek Across the Arctic,* written by Will Steger and John Bowermaster and illustrated with photographs (Scholastic, 1997). This well-written journal account of a six-person team's exploration across the Arctic reads like an adventure story, and I found I was so anxious to see how they overcame their many challenges that I continued to read the journal entries nonstop. Only after I had finished reading them and heaved a sigh of relief when I realized the explorers had achieved their goals safely, did I go back to read the many sidebars included throughout the book. Each sidebar is filled with fascinating information: profiles of the individual sled dogs, a brief history of Arctic explorations, biographical sketches of the original six team members of the expedition, keeping warm in the Arctic, preparation of food and disposal of garbage, construction of the canoe sleds, communicating via the Internet with schools all over the world, and transmitting the expedition's daily progress reports (through words and photographs) via one of the very few satellites that orbit the earth around the poles. The sidebars in *Ghost Liners: Exploring the World's Greatest Lost Ships,* written by Robert D. Ballard and Rick Archbold and illustrated by Ken Marschall (Madison Press/Little, Brown, 1998), add more details about specific ships and their passengers, humanizing the tragic and highly dramatic stories. (See illustration 1.)

Sidebars are also used by Cheryl Harness, author and illustrator of *Mark Twain and the Queens of the Mississippi* (Simon & Schuster, 1998)—but perhaps not as successfully. At one point in this partial biog-

NEARLY LOST BECAUSE OF A HAT

Willie Coutts's hat nearly cost him his life. When the *Titanic* hit the iceberg, his mother Minnie roused eleven-year-old Willie and his baby brother Neville (right), got them dressed, and put on their lifebelts. Through the swirl of panicking passengers Minnie led her children out of third class toward what she hoped was safety. One officer handed his own lifebelt to Minnie, saying, "If the boat goes down you'll remember me." Another crewman led them to the boat deck. Minnie and Neville got in one of the last boats — but the officer in charge held Willie back. The rule was women and children first, and the hat Willie was wearing made him look too old. Willie's mother insisted but the officer refused again. Finally, good sense prevailed and Willie, too, stepped to safety.

ILLUSTRATION 1   Sidebar (photo of Willie Coutts and his brother and the accompanying text) from in *Ghost Liners: Exploring The World's Greatest Lost Ships*, written by Robert Ballard and Rick Archbold. Illustrated by Ken Marschall. Madison Press/Little, Brown, 1998. Copyright © 1998, The Madison Press Limited.

raphy, the author tells her readers that as a young boy, Clemens (Twain) would rush down to the river to see the steamboats, "looking like a floating wedding cake." Not only did he wish he could go along, but he thought he would like to be "a steamboatman" more than anything else. The text includes a double-page painting of the *Eula Belle* (which does indeed look like a floating wedding cake!); seventeen parts of the boat are numbered in bold type and a sidebar describes the function of each one. Most readers will no doubt assume from this that the *Eula Belle* was the vessel that fired Clemens's dream of becoming a steamboat pilot or at least that it epitomizes the kind of boat that did. There is no hint of this in the text *per se,* however. In fact, the *Eula Belle* is never mentioned. Interesting as the information in the sidebar might well be to some readers, this is an awkward way of using sidebars to imply information that is never specifically presented in the text. Unfortunately, Harness is not the only author to use sidebars in this way.

■ *There is a vast increase in the number of picture-book biographies addressed to juvenile readers.*

This increase in the number of picture-book and profusely illustrated biographies (and some picture-book autobiographies) seemed to be well on its way when I was preparing the manuscript for *Picture Books for Children,* fourth edition (American Library Association, 1997) and is even more firmly established now. (I have included in this publication very few of the informational picture books that were described in the latest edition of *Picture Books for Children.* Those who are interested in identifying more picture-book biographies may wish to refer to that book as well.) In the main, the picture-book biographies I have described in both books are well written, adequately detailed, and authentic; they also tend to be effectively illustrated. Problems relating to authenticity or accuracy seem to be found largely in picture-book biographies geared to children in the age range of approximately five to seven. All too often, the lack of credibility in these biographies for younger readers appears to be due to one or more of the following reasons: First, the authors engage in far too much fictionalization, especially in the use of invented dialogue and concocted incidents. They may feel that this practice allows the readers to "see themselves" in and identify with the subject's motivation and achievements. Indeed, some reading experts suggest that it makes a book easier to read and motivates children to be interested in reading (especially biographies and historical fiction). Second, authors tend to romanticize and idealize well-known political personalities, social reformers, writers of literary classics, famous composers, celebrated athletes, and great inventors. These tend to be names children have heard often, and even though they are not really mature enough to realize the significance of these persons' contributions they want to read biographies about them—or, more likely, adults think children *should* read about them. In some instances, the authors (and some parents, teachers, and book selectors) think children are too young to read about some personal aspects of their life stories. In their attempt to satisfy the real or imposed need for biographies of these people, authors tend to oversimplify or omit some of their achievements or personal activities. The result is a biography that is romanticized and idealized.

Seldom does one find such weaknesses and flaws in picture-book biographies or full biographies addressed to children eight years of age or older. There are fine picture-book biographies telling the life stories of people whose lifestyles, involvements, and accomplishments are varied, and they cover almost every time period and every facet of the human condition. There are picture-book biographies of visual artists (i.e., the "masters" of the past and current notable gallery artists, sculptors, and book illustrators), literary greats, musicians, sports personalities, politicians, statesmen, military leaders, social reformers, stars of stage and screen, pacesetters in journalism, industry, medicine, and science. Oftentimes the personalities are made vital and immediate. Because the picture-book format in-and-of itself imposes restrictions on length (especially when compared to what can and should be accomplished in a full-length biography), one would probably have to say the breadth and depth of treatment in most of these books is quite skeletal and usually amounts to a partial biography at best.

With the enthusiasm that children and adults seem to have currently for folk and country music, the picture-book biography entitled *This Land Is Your Land* (Little, Brown, 1998) will probably be very popular. It is based on the words and music of Woody Guthrie's classic song with the same title and is illustrated with reproductions of naive-styled paintings by Kathy Jacobsen; the scrapbook text is written by Janell Yates. Although the book deals very briefly and superficially with Guthrie's life story, the readers can actually glean a generous amount of information from the sidebars in this book. These sidebars (printed in tiny type and frequently on dark-colored areas of a page) provide major events of Guthrie's life story as well as considerable insight into his appreciation of the varied and beautiful landscapes throughout our nation, his opinions about the social and political events and economic conditions that prevailed during much of his lifetime, and some of the major technological inventions and accomplishments that were having an impact on the lifestyles of his day. Most of this information pertains to topics mentioned in Guthrie's famous songs.

One of the most outstanding of the current picture-book biographies is *Leonardo da Vinci,* written and illustrated by Diane Stanley (Morrow,

1996). Seldom is excellence popular, and with that in mind, I suspect this book will not be among the most popular books in a children's library. Nonetheless, I have little doubt it is one that will be enjoyed and appreciated and probably long remembered by those readers who are already interested in visual art or the "great masters" or by those who are "ready" for this kind of literature and need only that extra little nudge to be connected with it. Stanley's carefully written text details, but not too overwhelmingly for young readers, major aspects of da Vinci's successes and failures. His diverse talents as a well as his human weaknesses are described. She makes quite clear his place in the history of art in general and his status and artistic accomplishments in relation to other noted artists of his time. Stanley's full-color, full-page paintings competently support and extend and make so much more concrete the specific paintings, frescoes, and sculptures discussed in the text. Reproductions of many of the study sketches found in da Vinci's notebooks are discussed in the book and shown in her colorful paintings.

■ *Informational material is frequently presented in skeletal fictional writing or in narrative or lyrical verse rather than in an expository style.*

Not too many years ago it was almost unheard of for informational books to be presented in anything other than an expository writing style. Occasionally, informational material for children was couched in slight (skeletal) stories whose animal characters emoted and talked like humans and were shown wearing the same kinds of clothes as humans. ("Ourselves-in-fur," as May Hill Arbuthnot, the author of seven editions of the classic text *Children and Books* [first published by Scott, Foresman in 1947] so astutely characterized them.) Interestingly, and in many respects amazingly in this supposedly "enlightened" and sophisticated age, this approach to writing informational books is still widely used, especially in informational picture books for children ages three to five. Only if the story elements (characters, plot, etc.) are indeed skeletal, so that they do not distract from the author's primary and basic purpose (which should be to inform the reader) does it seem acceptable to couch information in a story (especially a fanciful one) or narrative verse. There are, however, a few examples in which a wealth of excellent information is introduced artfully and effectively to children within a skeletal story or through verse. Nan Parson Rossiter's slight fiction and attractive full-color realistic illustrations are combined in *Rugby and Rosie* (Dutton, 1997) to inform her young readers about how a family took an exuberant golden retriever puppy into their home during the first year of her life and taught her the early lessons of being a guide dog for the visually impaired to prepare her for attending a special training school. Upon "graduation" from the program, Rosie became a working guide dog for a young blind woman.

Fascinating and informative facts about the social behavior of wolves and the whelping and weaning of wolf pups are presented in *Wolf Watch* through rich narrative verse written by Kay Winter and realistic oil paintings created by Laura Regan (Simon & Schuster, 1997). An exceptionally elegant aesthetic encounter with the many different forms of water (liquid, vapor, ice) seen in rain, a mountain stream, a waterfall, a lake, a river, the sea, the mist, clouds, a storm front, a thunderhead, a rainbow, and a colorful sunset is offered to readers by Thomas Locker in the simple lyrical free verse and impressionistic landscape oil paintings of *Water Dance* (Harcourt Brace, 1997). In the back matter is a section entitled "The Water Cycle" written by Candace Christiansen. This section provides easy-to-understand scientific facts about each of these forms of water; small reproductions of Locker's paintings are placed alongside Christiansen's discussion of each one.

■ *An increasing number of authors of informational picture books about aspects of science and arithmetic encourage their readers to interact and make personal connections.*

Children enjoy participating in activities that enable them to interact and make personal connections with the informational books. When these activities are specifically designed and carefully planned, and are implemented in a manner that will enable students to add breadth and depth to their understanding of a subject matter discipline, participating in hands-on learning experiences related to the principles and facts under study will prove invaluable. Students are more likely to understand, to retain longer what they have learned, and to be more capable of using the facts and concepts and principles in everyday situations, if and when they use them in hands-on, real-life conditions. The Discovery Box series published in the United States in 1997 by Scholastic, Inc., provides excellent examples of books that contain activities designed to help readers understand and apply fundamental principles of the physical and natural sciences. In each case, directions for the easy-to-implement activities are given and the inexpensive and usually replaceable equipment needed to engage in these activities are provided in the accompanying kits. All of the books in the series were originally published in France by Editions Gallimard Jeunesse in 1996 and translated from the French by Scholastic. The recommended science titles include: *Weather,* adapted by Claudia Logan; *Time,* adapted by Lorraine Hopping Egan; *Light,* adapted by Robin Bromley; and *Plants,* adapted by Randi Hacker. Several arithmetic and mathematics books written by David A. Adler demonstrate this author's practice of encouraging his readers to interact and make personal connections with the subject matter. More specifically, in his book *Shape Up! Fun with Triangles and Other Polygons,* illustrated by Nancy Tobin (Holiday House, 1998), Adler helps his readers learn some simple and complex concepts about polygons by guiding them through hands-on activities that involve such items as slices of cheese, pretzels, bread, pencils, graph paper, unlined paper, and plastic knives.

■ *A large proportion of the current informational picture books give evidence of scholarship and research on the part of the authors and illustrators.*

That the information provided in so many of the contemporary informational picture books is accurate and based on valid interpretation of the facts is due to the authors' knowledge about their subject matter, knowledge that is acquired through scholarship and research. Oftentimes the authors not only have vast "book knowledge" and have researched their subject thoroughly, but they actually share their first-hand experiences with their readers, describing how they lived, what they learned, and how they applied that knowledge "in the field" in real-life situations. Most of these experts have a refreshing enthusiasm for the subject they have studied and researched and worked with. That enthusiasm seems to permeate every facet of the books they have written on these subjects. Many writers delight in learning about topics previously unfamiliar to them and in sharing their delight and enthusiasm about their learning experiences. I find it especially interesting that this enthusiasm for learning is very much evidenced both in the tone and content of some book creators who have just learned about their subjects and by the experts they interviewed and observed. Such enthusiasm is particularly evident in books by the husband-and-wife writing team of Kathryn Lasky and Christopher G. Knight, e.g., *Shadows in the Dawn: The Lemurs of Madagascar* (Gulliver/Harcourt Brace, 1998) and *The Most Beautiful Roof in the World: Exploring the Rainforest Canopy* (Gulliver/Harcourt Brace, 1997) and in George Ancona's books, e.g., *The Golden Lion Tamarin Comes Home* (Macmillan, 1994), *Man and Mustang* (Macmillan, 1992), and *The Piñata Maker/El Piñatero* (Harcourt Brace, 1994).

I have discussed several of the positive trends; in fact, I tried not to dwell on the negative trends, although I felt obliged to identify the potential problem sidebars might pose to young readers. There is one negative trend I would like to identify and discuss briefly at this point, and that is the decided drop in the number of informational books (especially concept books) currently being published for infants and children in the early childhood (nursery and kindergarten) age range. I find this negative trend quite surprising, especially when one considers the substantial body of recent research that solidly demonstrates the huge role that this kind of literature plays in the development of children's language ability and experiential background. Both of these factors play crucial roles in children's ability to learn to read and, in large measure, determine their overall level of achievement and success throughout their entire academic career (thus affecting their potential social and economic status as well). This trend is even more confounding when one considers all the attention the media has given in the last few years to the dire need for improvement in quality parenting skills, more day care centers, all-day kindergartens, and educational programs comparable to the Headstart programs of the not too distant past.

I have long operated on the conviction that if it is a good book for children, there must be something in that book an adult will find engaging and will gain some pleasure from. Working on this project of identifying quality informational books has established the credibility of this *modus operandi* even more. Not only are these books well written, but the all-around scholarliness and the breadth and depth of the content and the laudable, often distinguished quality of the illustrations in these books provided captivating reading fare in-and-of themselves. Even more pleasing and exhilarating was the fact that in many instances I acquired a great deal of new knowledge about unfamiliar topics or gained a greater depth of knowledge and new perspectives on topics I thought I knew quite a bit about. These books provided me with many hours of pleasant, informative, satisfying, and engaging reading fare. Children who shared their responses to many of these same books have demonstrated they too acquired new or additional knowledge and found them satisfying and intriguing. Obviously, the aspects that impressed them were not always the same ones that affected me. In some cases both the children and I were motivated by the text or illustrations to explore a subject further, searching for other books that would expand upon the topic or view it from a different perspective. The very multidimensional qualities of these books, I think, speak to their overall merit and their potential to provide informative, intellectually stimulating, and gratifying reading for a wide audience, whether it be children or educated adults.

NOTES

1. David Macaulay, "The Truth About Nonfiction," in *The Zena Sutherland Lectures, 1982–1992,* ed. Betsy Hearne (New York: Clarion/Houghton Mifflin, 1993), 141–59.

2. Margery Fisher, *Matters of Fact: Aspects of Non-Fiction for Children* (New York: Crowell, 1972).

3. Jean Fritz, "The Known and the Unknown: An Exploration into Nonfiction," in *The Zena Sutherland Lectures, 1982–1992,* ed. Betsy Hearne (New York: Clarion/Houghton Mifflin, 1993), 164–82.

4. For information about a five-year study devoted to the teaching and learning of the critical reading of literature in the elementary grades, see Patricia Cianciolo, "University Personnel and K-5 Teachers Collaborate to Study How to Improve the Teaching and Learning of Literature," *Journal of Youth Services in Libraries* 7 (summer 1994): 406–12.

The Natural
World

ANIMALS

Bateman, Robert, and Rick Archbold

SAFARI   *7–10 YEARS*

Illustrated by Robert Bateman. Boston: Madison Press/Little, Brown, 1998.

The oversized illustrations in this book are reproductions of magnificently detailed paintings of African animals in their natural environment; they are so realistic they look like expertly accomplished candid photographs. The information provided about each animal includes its major behavioral characteristics, habitat, height, weight, food, and range. Some of the animals introduced include the Cape buffalo, wildebeest, lion, zebra and lesser kudu, dik-dik and impala, and giraffe. Bateman's study sketches of the animals shown on the endpapers provide excellent examples one might use to demonstrate the variety of ever changing positions and actions an artist might capture before deciding on "the one" to depict in the complete and polished painting of his or her subject, in this case a wild animal of Africa. The authors conclude this beautiful book by making an appeal for people to work together to protect the wilderness that is left in Africa, so that plants and animals can live as they always have. They also emphasize that the uncontrolled killing of animals must be stopped and people should live in harmony with nature.

Bishop, Nic

THE SECRETS OF ANIMAL FLIGHT   *8–11 YEARS*

Illustrated with photographs by Nic Bishop and drawings
by Amy Bartlett Wright. Boston: Houghton Mifflin, 1997.

Nic Bishop developed a high-speed technique for photographing insects on the wing, and his accomplishments have put him in the forefront of insect photography internationally. He used the same technique for photographing birds and bats as well as insects for the illustrations in *The Secrets of Animal Flight*. The text is easy to understand, and the concepts and the facts about the animals' structure and their unique processes of flying are presented in a manner that captures and extends children's interest and curiosity. The combination of the knowledge revealed in Bishop's high-speed photographs and his accomplished writing results in a picture book that is exquisitely beautiful and informative. There is no table of contents or index, but the topics discussed are highlighted in large, bold-faced type. There are no captions under pictures or diagrams, but each is referred to and explained within the body of the text. The author stretches the perspectives of his readers by asking them to identify some of the advantages of flying, some of the disadvantages, some of the mysteries, and so forth. (See illustration 2.)

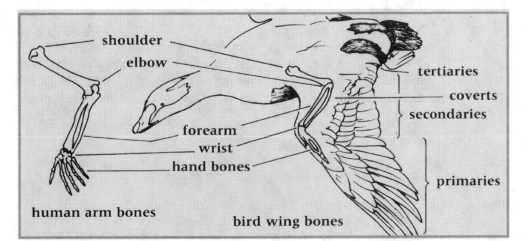

ILLUSTRATION 2   Line diagram from *The Secrets of Animal Flight* by Nic Bishop. Jacket photograph
© 1997 by Nic Bishop. Reprinted by permission of Houghton Mifflin Company. All rights reserved.

Bowen, Betsy
TRACKS IN THE WILD   *7–10 YEARS*
Illustrated by Betsy Bowen. Boston: Houghton Mifflin, 1998.

> The habits and behavior of thirteen northwoods animals are discussed in
> terms of the life-size and unique footprints (track) and in other signs each
> animal leaves behind. In brief discussions, Bowen tells why each animal
> was important traditionally, and is currently, to humankind in general
> and to the people of Native American nations, hunters and trappers,
> merchants, and farmers in particular. She states that the tracks of each
> animal provide the observer with a specific and unmistakable record of
> its wanderings—where it goes, what it eats, when it runs and why.
>
> Distinctive, sophisticated and expertly crafted bold multiple-block
> woodcut prints illustrating profound and mind-stretching concepts and
> philosophical statements made by well-known Native American leaders
> and literary and religious personalities appear throughout this mind-
> stretching informational book. The individuals quoted include Stalking
> Wolf (an Apache tracker), Black Elk (an Oglala Sioux), Crowfoot (Orator
> of the Blackfoot Confederacy), Brave Buffalo (an Oglala Sioux), Chief
> Seattle (Suguamish), Old uncle of Ohiyesa (Charles Eastman); A. A.
> Milne (author of *Winnie-the-Pooh*), and Ernest Thompson Seton (nat-
> uralist and artist). The sources used in creating this book are listed on
> the copyright page.

Collard, Sneed B. Jr.
ANIMAL DADS   *5–8 YEARS*
Illustrated by Steve Jenkins. Boston: Houghton Mifflin, 1997.

> The text about how the males of each of twenty species (such as the
> male western meadowlark, lion, emperor penguin, and the stickleback)
> help in raising their offspring is informative, but minimal. The large
> paper collages in rich, full color not only clearly depict these verbal
> descriptions but masterfully enrich and embellish them. (See illustra-
> tion 3.)

Darling, Kathy
DESERT BABIES   *6–10 YEARS*
Illustrated with photographs by Tara Darling. New York: Walker, 1997.

> Readers are introduced to fourteen remarkable species of baby animals
> that inhabit desert lands throughout the world. The map on the first page
> indicates the desert landscape areas located in North America, South

America, Africa, Arabia, Asia, and Australia. Symbols denoting whether the landscapes of the desert the animals inhabit are pan, sandy, or rocky are also introduced on the first page. There is an additional symbol which indicates that a particular species is endangered; this symbol is not introduced with the others, but appears occasionally throughout the text in the sidebars that focus on each desert animal baby. These sidebars indicate the common and scientific names of the animal and include a small photo of an adult member of the species. They also include ready reference data as baby name, birthplace, birth size, adult size, number of littermates, favorite food, parents' care, enemies, and home deserts. Two pages are devoted to each animal baby: one page is a full-page, close-up picture of the animal baby and the other page contains a few paragraphs about it plus a sidebar containing the data described above. Additional information about the desert environment is found on the last page. The same approach to baby sea animals is used effectively in *Seashore Babies,* written by Kathy Darling and illustrated by Tara Darling (Walker, 1997).

George, Jean Craighead
MORNING, NOON, AND NIGHT   *5–8 YEARS*
Illustrated by Wendell Minor. New York: HarperCollins, 1999.

Lyrical prose describes the daily activities of wild animals from dawn to dusk as the sun rises on the eastern coast and moves westward to set on the Pacific coast. Brightly colored full-page paintings depict creatures large and small (such as a cardinal, mallard ducks, bats, an opossum and raccoon, an owlet, and an elephant) in their natural habitat engaging in their daily routines. The common names of the creatures shown in these paintings and the page numbers on which they appear are given in the end matter.

Hunt, Jonathan
BESTIARY: AN ILLUMINATED ALPHABET OF MEDIEVAL BEASTS   *9–13 YEARS*
Illustrated by Jonathan Hunt. New York: Simon & Schuster, 1998.

A fascinating array of creatures from fact, myths, and story portrayed in bestiaries written by medieval scholars are described and dramatically pictured in this oversized alphabet book. A very helpful pronuncia-tion guide precedes the alphabetical presentation of each creature. The bright, clean colors of the ink and dyes used in the line and wash paint-ings picturing the beasts, the ornamented letters, and decorative borders on the pages throughout the book are strongly suggestive of medieval illuminations and are certainly in keeping with the content and theme of the book. I am quite certain that after seeing these illustrations and reading through this book children would want to find out more about these creatures and would be motivated to seek out the titles that appear in the excellent bibliography on the last page of the book. The map on the endpapers denoting specific places where the beasts were said to have lived lends greater credibility to their existence.

Rotner, Shelly
PICK A PET   *3–7 YEARS*
Illustrated with photographs by Cheo Garcia. New York: Orchard, 1999.

Patty wants a pet of her own, but has not decided which kind of animal would make the best pet for her. She visits her young friends, relatives, and neighbors, each of whom has a different kind of pet and is very happy with the kind of animal he or she has chosen: a rabbit, a mouse, a frog, a tortoise, a kid, two pigs, a bird, a horse, a lizard, a cat. Patty even dreams about pets—the real animals like those she visited and make-believe ones that neither she nor anyone else ever saw before. None of these seem to be the right kind of animal for Patty. One morning after dreaming all night about pets, she wakes up knowing exactly what kind of pet she wants! The perky photographs depicting happy children with their much loved pets and Patty's way-out menagerie of fanciful animals are reproduced in rich, full color; the text is easy to read and printed in primary-sized type.

Sayre, April Pulley
HOME AT LAST: A SONG OF MIGRATION   *5–10 YEARS*
Illustrated by Alex Berenzy. New York: Henry Holt, 1998.

The instinct that drives nine animals to go to great lengths to swim, fly, or crawl in order to migrate, that is to spend part of their lives in one "home" and part in another, is described aptly and briefly in this easy-to-read text, which is embellished considerably by attractive jewel-toned paintings, done in soft pastels on black paper. Each animal is pictured during the course of its migration and when it has reached "home at last." The last two pages add a bit more information about the migrating practices of each animal to that presented in the body of the book.

33

Settel, Joanne

EXPLODING ANTS: AMAZING FACTS   *7–10 YEARS*
ABOUT HOW ANIMALS ADAPT

Illustrated with photographs from various sources.
New York: Atheneum, 1999.

> Only the subtitle presents an accurate indication of what this profusely illustrated informational book is about. The book provides a fascinating discussion of the ways animals live and thrive on Earth. (Keep in mind that while the ways these creatures find food, shelter, and safety in the natural world may be considered "unusual" or "gross" when compared to humans, they are very true and common to the creatures themselves!) The readers will surely be impressed with how the different animal species make use of every kind of matter and space that has the potential to provide them with the shelter and food that enable them to survive. In the end, nothing is wasted. A detailed and cleverly labeled table of contents identifies the wide range of topics about how animals discussed in this book survive, and a comprehensive and precise index is appended. The list of suggested readings in the back has the potential to lead the readers to additional interesting reading fare. The large full-color photographs that enhance and clarify the text were taken by numerous photographers. The captions accompanying each photograph supplement and dramatize aspects of the text.

Simon, Seymour

THEY SWIM THE SEAS: THE MYSTERY OF ANIMAL MIGRATION   *9–12 YEARS*

Illustrated by Elsa Warnick. San Diego: Browndeer/Harcourt Brace, 1998.

> The diverse migration and mating practices of oceanic animals are documented quite thoroughly in an understandable manner in this book. Among the marine animals whose migration practices are described are plankton, green sea turtles, tuna, eel, salmon, seals, whales, and lobsters. Simon alerts his readers to the fact that many questions remain about some of these creatures and their journeys. For example, scientists have yet to find out how salmon and tuna find their way to the same spawning ground where they were born and return to it after years at sea; they have yet to determine how eels reproduce. The full-page illustrations, done in watercolor, are in a simplified expressionistic style and reveal the vast diversity of creatures that often travel the same areas of the sea simultaneously. Unfortunately, there is no table of contents, glossary, or bibliography of books recommended for further reading.

Singer, Marilyn

BOTTOMS UP! A BOOK ABOUT REAR ENDS   *5–10 YEARS*

Illustrated by Patrick O'Brien. New York: Henry Holt, 1997.

> Assuredly, the title itself will attract children to this book, but despite what they might assume, the content is not the least bit gross or risqué. This is a collection of facts about how animals use their hindquarters to survive, breed, and achieve and maintain power. For example, one can tell what kinds of tasks a horse is best qualified to do by looking at its rear end. Well-developed muscles at the race horse's rear end are bunched up high at the top of its long slender legs, helping it achieve great speed. Draft horses used to pull wagons, carriages, and plows have wider rear ends, legs, and necks and broader chests. Horses used for riding and jumping have heavier hindquarters. Information that the horse's bottom provides to fellow horses includes its age, sex, and desire to mate. Cats, dogs, and many other mammals will also sniff another's bottom in greeting to get this information. A horse will sometimes present its backside to warn a person or another animal that it thinks it is being annoyed and may well retaliate with a kick.
>
> Skunks and all animals in the weasel family have glands in their rear ends that produce a strong-smelling musk, but only skunks use their musk for defense. A full-page, realistic picture of each animal discussed is included; occasionally a smaller picture will show another animal of the same kind responding to the shape, smell, or color of the animal's rear end or the spray released from that animal's rear end.

Singer, Marilyn

PRAIRIE DOGS KISS AND LOBSTERS WAVE: *4–9 YEARS*

HOW ANIMALS SAY HELLO

Illustrated by Normand Charter. New York: Henry Holt, 1998.

> Animals' greetings to their own kind are as many and varied as the variety of species themselves. Rather casual, somewhat sentimental impressionistic paintings depict animals when they meet others of their kind. Some of these greetings are welcoming and some are not. Often their body language indicates which animal is dominant, or if they are equals. For example, dogs (and other members of the canine family, such as wolves and coyotes) smell each other's faces and hindquarters. Dogs who are equal do not threaten or act defenseless. If they are friendly, they will wag their tails, put their ears upright or forward, bow, and bark happily. If they are unfriendly, their tails will droop or stiffen, they will flatten their ears and growl. A dominant dog or leader will stand tall and straight and stare at the other dog or put its head or neck on the

other dog's shoulders, whereas an underdog will bow its head, lower its body and look away, or lie down on its side or back.

Using chemicals or chemical-producing bacteria in their bodies, each kind of luminous fish will create and flash its own light signal that has its own pattern, odor, and color; each kind of fish can recognize its own species from these signals. A flashlight fish has greenish "head-lights" on its face. These "headlights" help the fish navigate through dark water, see and catch prey, and defend its territory. To escape an enemy, it will zigzag away and confuse the predator by rapidly blinking its lights on and off; when greeting a friend or its mate it will remain still and blink its lights quickly. When another fish swims near its home, the female flashlight fish will turn off her lights, swim close to the other fish, and suddenly flash her lights. Children were thoroughly fascinated by this book. Unfortunately, there is no table of contents or index to help more sophisticated or experienced readers use the book as a reference tool. The beautiful watercolor paintings depicting each of the animals discussed are reproduced in full color.

Yolen, Jane
THE ORIGINALS: ANIMALS THAT TIME FORGOT   *9–14+ YEARS*
Illustrated by Ted Lewin. New York: Philomel, 1998.

This is a very special and high-quality book! It is elegant in terms of Yolen's poetic comments about these animals from the past, some of whom looked and behaved much like their descendants today, and some of whose characteristics have dramatically changed during their evolution. It is elegant in terms of Ted Lewin's accomplished illustrations, all of which are perfectly suited to the almost ethereal and reverent tone and mood of Yolen's text. The glossary at the back of the book, headed "Notes About the Originals," gives additional insights. Unfortunately the size of the print in this section is so small and the reading level so advanced that younger readers will probably need to have an older child or an interested adult read and explain it to them.

Extinct Animals

Dixon, Dougal
DOUGAL DIXON'S DINOSAURS   *8–12 YEARS*
Illustrated. Honesdale, Penn.: Boyds Mills, 1998.

This book provides a comprehensive discussion on the life and times of more than twenty-five kinds of dinosaurs covering 160 million years of survival—from about 225 to about 65 million years ago. There are five sections: Giants of the Earth, The Real Monsters, All Shapes and Sizes, A Closer Look, and Fossil Hunters. Each section focuses on thirteen specific dinosaurs or topics and is illustrated with photographs, realistic paintings in full color, and diagrams. Many of the illustrations are double-page spreads depicting the dinosaurs in action and in their habitats. There is a full-page, portraitlike painting of each of the twenty-five dinosaurs discussed. The diagrams are small (3"x 5¼"or 3"x 4½"); they are simple, precise sketches, clearly labeled, and easy to interpret. Photographs very in size and function. Some are of well-known paleontologists who hunted dinosaur fossils or prepared the fossils for display in museums; others are of animals living today that are similar to dinosaurs in their bone structure, size, feeding habits, or the ways they communicate with one another or capture their prey. The captions that accompany each illustration provide significant information. The extensive back matter provides facts and figures about dinosaurs not covered within the text and contains a bibliography of related titles, thus encouraging readers to supplement and expand upon what they learned from this book. An excellent glossary and index are appended.

Gillette, J. Lynett
DINOSAUR GHOSTS: THE MYSTERY OF COELOPHYSIS   *8–12 YEARS*
Illustrated with photographs by Douglas Henderson and others.
New York: Dial, 1997.

Written like a mystery and demonstrating effectively the scientific method of inquiry typically used by paleontologists to determine what catastrophe killed several hundred of Coelophysis dinosaurs together and so suddenly, this well-written and beautifully illustrated book is bound to enthrall young readers. The author identifies some of the hypotheses scientists put forth to explain the dinosaurs' demise and the procedures they used to test them. The only hypothesis (explanation) the scientists can substantiate so far suggests that a drought was followed by a sudden rainstorm.

The readers are reminded that this decision is not necessarily conclusive. The site is still being studied and more information might turn up that might point to a whole new hypothesis. All of the full-page pictures and smaller pictures throughout the book are reproductions of full-color paintings rendered in pastels; only two illustrations—the one used on the cover and the one of the clusters of skeletons with separated bones—were done in pen and ink. A comprehensive index and pronunciation guide are included in the back matter.

Tanaka, Shelley

GRAVEYARDS OF THE DINOSAURS: WHAT IT'S LIKE   *9–14 YEARS*
TO DISCOVER PREHISTORIC CREATURES

Paleontological consultation by Philip J. Currie, Mark Norell, and Paul Sereno.
Illustrations by Alan Barnard. New York: Hyperion/Madison Press, 1998.

> One of many books in the I Was There series, this is a very special book.
> It is special in depth and breadth of content covered, viewpoint, style of
> presentation, and format and book design! The stories about some of the
> scientific discoveries about how dinosaurs lived and died, what they can
> tell us about life on our planet today, and the mysteries about dinosaurs
> that still remain unsolved are arranged in six sections. The prologue
> and epilogue are important components of this fine book. The captions
> for each of the numerous colorful paintings, photographs, sketches,
> diagrams, and maps significantly extend and embellish the information
> presented in the body of the text. Be certain to bring the students'
> attention to the monochromatic green illustration on the endpapers,
> which depicts the badlands of Dinosaur Provincial Park in Alberta,
> Canada. Not to be ignored are the illustrations that appear on the title
> page and accompany the table of contents, prologue, and epilogue.
> The glossary, bibliography of titles recommended for further reading,
> and listing of new dinosaur finds around the world offer the readers
> invaluable but subtle suggestions ("teasers") for further study of theories
> and facts about dinosaurs.

Birds

Gibbons, Gail

PENGUINS   *5–9 YEARS*

Illustrated by Gail Gibbons. New York: Holiday House, 1998.

> As is typical of this prolific author-illustrator's informational picture
> books, the readers are offered a fine introduction about penguins in
> a straightforward style. They learn from the very beginning that the
> penguin is actually a bird that no longer flies; what millions of years
> ago used to serve as wings have evolved into powerful, rigid flippers for
> swimming. Penguins eat under water on krill, fish, and other creatures
> of the sea. Although they may stay at sea for weeks at a time, they leave
> the water, climb onto a rocky shore, and can speed over snow and ice
> by sliding on their bellies. The author describes the penguins' annual
> courting and mating patterns and the manner in which the female and
> male parents share in incubating the eggs and taking care of their chicks.
> Young readers will be intrigued with the way fledgling penguins learn
> how to hunt for food and survive on their own without the help of their

parents. A concise summary of the information presented throughout the book appears on the back page. The simple full-page sketches, done in ink line and watercolor wash, clarify, support, and extend very well what is so aptly presented in the easy-to-read text printed in crisp primary type.

Kurtz, Jane, and Christopher Kurtz

ONLY A PIGEON   *6–9 YEARS*

Illustrated by E. B. Lewis. New York: Simon & Schuster, 1997.

Ondu-ahlem, an impoverished boy living in Addis Ababa, a modern-day city of Ethiopia, raises and trains homing pigeons. He builds up his flock through breeding or sending up one of his birds to lure an unattached pigeon back to his cage. Accounts of how Ondu-ahlem guards his birds from the attacks of hungry stray cats and a wild mongoose are vivid and grim. The description of what happens when he sets his favorite pigeon, Chinkay, free to fly with a pigeon owned by his friend in a game designed to test the birds' homing instinct and loyalty, reveals the tension Ondu-ahlem feels. The illustrator, who traveled to Addis Ababa so he could represent the city authentically, has created accomplished, detailed impressionistic paintings done in watercolor to illustrate this story. They reveal the beauty of life as well as the impoverished conditions under which Ondu-ahlem and his family live on the outskirts of town, his overcrowded school, the boys' games and after-school jobs shining the shoes of businessmen or selling roasted chickpeas. Most impressive are the illustrations depicting Ondu-ahlem caring for and training his pigeons. A glossary at the back of the book provides the pronunciation and meaning of the Ethiopian words used throughout the book. The author's note, also in the back matter, offers considerable additional information about how Ethiopian children like Ondu-ahlem start pigeon raising, how they increase the size of their flock, and how homing pigeons can find their way back to their flock.

Morrison, Gordon

BALD EAGLE   *7–10 YEARS*

Illustrated by Gordon Morrison. Boston: Walter Lorraine/Houghton Mifflin, 1998.

This picture book is a testimony to Morrison's insightful observations and his selective and precise in-depth portrayal of the biology, life cycle, and behavior of two baby bald eagles. The text, albeit brief, is well written in a straightforward style; it is factual, interesting and informative, and easy to read. Information verifying and vastly extending the text is included in the full-color pictures and in the sidebars. The large, detailed, action-filled sketches, done in fine line, crosshatching, and full-color watercolor wash support and enrich the text. The numerous sidebars, which consist of close-up sketches, verbal explanations, labels, and captions add a vast amount of information about the bald eagles that is not specifically covered in the text or illustrations. The sketches in the sidebars are done in fine line, crosshatching, and gray watercolor wash. They provide close-ups of such things as bird topography, the anatomy of the bald eagle's wings and legs, stages the down develops to form the base for growing feathers, sketches of the bird's egg tooth, eye shield, and the five different kinds of basic feathers. Readers will probably read the book straight through and then go back many times over to reexamine the sidebars.

Insects

Berger, Melvin

CHIRPING CRICKETS   *5–9 YEARS*

Illustrated by Megan Lloyd. New York: Harper Collins, 1998.

> Part of the Let's Read-and-Find-Out Science series, this is an excellent straightforward, factual introduction to the physical characteristics, behavior, and life cycle of several kinds of crickets, including field crickets, ground crickets, tree crickets, and house crickets. Children were intrigued with the array of facts the author provided about how the male crickets make their chirping sounds, the placement of crickets' "ears," the construction of their eyes, and how one can tell the temperature by counting a cricket's chirps for fifteen seconds. They were able to follow and thoroughly enjoyed implementing Berger's directions for making a sound almost the same as a male cricket's chirp using a piece of stiff paper and a nail file, and how to catch, care for, and study a pet cricket. This book is suitably illustrated with double-page reproductions of realistic paintings done with watercolor and pen and ink. Compare with *The Very Quiet Cricket,* written and illustrated by Eric Carle (Philomel, 1990).

Caffey, Donna

YIKES—LICE!   *5–10 YEARS*

Illustrated by Patrick Girouard. Morton Grove, Ill.: Albert Whitman, 1998.

> The author of this book emphasizes that head lice are not a sign of uncleanliness and are not known to carry human disease. Yet most people

consider head lice as something to be ashamed of and are frightened if and when they are found to have lice. Two lines of rhyming text on each page describe how a family responds when one of the children in their home gets lice and identify the steps one should take to get rid of them. Each couplet is followed by a paragraph of factual information about how lice live, multiply, spread from one person to another, and can be eradicated. The text and the zany cartoon-styled illustrations make light of a situation that most people continue to find less than humorous.

High, Linda Oatman

THE BEEKEEPERS   *4–9 YEARS*

Illustrated by Doug Chayka. Honesdale, Penn.: Boyds Mills, 1998.

> A grandfather teaches his granddaughter how to tend his beehives and thereby allows young readers to get a superb glimpse of how swarming bees are dislodged from a tree with a swarm-gathering tool (a long pole with a hook at the end) and led into an empty hive placed on the ground directly below the tree. The illustrations are full-page reproductions of paintings done in oil. They capture this rare and endearing experience between a grandparent and a child. The age-old folk wisdom of beekeepers is introduced: "A swarm in May is worth a load of hay. A swarm in June is worth a silver spoon. A swarm in July isn't worth a fly."

Mammals

Onish, Liane B., *Adapter*

MAMMALS   *8–11 YEARS*

Translated from the French by Nicole Valaire. Illustrated. New York: Scholastic, 1995.

> One of many books in the innovative Scholastic Voyages of Discovery series, this book was originally published in France under the title *Sur le trace des mammals ferers* by Éditions Gallimard Jeunesse. *Mammals* is a fine example of a studied combination of amazing book art and informed text that actively involve young readers in the scientific exploration of what is known about mammals of long past and present. It suggests there are certain to be new animals discovered in the future. The content of the book is well organized, and a short descriptive phrase is included under each of the category headings listed in the table of contents. Thanks to clever paper engineering techniques, the readers can participate and interact with a variety of elements in the book: they can feel the hoof prints of a giraffe and an impala, the footprints of a kangaroo, and the paw prints of a cheetah and a hare. They can

mix and match, comparing and contrasting the sizes and shapes of teeth various animals have, and thus gain a clear understanding of how these aspects of an animal's teeth determine what they eat and the role their teeth play in killing prey and in cutting and grinding up their food into digestible pieces. Additional information is found when the readers lift the flaps or turn over transparent pages. There are extensive invaluable learning aids offered in the back matter: titles of books recommended for further reading, names and addresses of museums and zoos throughout the United States, and profiles of scientists known for their research on specific kinds of animals. Folk beliefs about mammals held by various ethnic and cultural groups are identified. An extensive glossary defines words about mammals one should know. Species of mammals discussed in this book are listed according to scientific order. An extensive and comprehensive index is provided. Students might enjoy completing the illustrations with the reusable vinyl stickers found in the pocket attached to the inside of the back cover.

CATS AND DOGS

Darling, Kathy

ABC CATS   *4–10+ YEARS*

Illustrated with photographs by Tara Darling. New York: Walker, 1998.

This introduction to cats and the alphabet is bound to be a favorite with almost everyone who takes the time to read and think about the content of the brief, easy-to-read, informative text and to look at the engaging, large, full-color photographs of an adult cat and a small photographs of a kitten for each of the twenty-six feline breeds identified. Information about each breed (e.g., country of origin, texture of hair, type of ears, range of color and fur patterns) is offered in a paw-print-shaped sidebar for each of the twenty-six kinds of cats. The photographs capture most effectively the distinctive physical and personality traits of each kind of cat. A special section at the end of the book contains photographs of eight cats and a brief description of the distinctive color and color combinations of each. The reader is informed that this alphabetical introduction to twenty-six breeds of cats is just the beginning: "There are twenty-six letters, but there are more than a hundred different breeds of cats. Cats come in hundreds of colors and patterns. . . . [T]he color of a cat's fur can tell you some important things. If a cat is solid orange it is almost always a male cat. And if it is calico or tortoiseshell, it is probably a female cat."

Hindley, Judy

THE BEST THING ABOUT A PUPPY   *3–6 YEARS*

Illustrated by Patricia Casey. Cambridge, Mass. Candlewick, 1998.

> A concept book that is bound to evoke gales of laughter from preschool-ers and offer a satisfying, fun-filled, independent reading experience on the part of a beginning reader. The pictures, done in line and watercolor wash, definitely add to the humor of the litany of "good" and "bad" things about a puppy.

Rossiter, Nan Parson

RUGBY AND ROSIE   *4–7 YEARS*

Illustrated by Nan Parson Rossiter. New York: Dutton, 1997.

> Couching the facts in slight fiction, this attractive informational picture book alerts young readers how carefully bred dogs (like Rosie, the golden labrador retriever puppy in this book) that have the potential to be guide dogs spend the first year of their lives with families who take them into their homes and provide them with early lessons in being a guide dog. The full-color illustrations realistically and sensitively dramatize how the family and their old dog (Rugby) responded to the exuberant Rosie. They portray most aptly Rosie's gradual maturing over time, showing convincingly the family's (and Rugby's) responses as she departs from their home to attend a special training school, completes the program successfully, and becomes a working guide dog for a young blind woman.

WILD ANIMALS

Ford, Miela

WATCH US PLAY   *3–6 YEARS*

Illustrated with photographs by Miela Ford. New York: Greenwillow, 1998.

> Delightfully action-oriented, sharply focused full-color photographs re-produced as full-page illustrations detail the antics of two lion cubs as they wake up from a nap, romp and frolic with each other, and then (predictable only to adults) flop down in exhaustion for another nap. The very brief text is printed in large, heavy primary-sized type.

George, Jean Craighead
LOOK TO THE NORTH: A WOLF PUP DIARY   *7–10 YEARS*
Illustrated by Lucia Washburn. New York: HarperCollins, 1997.

Large, impressive realistic paintings done in acrylic on watercolor paper dramatize and extend the accomplished and heartfelt poetic prose that describes each of the fifteen developmental stages the three wolf pups go through from the time they are one day old through the time they are young adults. George relates each significant developmental stage to the seasonal changes occurring in the lower forty-eight states, having her readers "look to the north" to watch the wolf pups mature during that same span of time. (See illustration 4.)

ILLUSTRATION 4   From *Look to the North: A Wolf Pup Diary*. Illustrations copyright © 1997 by Lucia Washburn. Used by permission of HarperCollins Publishers.

Lasky, Kathryn

SHADOWS IN THE DAWN: THE LEMURS OF MADAGASCAR   *9–13 YEARS*

Illustrated with photographs by Christopher G. Knight. San Diego:
Gulliver/Harcourt Brace, 1998.

> This famous author-illustrator team has created a collection of captivating glimpses designed to introduce young readers to the complex society of ring-tailed lemurs that live in the canopy of the rain forests on the tropical island of Madagascar. The back matter includes an afterword with information about the primatologist who guided Lasky and Knight during their visit to Madagascar and their research on ring-tailed lemurs in preparation for this book. It also contains information about the cooperative efforts of the Malagasy government and the Wildlife Preservation Trust International to provide the space people and the animals, such as the lemurs, will need in the not-too-distant future to live together in a supportive environment. A map of this small island off the coast of Africa and a short but excellent list of titles recommended for further reading are also included.

Moss, Cynthia

LITTLE BIG EARS: THE STORY OF ELY   *5–10 YEARS*

Illustrated with photographs by Martyn Colbeck. New York:
Simon & Schuster, 1997.

> Less than an hour after his birth, it became apparent to his mother Echo and sister Enid that Ely, a bull elephant calf, was born with a handicap that made his chances for survival very slim. An elephant can usually walk when it is less than an hour old. Ely could stand on his hind legs, but because the first joints of his front legs were bent back and completely stiff, he could not straighten his front legs. Two hours later he was able to take a few shuffling steps on his knees and move out of the sun to a nearby pool. With great strain he could stretch up to his mother's breasts but did not manage to reach the nipple and get the life-saving milk he so desperately needed. That Ely taught himself how to stand with the soles of his feet on the ground, to take one step then another, and eventually to learn how to walk, is a story of true grit—determination, great effort, practice, and eventually progress. But he had to learn how to do more than "just" walk. Each new thing he had to learn made him less dependent on his mother and meant new challenges. Slowly but surely, with the help of his mother and sister, always with considerable effort and practice, he learned things that meant he could eventually survive on his own. For example, he had to learn how to control his trunk well enough so he could eat grass and drink water,

both of which were very difficult for him. Other lessons he had to learn were to look out for natural enemies and predators and how to survive in a drought when grasses and other plants are scarce or simply gone. The epilogue reveals that almost five years have passed since Ely's first birthday. He is completely weaned from his mother and gets all his nourishment from the grasses and plants that he finds on his own. He is over five feet tall at the shoulder and weighs nearly 2,000 pounds, and his tusks are eight inches long. Shortly after his fourth birthday his mother gave birth to a female calf named Ebony. Moss and Colbeck collaborated on a film documentary entitled *Echo of the Elephants,* which features Ely's story. They also collaborated on a second award-winning documentary film entitled *Echo of the Elephants: The Next Generation.*

Ryden, Hope

WILD HORSES I HAVE KNOWN   *8–11 YEARS*

Illustrated by Hope Ryden. New York: Clarion, 1999.

Three decades of observations of wild mustangs by the author combined with numerous photographs enable young readers to reap the benefits of an exceptionally thoughtful, informative, and attractive picture book. The author's conversational tone and the numerous crisp, close-up photographs reproduced in full color bring the author's personal adventures, some of which are humorous, others terrifying, even mysterious, convincingly to life. Readers will learn about the social hierarchies of the wild mustangs and the survival strategies and habits of these free-roaming horses. They will learn about various long-standing questions and controversial issues concerning the wild horses that once roamed all over Europe, Asia, and North America, especially those that still inhabit the American West. What about the tarpan that lived in Poland and may still run wild in remote parts of Asia, but is so endangered some are now being bred in zoos? Should the mustang more accurately be referred to as a feral animal rather than a wild animal since it was once domesticated and began returning to the wild state around four hundred years ago? In other words, how valid is the argument that "an animal that acts wild, looks wild, and breeds in the wild is wild?" (p. 2) Ryden provides considerable support for her position on this issue. Her readers will have to decide whether they agree with her. The final question that Ryden raises focuses on the significance of the coloring and markings of the mustangs. An extensive bibliography with titles of books, booklets, and articles recommended for further reading is appended.

Winter, Kay
WOLF WATCH
Illustrated by Laura Regan. New York: Simon & Schuster, 1997.

Rich verse and detailed realistic pictures rendered in oil paint meld
together to tell an interesting and informative tale about the social
behavior of wolves and the whelping and weaning of wolf pups. This
tale builds up to a resounding tension and leads to a credible and
satisfying conclusion. Readers are certain to be totally absorbed as the
array of double-page and full-page pictures move back-and-forth from
distance to close images of the four wolf pups from the moment of
their birth in the warm, dark den. Eventually the mother wolf pushes
them out of the tunnel so they can meet the rest of the pack and
explore the smells and sounds of their new surroundings. One of the
pups, in pursuit of a cricket, wanders away from the pack unaware
that a watching eagle is plunging toward him. Readers are bound to
be fascinated with the father wolf's behavior when he recognizes the
need to protect the pup from the eagle. This book does not include
the aids one would find in most informational books (i.e., table of
contents, glossary, index, and bibliography of sources used by the author
or titles recommended for further reading), but it is indeed an excellent
informational book told in the form of a narrative verse, and good verse
at that.

Amphibians

Martin, James
FROGS
Illustrated with photographs by Art Wolfe. New York: Crown, 1997.

Not only is this book illustrated with crisp, large photographs reproduced in brilliant full colors, the text is written in a manner that instills
wonderment about the huge variety of frogs that inhabit all parts of
the world, and admiration for their almost magical ability to adapt
to changing conditions. The author shares his vast knowledge about
the physical characteristics and behavior patterns of many kinds of
frogs in a way that will thoroughly intrigue his readers. Unfortunately,
although he seems to put forth the idea that the information presented
here—however vast and interesting—is only the beginning, there is no
bibliography of books for further reading. There is no table of contents,
but the breaks between the discussions about different topics (structure,
survival techniques, mating practices, etc.) are obvious. The common
and scientific name of a frog pictured is usually given; occasionally sage

comments about a specific physical characteristic or behavior pattern of a particular kind of frog is included in a picture caption. An index is appended.

Fish

Ryder, Joanne

SHARKS IN THE SEA   *7–10 YEARS*

Illustrated by Michael Rothman. New York: Morrow, 1997.

> The setting for this day with a white shark is in the Pacific Ocean near the South Farallon Islands, about thirty miles west of San Francisco. Poetic prose, filled with sensory images and supported and embellished with action-filled, realistic acrylic paintings in full color, enables young readers to experience the natural habitat and ways of the white shark, the largest predatory fish found in all the world's temperate seas. Like all of the other excellent informational picture books included in the Just for a Day series, the scientific information included in the content of the text and illustrations in *Sharks in the Sea* has been evaluated, validated, and endorsed by an expert in marine animal behavior.

Reptiles

Ling, Mary, and Mary Atkinson

THE SNAKE BOOK: A BREATHTAKING CLOSE-UP LOOK AT   *8–13 YEARS*
SPLENDID, SCALY, SLITHERY SNAKES

Illustrated with photographs by Frank Greenaway and Dave King.
New York: DK Publishing, 1997.

> What a book! Dramatic photographs of sensationally beautiful snakes, some of which can be lethal, illustrate this oversized book. The book designer obviously was given free rein and did an exquisite job of employing his or her knowledge and creative skill, so that the textual matter about each of these unique snakes appears as smashingly beautiful as the oversized double-spread illustrations of eleven of them and the one truly sensationalistic and extravagant illustration of the "giant among serpents" (the reticulated python), which is shown in all its glory in a four-page foldout. The authors' comments about each of the twelve reptiles are brief and offer tidbits of information that are as intriguing as the pictures and will serve nicely to motivate readers to check into other sources to find out more about them. At the back of the book is a full page of "Special Statistics," which includes a miniature replica of each snake pictured in the book, plus data about its common and scientific names, distribution, food, method of hunting, and length.

Markle, Sandra

ALLIGATORS: OUTSIDE AND INSIDE   *7–11 YEARS*

New York: Atheneum, 1998.

Illustrated with photographs by Sandra Markle.

> This is a fairly in-depth description of many aspects of alligators: their habitats, structure (internal and external), natural enemies, food sources, mating practices, and much more. The full-color photographs, many of which are close-up views, effectively clarify and expand upon the behavior described in the well-written and carefully prepared text. Of special note is the author's practice of involving the reader directly by posing thought-provoking, mind-stretching questions before presenting the facts about some significant behavior that is characteristic of this animal. The illustrations are placed on the same page or facing the relevant text. The index and comprehensive glossary (which includes a pronunciation guide) are combined and presented on two pages at the end of the book. On the last page, in the section entitled "Looking Back," the author highlights five major questions for readers to think about, referring them to specific pages in the book to refresh their memories if they have forgotten the answers.

PLANTS AND GARDENING

Plants

Arnold, Katya, with Sam Swope

KATYA'S BOOK OF MUSHROOMS   *9–11 YEARS*

Illustrated by Katya Arnold. New York: Henry Holt, 1997.

> This is a comprehensive introduction to the world of mushrooms. Many types of mushrooms are discussed. Each mushroom pictured is clearly labeled with its common name and scientific name and accompanied by a short comment or significant caption. Readers are told when and where each kind of mushroom grows and how to find them; the distinguishing characteristics are described. Arnold states emphatically that this book is *not* intended as a field guide for use in identifying mushrooms. For that kind of information she urges readers to consult the books listed in the bibliography included in the back matter and to contact their local mycological society for expert identification.
>
> There is a separate section devoted to particularly precise verbal descriptions and visual images of poisonous mushrooms. In this section and in several other places throughout the book Arnold warns her readers to "never, never, never eat a mushroom you do not recognize."

49

There is no table of contents, but throughout the book sectional topics are highlighted in bold-faced type. Directions for a few activities and a project for growing mushrooms at home are included. The glossary and index are extensive and should prove helpful aids. That the author is "passionate" about mushrooms, a stance she proudly admits, is clearly apparent throughout her captivating discussions about them and in her detailed, double-page illustrations of them. Much of what she writes about and depicts in her dramatic illustrations, done in linocuts that combine bold colors with heavy black outlines, is based on her personal experiences both as a child and as an adult.

Hacker, Randi, *Adapter*
PLANTS   *6–10 YEARS*
Translated from the French. Illustrated. New York: Scholastic, 1997.

Part of the Discovery Box series, this is an efficiently boxed picture book and activity kit. It provides just enough information to intrigue readers about some fundamental aspects of plants so they can engage in some of the activities (e.g., watch for plants that are harmful or endangered, or collect plants and press and dry them). The pieces needed for the leaf and flower drying press are included. Should readers want to make a larger drying press than the one included in the activity kit, or need replacement pieces for the small press kit provided, the necessary materials are inexpensive and readily available in the home or hardware store. The full-color drawings, photographs, maps, and diagrams and the captions that accompany them add considerably more information to the text. Although some of these illustrations are small, they are clear and sharp enough so the significant details in them can be identified. A table of contents and glossary are included, but a bibliography recommending titles for further reading is not. Originally published in France by Éditions Gallimard Jeunesse in 1996 under the title *Secrets de l'herbier.*

Micucci, Charles
THE LIFE AND TIMES OF THE PEANUT   *7–10 YEARS*
Illustrated by Charles Micucci. Boston: Houghton Mifflin, 1997.

A wealth of information about the peanut is included in this enthusiastic and fairly comprehensive overview illustrated with explanatory cartoon-styled sketches done in watercolor. Fourteen topics, which are listed in a table of contents, explain clearly where and when the peanut first grew, how peanuts grow and are harvested, the location of the main peanut-growing areas in the United States and other parts of the world, the uses of the peanut in food and in industry, and so on. Children will undoubtedly be intrigued with the fact that its name is a misnomer—the peanut is not a nut. It is a seed from a flower that blossoms above the ground and produces its seeds (peanuts) below ground. A major asset of this book is its coverage of the peanut's historical significance, including the role played by George Washington Carver as "father of the peanut industry" and the importance of peanuts as a major source of food for both Northern and Southern soldiers during the Civil War. The words and music for a Civil-War-era song about peanuts, "The Goober Peas," are included in the book. March is "National Peanut Month" and March 4 is "Peanut Butter Lovers' Day," and a fun spin-off of the reading of this book might be to have the students sing this little ditty, especially on or around March 4. (*Warning:* Be certain to find out if anyone is allergic to peanuts before allowing children to eat them.) Micucci's book could be supplemented by *A Picture Book of George Washington Carver,* written by David A. Adler and illustrated by Dan Brown (Holiday House, 1999).

Rockwell, Anne
ONE BEAN   *3–6 YEARS*
Illustrated by Megan Halsey. New York: Walker, 1998.

The easy-to-read text is printed in crisp, primary-sized type and accompanied by simple, brightly colored line and wash illustrations, providing excellent step-by-step directions for germinating a lima bean. Young readers will probably grasp the concept of the life cycle of this kind of plant by reading the book and may also be motivated to engage in the same activities as the characters in the book. At the back of the book readers will find worthwhile information: The author offers a list of "More Activities" one can engage in with seeds, and in the section entitled "More About Beans," answers basic questions as What is a bean? Why is a bean a perfect seed to grow? Why does the bean in this book look different from the beans you eat for dinner? How do plants grow? and What else can you discover from watching seeds turn into plants?

Gardening

Godkin, Celia
WHAT ABOUT LADYBUGS?   *5–8 YEARS*
Illustrated by Celia Godkin. San Francisco: Sierra Club
Books for Children, 1995.

In this cautionary tale, the author presents clearly, albeit in a way some adults will deem a bit too simplistic and overly dramatic, what happens when one sprays all the plants with bug killer to rid a garden of "bad" insects. Young readers learn how such measures cause an imbalance in nature and this ultimately leads to the ruin of the garden. They will understand and appreciate how plants and insects are linked, depending on one another to survive. They will also learn there are preventive measures one can take to maintain a balance in nature and ways of undoing the damage caused when an imbalance of nature does occur. This story demonstrates that ladybugs are nature's way of controlling aphids. In turn, what the gardener in this story labelled as "bad" insects (i.e., caterpillars, ants, and wasps) will not overmultiply to the point of creating havoc in the garden, and the "good" insects (i.e., butterflies, bees, and ladybugs), flowers, and vegetables will flourish and fruit trees will bear juicy fruit. Large, colorful, and simple impressionistic paintings aptly clarify and dramatize the details and message of the text. This book is appropriate to read when studying gardening, ecology, biological control, or ladybugs.

Heck, Alice

THE ENCHANTED GARDENING BOOK: IDEAS FOR USING *5–10+ YEARS*
PLANTS TO BEAUTIFY YOUR WORLD, BOTH INDOORS AND OUT

Illustrated by Linda Dockey Graves. New York: Random House, 1997.

A plethora of charming paintings (albeit at times sentimentalized) show children engaging in basic gardening activities and creating decorative items with flowers. Some of the full-page illustrations depict children in these activities or simply show them romping about in a "butterfly and bird garden," enjoying not only the beautiful flowers, but the butterflies and birds they attract. Numerous other illustrations demonstrate the steps in planting and tending the right kinds of grasses and weeds, flowers, aromatic herbs, leaves, seed pods, etc., and using them to create such things as a Roman bath and sachet or herbal bath powder, "everlastings," "a lavender wand," a miniature rain forest, and more. This is a joyful book, one that will no doubt be referred to many times over. Readers who grow the plants and make some of the items the author recommends are certain to find a special kind of satisfaction and enjoyment from this book. The endpapers are beautifully decorated with various items described in the text.

Rosen, Michael J., *Compiler* and forty-one children's
book authors and illustrators

DOWN TO EARTH: GARDEN SECRETS! GARDEN STORIES! *7–12 YEARS*
GARDEN PROJECTS YOU CAN DO!

Illustrated. San Diego: Harcourt Brace, 1998.

Forty-one authors and illustrators have each written about a memorable experience associated with a favorite flower, fruit, vegetable, weed, or seeds. Most of the illustrations are by Rosen, but a few are by illustrators who relate their memorable experiences. The result is a delightful book that one will want to flip through, stop to read one entry, really "look" at the illustration that accompanies it, think about the significance of the person's experience and the accompanying illustration, and then move on to another that strikes his or her fancy. It is not a book children are likely to read in one sitting; it is one they will no doubt return to again and again, each time finding some idea or image of beauty, wisdom, insight, inspiration to ponder over. There are thirty-two intriguing activities or projects inspired by the stories in this collection. None of them are expensive, elaborate, or difficult. A few of them involve sharp objects and some recipes require the use of a stove or oven; in each case Rosen reminds the reader to ask for an adult's permission or participation before beginning them. I tried some of the recipes and they proved to be not only of the "no-fail" variety, but were easy to follow and tasty! (Each of the contributors donated his or her story and illustrations; all proceeds from the book will go to support of the community garden projects of Share Our Strength, a leading antihunger organization.)

OCEANS

Faulkner, Keith
A 3-D LOOK AT OCEANS   5–9 YEARS
Illustrated by Robert Morton. Boston: Little Simon/Simon & Schuster, 1996.

This book provides a cursory introduction to the dramatic and awesome wonders of ocean life, ranging from microscopic plankton to the majestic blue whale, the largest creature known to have lived on our planet. A clever 3-D viewer is mounted inside the back cover. The viewer is easily assembled by folding it along the creases and locking the tabs into the corresponding slots. The viewer can then be folded back so a page can be turned and the viewer flipped forward into place over the 3-D images. The reader looks down through the lenses at three-dimensional views of the terrain of the sea and ocean waters as well as the creatures and vegetation that live in it. A wealth of information about the underwater mountains and ranges that make up the ocean bottom and the thousands of different kinds of creatures that inhabit these waters is briefly but clearly presented, as are the rich deposits of oil, gas, metals, diamonds, and coal. Realistic paintings in full color supplement the wealth of information provided in the text, and almost every picture is accompanied by an explanatory caption or label. See also *A 3-D Look at Outer Space* (Little Simon/Simon & Schuster, 1996), also created by Faulkner and Morton.

Frasier, Debra

OUT OF THE OCEAN   *8–11 YEARS*

Illustrated by Debra Frasier. San Diego: Harcourt Brace, 1998.

Lyrical poetic prose alerts the readers to look to the wonders of their surroundings, for "if you look, you might find it"—the big things that are there and the small, the things that are always there and the things that are totally unexpected, but turn out to be just what you wanted." The double-page, mixed-media collage pictures are unique and inspiring; they leave no room for doubt about the multiple moods of the ocean, its trove of treasures, and its constantly changing scenes. A variety of kinds of flowers, clouds, vast spans of sky and water are cut out of flat colored paper, still-life photographs of "ocean treasures" (e.g., an incredible variety of shells, sea glass, skate egg pouches) are arranged in sand or placed amidst the ocean waves made with hand-embellished paste paper. Silhouette images of people are superimposed amid black-framed photographs of the sun setting on the water, or the churning, foaming, and frothing waves rolling into shore, or silver moonlight reflected on the rolling water. In the back matter the creator of this exquisite picture book offers a wealth of information that supplements the brief but profound text and the numerous still-life photos of the ocean's treasures the author and her mother found over many years along the shore of the Atlantic Ocean near their family home. The Illustration Notes give a detailed explanation of how the mixed media were prepared.

Lember, Barbara Hirsch

THE SHELL BOOK   *5–9 YEARS*

Illustrated with photographs by Barbara Hirsch Lember. Boston: Houghton Mifflin, 1997.

Each of the beautiful, full-page photographs of the sixteen kinds of shells commonly found along the seashores throughout the United States was taken with black-and-white infrared film, then hand tinted and reproduced in full color. A short description of each shell includes information about the mollusk family to which it belongs, where in the United States or other parts of the world it can be found, the creature's main source of food and how it obtains it, where its eggs can be found and what they look like, its size as an adult, and the uses made of shells now and in the past (e.g., currency, ornaments, religious symbols, food). Compare this book with the classic *Houses from the Sea,* written by Alice E. Goudey and illustrated by Adrienne Adams (Scribner, 1959).

Locker, Thomas
WATER DANCE   *5–11 YEARS*
Illustrated by Thomas Locker. San Diego: Harcourt Brace, 1997.

> Combining simple lyrical free verse and stunning landscape scenes rendered in full-color oil paintings, Thomas Locker speaks eloquently and aesthetically of the existence of the many forms of water: rain, a mountain stream, a waterfall, a lake, a river, the sea, the mist, the clouds, a storm front, a thunderhead, a storm, a rainbow, and a colorful sunset. I suspect young readers would benefit more from Candace Christiansen's highly informative factual comments about aspects of each of these forms of water if they had been placed with Locker's poetic prose and landscape pictures instead of in the back matter as an appendix-like addition entitled "The Water Cycle" alongside small reproductions of each of the paintings. As it is, the reader is presented with Locker's aesthetic or affective response to the beauties of the forms of water apart from Christiansen's straightforward factual comments. This implies, far from subtly, that one is not likely to acquire information by reading aesthetically oriented factual material.

ECOLOGY AND CONSERVATION

Allen, Judy, *Compiler and editor*
ANTHOLOGY FOR THE EARTH   *10 YEARS–ADULTHOOD*
Illustrated. Cambridge, Mass.: Candlewick, 1997.

> A fabulous book! The mind-stretching literary selections included in this anthology of essays, folktales, and poetry (by such authors as Anton Chekhov, Willa Cather, John Bierhorst, John Muir, Leo Tolstoy, and Judy Allen and from the scriptures of various religions) are about the wonders, the beauty, and the abuses of the earth. They are illustrated with full-page or even larger full-color (and a few black-and-white) reproductions of superb photographs, beautifully crafted etchings, and paintings by artists as Quentin Blake, Barbara Frith, Peter Sis, Michael Foreman, Wayne Anderson, David Stephen, Nicola Bayley, Jean-Paul Tibbles, and George Snow. This is a great book to reread, to pick out favorite selections and illustrations and ponder over and refer to again and again. It is a "must purchase" for inclusion in elementary, middle school and secondary school libraries, public libraries and personal

libraries in the home. The table of contents listing the title of each selection and its author and illustrator is attractively formatted, as are the biographical sketches of the authors and illustrators whose works appear in this anthology. An index of authors and illustrators is included.

Anderson, Joan
EARTH KEEPERS   *8–14 YEARS*
Illustrated with photographs by George Ancona.
San Diego: Harcourt Brace, 1993.

> In this three-part documentary, an award-winning author-photographer team describes three instances in which committed individuals of various ages assumed responsibility for helping save our earth, water, plants, and animals from destruction. The three projects focused on in this book depict how (1) the crew of the sloop *Clearwater* campaigned for the clean-up of the Hudson River, (2) a group of 105 "urban farmers" transformed a New York City-owned vacant lot from a garbage dump and a home to drug dealers and addicts to cultivated garden plots, and (3) a team of researchers from the Forest Service worked to ensure the protection of the black bears' habitat in the Minnesota wilderness by careful and responsible management and to save hundreds of plants and animals in the same area.

Ecosystems

Darling, Kathy
RAIN FOREST BABIES   *6–9 YEARS*
Illustrated by Tara Darling. New York: Walker, 1996.

> This prolific mother-daughter naturalist and photographer team have collaborated in creating many fine science books for children and this one is their best thus far. The fourteen rain-forest animal babies discussed in this book are arranged alphabetically; the information provided about each animal features facts about the environment in the particular layer of the rain forest they inhabit, their birthplace, birth weight, adult weight, number of littermates, favorite food, parent care, and enemies. The text is easy to read and informal and will interest children. The crisp, clear, full-color photographs were taken "on location" throughout the tropics from Brazil to Madagascar. At the beginning of the book there is an easy-to-decipher map clearly indicating where the tropical rain forests of the world are located and in which of the three layers of the rain forest the animal babies discussed in the book live.

Lasky, Kathryn

THE MOST BEAUTIFUL ROOF IN THE WORLD: 8–11 YEARS
EXPLORING THE RAINFOREST CANOPY

Photographs by Christopher G. Knight. Gulliver/Harcourt Brace, 1997.

This award-winning children's book team provides their readers with a fascinating glimpse of the rainforest canopy, the upper layer of foliage of a rain forest. Lasky's use of language is concise and information laden, but easily understood. Knight's full-color photographs, characterized by artistic sensibility to content, theme, and mood, masterfully illustrate the arduous work of pioneer rain-forest scientist Dr. Meg Lowman, her two sons, her brother, and her graduate assistants as they explore this previously uncharted world at the very top of the rain forest at Blue Creek, Belize.

The book is divided into three sections. In the first, entitled "Pioneer in the Rainforest," the author and photographer briefly inform their readers about how about Lowman's interest in plants, flowers, and insects developed during her childhood and about her present responsibilities as director of research and conservation at the Marie Selby Botanical Gardens, a research center in Sarasota, Florida. Lasky mentions briefly how Rachel Carson and Harriet Tubman, pioneer naturalists attuned to the environment in different ways and for different purposes, heightened and inspired Dr. Lowman's fascination and interests in the natural world when she was ten years old. This knowledge might well encourage the readers of this beautiful information book to read more about these women as well.

The second section, entitled "Out of the Shadow and into the Light," is devoted primarily to describing Lowman's efforts to record the canopy of the rain forest deep in Blue Creek, Belize, "one of the most humid places on the entire planet [and] where one can find more varieties of living things perhaps than any other place on earth." The third section is entitled "A Column of Life." This section follows Dr. Lowman, as she and her companions conduct an inventory of the different species of trees, plants, and insects that are found from the ground up to the canopy within the confines of several sixteen-foot squares they marked on the forest floor. Readers will be intrigued, as were Dr. Lowman's sons, to discover what happens when the team observes an insect they had never seen or heard of before. Although the author clearly defines the technical terms and describes the complex processes in the context of their use, the glossary should prove helpful.

Lessen, Don

INSIDE THE AMAZING AMAZON   *7–10 YEARS*

Illustrated by Michael Rothman. New York: Crown, 1998.

> The major aspects of the Amazon River rain forest discussed in this excellent informational picture book include the ecology, climate, animal and insect inhabitants, and vegetation found in each of its three layers. Some of the full-color illustrations are especially worthy of note; one is the full-page picture depicting the cross section of a typical patch of the Amazon rain forest showing each of eight different species of trees that start their growth on the forest floor and reach into one of the other layers, and the epiphytes (plants that do not live in the soil, but in another plant). Also noteworthy are the triple-page foldouts picturing a view of a few square feet of each layer of the rain forest (the understory, the canopy, and the emergent layer). Preceding each foldout the life in, on, and near each layer is described. Following each foldout are three pages of beautiful full-color pictures and a brief description of some of the animals and plants typically found in that layer of the forest. Each animal and plant shown in the foldouts is also reduced, shown in silhouette, and numbered. The numbers of each of these animals and plants are repeated in the back matter, which gives the scientific name of each one. A listing of the names and addresses of organizations that can provide information about things readers can do to help prevent the disappearance of the rain forest is also provided at the back of the book.

Paladino, Catherine

ONE GOOD APPLE: GROWING OUR FOODS   *8–11 YEARS*
FOR THE SAKE OF THE EARTH

Illustrated with photographs by Catherine Paladino. Boston:
Houghton Mifflin, 1999.

> From the very start, the author of this profusely illustrated book informs her readers that perfect-looking fruits and vegetables are not usually as pure and wholesome as they look. Their appearance may indicate that farmers have relied on poison or pesticides to kill insects, weeds, fungi, and other things that might damage crops, so they look as attractive as possible and thus sell for more money. Paladino then provides a short history of the use of pesticides, especially natural poisons farmers used as early as 1891, when the fungicide copper sulfate powder was used on grapes, and in the early 1900s when apple orchards were sprayed with lead arsenate to control the codling moth because its caterpillar was the number one apple eater. She then identifies some of the medical problems that are partly caused by synthetic chemicals such as

DDT and about 325 pesticides that are currently allowed within specific limits by the Environmental Protection Agency. Paladino praises some practices employed by organic farmers and gardeners, who grow fruits and vegetables without the use of pesticides. For example, she discusses the practice of growing old-fashioned or heirloom varieties of fruits and vegetables that help to preserve biodiversity, especially such traits as the ability to fight off certain diseases or insects or to survive drought conditions. She lauds the practice of growing a variety of crops—often in the same field or row, thus making it harder for the insects to find food. She discusses the practice of encouraging the population of certain beneficial insects by providing a suitable habitat for them. Sprinkled throughout this persuasive photo-essay are crisp, full-color photographs, most of which are accompanied with informative captions that expand most aptly upon the text. Appended are eleven easy-to-implement activities readers can do to help grow good food for the sake of the earth, a bibliography of the sources consulted in the preparation of this book, and a comprehensive index.

Swinburne, Stephen R.

ONCE A WOLF: HOW WILDLIFE BIOLOGISTS FOUGHT TO BRING BACK THE GRAY WOLF   *9–11 YEARS*

Illustrated with photographs by Jim Brandenburg.
Boston: Houghton Mifflin, 1999.

Students are certain to be impressed with the many facets of the long and troubled relationship between the wolf (especially the gray wolf) and humans, and more recently the results of the conservation movement to restore the wolves to the wild. Some of the issues explored by Swinburne and Brandenburg are the negative image and persecution of the wolf throughout history, the role scientists have played since 1920 in saving and protecting the wolf, and the important function the wolf plays as a predator in the ecosystem. The full-color photographs in this well-written, profusely illustrated book expand and enhance most effectively the information and issues the author discusses. The table of contents makes very clear the kinds of topics examined in this book. An excellent two-color map at the back of the book depicts both the historical range and the current range of the gray wolf in North America. Appended is a list of sources that includes an excellent bibliography of books about the topics focused on in this photo-essay. Quite a few of the titles listed are by authors who have written other well-known children's books. This bibliography also identifies Web sites computer-literate children can access to learn more about the issues related to the gray wolf. A comprehensive index is also appended.

Wright-Frierson, Virginia

A DESERT SCRAPBOOK: DAWN TO DUSK   *7–10+ YEARS*
IN THE SONORAN DESERT

Illustrated by Virginia Wright-Frierson.
New York: Simon & Schuster, 1996.

> Carefully and accurately detailed and truly accomplished full-color watercolor paintings combined with well-written informative text provide readers an aesthetic and scientific introduction to the ecosystem of the Sonoran Desert. The author obviously spent many thoughtful and enraptured hours observing and studying the desert plants and animals. Luckily for young readers, one major outcome of her efforts is that she has managed to capture the aura and reality of the unique beauty in the desert flora and fauna and the relationship between them in this "scrapbook." Rarely does one have an opportunity to offer children such a top-notch informational picture book as this! Be certain to notice the linoleum-cut prints on the endpapers; they highlight the many desert creatures Wright-Frierson depicts so eloquently in her text and illustrations.

Wright-Frierson, Virginia

AN ISLAND SCRAPBOOK: DAWN TO DUSK   *7–10+ YEARS*
ON A BARRIER ISLAND

Illustrated by Virginia Wright-Frierson.
New York: Simon & Schuster, 1998.

> Wright-Frierson and her daughter combed the shore of a North Carolina barrier island off the Atlantic Ocean to identify and observe the many aspects of this unique ecosystem: the muddy salt marsh, the maritime forest along the ocean where the oak, pine, and magnolia trees form a canopy and protect the fragile and salt-sensitive plants (e.g., palmettos, young cedar, dogwoods, bays, and hollies); the slow sunrise; the sounds of the lapping tide; the calls of the many different kinds of salt marsh and ocean shorebirds (e.g., clapper rail, pelicans, snowy egrets, gulls, and double-crested cormorant). They also see small fish, claw-clicking fiddler crabs, two bottlenose dolphins, sea turtle hatchlings, and the innumerable shells washed up from the ocean floor during a hurricane that occurred a few weeks before. There is no doubt that Wright-Frierson is interested in alerting her readers to the hazards human carelessness presents for the creatures of this fragile ecosystem. She writes of finding a dead baby sperm whale washed up on the beach. A naturalist friend informed her that scientists had already examined the whale and discovered that its stomach had contained a marine oil bottle, nylon rope, a

black plastic trash bag, a plastic buoy, and some rubber and Styrofoam. It had starved because there was no room for food! The last page of her scrapbook contains a large sign that says: "Protect and preserve this fragile earth—our island." The endpapers in this book, like those in her Sonoran Desert scrapbook, consist of accomplished linoleum-cut prints depicting the many creatures the author and her daughter observed during their exploration of this barrier island. Compare this book with the observations of "ocean treasures" in Debra Frasier's *Out of the Ocean* (Harcourt Brace, 1998), described above.

Wildlife Conservation

Ancona, George

THE GOLDEN LION TAMARIN COMES HOME   *7–11 YEARS*

Illustrated with photographs by George Ancona. New York: Macmillan, 1994.

> Ancona's well-written text and crisp, full-color photographs provide an intriguing account of why and how golden lion tamarin monkeys are being reintroduced to Brazil by the cooperative efforts of wildlife conservationists from the National Zoological Park of the Smithsonian Institution in Washington, D. C., and from a reserve in the coastal rain forest near Silva Jardin, a farming community a short distance from Rio de Janiero. A listing of seventy-two zoos in the United States where this species of monkeys can be seen is included at the back of the book.

Ancona, George

MAN AND MUSTANG   *7–12 YEARS*

Illustrated with photographs by George Ancona. New York: Macmillan, 1992.

> Ancona's well-written text and black-and-white photographs are aptly combined to tell an informative and exciting story of how the Bureau of Land Management implements the Adopt-a-Horse (or Burro) Program designed to maintain an ecological balance among wild mustangs that overpopulate on the remote public lands of our western states. Children were awestruck when I read this fascinating photo-essay of how inmates from the Santa Fe Penitentiary volunteered to participate in this program and learned how to round up and train the wild mustangs so the horses could be given to people who wanted to adopt them. At the back of the book Ancona provides a list of the thirteen Bureau of Land Management's Wild Horse and Burro Adoption Centers in ten western states that readers can contact for further information. Supplement with

61

Black Cowboy, Wild Horses, written by Julius Lester and illustrated by Jerry Pinkney (Dial, 1998).

Bernhard, Emery
PRAIRIE DOGS   *6–9* YEARS
Illustrated by Durga Bernhard. San Diego: Gulliver/Harcourt Brace, 1997.

> This account of the social behavior and life cycle of the black-tailed prairie dog should prove intriguing to children. The author's chronicle of the ecological relationship between these fetching rodents, the prairie fauna, and more than 170 kinds of creatures that rely on prairie dogs for food or on their tunnels for living quarters should enlarge children's perspective about this species' contribution to the natural balance of nature. The large and colorful illustrations, done in gouache, reflect the tones and hues of the prairie landscape and skies. They do a fine job of interpreting and extending the text and the rather complicated and involved concepts pertaining to the prairie dogs' burrowing system, the ecological relationship between this species of rodents and other prairie creatures, and the long-running argument the conservationists and scientists have had with the ranchers about whether or not prairie dogs are pests. Ranchers feel that the prairie dogs and the cows actually compete for grass and there is not enough for both kinds of animals, and that the prairie dog's tunnels endanger horses and cattle. A small map showing the states in which the different species of prairie dogs live appears on the first page of the book and there is a glossary at the back of the book. Both aids provide a wealth of information and should prove useful to the reader.

Lasky, Kathryn
SHE'S WEARING A DEAD BIRD ON HER HEAD!   *5–10* YEARS
Illustrated by David Catrow. New York: Hyperion, 1997.

> In the Author's Note at the back of the book, Lasky informs readers that she mixed fact and fiction in this story and tells them which parts are based on historically substantiated information and which she made up. For example, she fabricated the account of how Harriet Hemenway (1858–1960) and her cousin Minna Hall (1859–1961), founders of the Massachusetts Audubon Society around the turn of the twentieth century, happened to find out how the proprietors of hat stores managed to obtain the illegal bird feathers to decorate ladies' hats. However, all of the other incidents in the story and the facts reported in connection with them are historically accurate, as are the names of the persons identified

as having been associated with the bird protection movement and its impact on legislation and education, and the heightening of the public's awareness of environmental concerns. The humorous expressionistic paintings that illustrate this informative story border on cartoon-styled art and were done with watercolor and ink; they add a bit of levity to this story, but their content is consistent with the geographical setting and the era during which the action of story takes place.

London, Jonathan

PHANTOM OF THE PRAIRIE: YEAR OF THE BLACK-FOOTED FERRET   *7–9 YEARS*

Illustrated by Barbara Bash. San Francisco: Sierra Club Books
for Children, 1998.

> Rarely is one fortunate enough to be able to read as fascinating a portrait of an animal's life cycle as this one created by the masterful union of Jonathan London's descriptive and poetic prose and Barbara Bash's accomplished sensitive, albeit romanticized paintings. The significance of the interrelationship of the black-footed ferret and the prairie dog is a dramatic phenomenon of nature in-and-of itself, as is the fact that this particular species of ferret came so close to extinction by the 1970s in the prairies of central and western Great Plains of North America. When you read aloud *Phantom of the Prairie* to the students or merely tell them about it, be certain to mention that there is considerable information about the near demise and subsequent survival of the black-footed ferret in *Prairie Dogs,* written by Emery Bernhard and illustrated by Durga Bernhard (Gulliver/Harcourt Brace, 1997), described above.

Mallory, Kenneth

A HOME BY THE SEA: PROTECTING COASTAL WILDLIFE   *9–12+ YEARS*

Illustrated with photographs by Kenneth Mallory and others.
San Diego: Gulliver/Harcourt Brace, 1998.

> This well-written text with its many informative, full-color photographs provides fascinating portraits of three programs in which New Zealand conservationists have banded together with scientists, animal activists, and members of the community at large to ensure (for the time being, at least) the survival of endangered species, proving that it is possible for animals and humans to share their living space.
>
> Program 1: During the 1980s the New Zealand Department of Conservation realized that an alarming number of Hector's dolphins were becoming entangled and killed in fishermen's nets. Fearing that the species would probably vanish from the area within fifteen years, they

called on New England Aquarium conservation biologist Greg Stone for help. Stone devised a pinger that could be attached to the commercial fishing nets to warn off the dolphins and thus prevent them from getting caught in the nets and drowning.

Program 2: As people moved into a stretch of the mainland coast of Otago Peninsula (near the city of Dunedin), clearing the land for sheep farming and for homes along the seashore, the nesting habitat of the yellow-eyed penguins was destroyed. With the human settlers came predators such as rats, opossums, and domesticated dogs and cats as well as the sheep that further altered nesting sites and trampled burrows. To provide them with suitable nesting sites protected from pests and prey, Penguin Place was established. Conservationists built makeshift camouflaged A-frames, snug hideaways backed by an assortment of bushes to provide the kind of shelter, shade, privacy, and safekeeping the penguins need for laying their eggs and raising their chicks. Thus far, the yellow-eyed penguin population has flourished in the makeshift nesting habitat at Penguin Place; without this sanctuary they all would have perished.

Program 3: The Eastern Bays Little Blue Penguin Foundation on the outskirts of Wellington in North Island, New Zealand, is a place for treating injured and sick penguins. Working from her home on the edge of Wellington harbor, Vivian Hextall enlists the volunteer efforts of her neighbors and works closely with representatives of the New Zealand Department of Conservation, who help her band the birds when they are eventually released. She frequently makes presentations in the local schools to help children appreciate the wildlife of the harbor.

There is no table of contents; as one pages through the book one will notice that there is a separate section devoted to each of the three conservation projects described above. An excellent and elaborate glossary of terms used in this book is appended.

Swinburne, Stephen R.

IN GOOD HANDS: BEHIND THE SCENES AT A CENTER   *9–13+ YEARS*
FOR ORPHANED AND INJURED BIRDS
Illustrated with photographs by Stephen R. Swinburne and sketches by
Rick Olson. San Francisco: Sierra Club Books for Children, 1998.

This photo-essay describes how teenage volunteers at the Vermont Raptor Center, and other places like it around the United States, capably care for injured and orphaned raptors (birds of prey) and eventually release them when they are able to survive on their own. Six main groups of raptors are found in North America: kites, hawks, eagles, vultures, falcons, and owls. Swinburne describes in words and photographs how the Vermont Raptor Center has attended to the needs of at least one raptor from each of these groups. Numerous full-color photographs that appear throughout the book support the text most effectively; these are supplemented by detailed pen-and-ink crosshatch sketches of eyes, wings, upper beaks, and claws of raptors that appear in sidebars. The captions that accompany most of the photographs and sketches clarify and explain aspects of the subject they depict, providing the reader with additional information.

The numerous sidebars throughout the book elaborate further upon aspects of the habitats, variety of species, and food chains that are mentioned only briefly in the body of the text; the sketches in the sidebars are noteworthy because they clarify most effectively how raptors are especially equipped for hunting. The glimpse of the behind-the-scenes work carried out by the center personnel should enlighten readers about the effects of human carelessness and the perils of nature that threaten wild animals in general and raptors in particular. This photo-essay might also alert readers to some roles they can play as volunteers (and later as professionals) in making this a better world for people and the wild animals that populate it.

Wadsworth, Ginger

JOHN BURROUGHS: THE SAGE OF SLABSIDES   *9–12+ YEARS*

Illustrated with photographs from various sources. New York: Clarion, 1997.

Rare archival black-and-white photographs, most of which are accompanied by informative captions, expand upon and enrich this profusely illustrated photo-biography of John Burroughs (1837–1921). Burroughs is best remembered as a pioneer of the conservation movement in the United States and was a highly respected naturalist, ornithologist, essayist, poet, teacher, and writer of short stories for children and full-length biographies of Walt Whitman and John James Audubon. In 1921 the John Burroughs Association (earlier called the John Burroughs Memorial Association) established a prestigious award for nature writing named after him. Some of the recipients of this award are Rachel Carson, Roger Peterson, Ann Zwinger, and Joseph Wood Krutch. Each year the John Burroughs Association also selects several outstanding nature books for children. This award is presented at the American Museum of Natural History on April 3 each year (John Burroughs' birthday).

Author/photographer Peter Lourie received this award for his informational River series book *Everglades: Buffalo Tiger and the River of Grass* (Boyds Mills, 1991). Appended are lists of the books written by Burroughs for adults and for young readers. Also appended is a helpful index.

WEATHER

Butler, Geoff

THE KILLICK: A NEWFOUNDLAND STORY   *9–13 YEARS*

Illustrated by Geoff Butler. Plattsburg, N.Y., and Toronto: Tundra, 1995.

> Full-page expressionistic illustrations, done in a style suggestive of Van Gogh and reproduced in full color, enhance and extend most aptly the sense of environment and horrendous circumstances of this tale based on a true heroic deed performed by a grandfather to save his grandson's life. Returning from an abandoned outport, where they went to visit the elderly man's wife's gravesite, they were caught in a fierce storm at sea. While waiting to be rescued they found shelter under their dory on an ice floe. The large full-color paintings and the small grease-pencil sketches scattered throughout contribute to the sense of place and terror so intrinsic to this powerful tale of courage and amazing sacrifice. Children will long remember the details of what it is like to be caught on an ice floe with the strong wind and blinding snow, the cracking sound of ice splitting up, the feeling of the ice pan (a small flat-topped piece of ice floating on the ice floe) moving under them, hearing the sound of the water lapping around the edges of the ice gradually become clearer and closer, the seals barking around them, and finally the boy's feeling of gratefulness yet intense misery when he realizes the ultimate sacrifice his grandfather made for him during the night while he (the boy) slept. The authenticity of the essential facts provided about the storm at sea, the experiences the boy and his grandfather had while they stayed on the ice floe hoping to be rescued, and the old man's heroic action provide the elements of this phenomenal informational picture book.

Logan, Claudia, *Adapter*

WEATHER   *6–10 YEARS*

Translated from the French. Illustrated. New York: Scholastic, 1997.

> A part of Scholastic's Discovery Box series, this is an efficiently boxed picture book and activity kit. It provides just enough information to intrigue readers about some fundamental aspects of weather so they

can engage in activities (e.g., build a weather station, determine the direction and speed of the wind, measure the amount of rainfall) that make use of a weather vane, thermometer, and rain gauge provided in the kit (all of which are easily and inexpensively replaceable should they "disappear" or get broken). The full-color drawings, photographs, maps, and diagrams and the captions that accompany them add considerably more information to the text. Although some of these illustrations are small, they are clear and sharp enough so the significant details in them can be identified. A table of contents and glossary are included, but there is no bibliography recommending titles for further reading. This book was originally published in France by Editions Gallimard Jeunesse in 1996 under the title *Secrets de la meteorologie.*

Martin, Jacqueline Briggs
SNOWFLAKE BENTLEY   *7–10 YEARS*
Illustrated by Mary Azarian.
Boston: Houghton Mifflin, 1998.

A multifaceted approach is used in this beautiful book to tell very briefly the biography of the "snowflake man," Wilson Alwyn Bentley, a self-taught scientist who developed a technique of microphotography and photographed thousands of individual snowflakes in order to demonstrate the unique formation of each one. He also explained that a snowflake is actually a form of water that has been transformed into a tiny six-pointed (or occasionally a three-pointed) crystal of ice that is an incomparably beautiful masterpiece of design. Some facts about Bentley's fascinating life story are told in a narrative style in an oversized picture-book format consisting of text and illustrations done with naive-styled woodblock prints hand-tinted with watercolors. Children (and most adults) will probably choose to read the traditional narrative version of Bentley's life story, which combines text and accompanying illustrations, in its entirety and then go back and read the factual information presented in the sidebars. Scattered throughout the book and on the jacket are reproductions of Wilson Bentley's snow crystal photographs. *Snowflake Bentley* was named the 1999 Caldecott Award Medal Winner. Readers (ages 8–10) of Johanna Hurwitz's historical novel *Faraway Summer* (Morrow, 1998) will be delighted with the authentic anecdotes about "Snowflake Bentley" and the several encounters the characters in this novel have with him.

ARCHAEOLOGY AND ANTHROPOLOGY

Deem, James M.

BODIES FROM THE BOG   *9–13 YEARS*

Illustrated. Boston: Houghton Mifflin, 1998.

A "bog body" is a type of natural mummy, the preserved body of a person who was buried in the bog perhaps thousands of years ago. The processes archaeologists and other scientists use enable them to determine the cause(s) of death, the age of the deceased, and approximately how many years the body had been in the bog, and even the season of the year in which the person died. Most of the "bog bodies" pictured and discussed in this book were found in bog peat and were mummified; other were skeletal remains found in fen peat. The author presents a thorough explanation as to why the one kind of peat mummifies the human body and why in the other kind of peat only the skeleton of the person remains. Adults who just flip through this book looking only at the illustrations might well get the impression that this is grim, morbid, or even macabre reading fare for children. When they examine the illustrations in the context of the text presentation of the scientific and anthropological theories about how these bodies got into the peat bogs or fen peat in the first place, they realize without doubt what a thoroughly informative and invaluable book *Bodies from the Bog* is.

Gerstein, Mordicai

THE WILD BOY: BASED ON A TRUE STORY   *9–12+ YEARS*
OF THE WILD BOY OF AVEYRON

Illustrated by Mordicai Gerstein. New York: Farrar, Straus & Giroux, 1998.

This picture-book version tells the true and poignant story of a child (about age twelve) found living alone in the mountain town of Saint-Sernin in the Aveyron district of southern France on January 8, 1800. Readers learn how the boy probably survived alone through all kinds of weather and among the fierce, unfriendly animals that roamed the mountains. The expressionistic line and watercolor-wash paintings effectively depict the emotional trauma the boy experienced when three people found him in the woods, captured him, and brought him to the city where he was studied by a local French naturalist and Parisian scientists, then by the scientists associated with the Institute for Deaf Mutes, and finally by Jean Marc Itard, a young doctor at the Institute who took him into his home to be cared for by himself and his housekeeper. I strongly recommend that this brief, yet wrenching picture book version of "the wild boy's" life be read before reading Gerstein's full-length historical novel *Victor* (Farrar, Straus & Giroux, 1998). Having the children compare and contrast the effectiveness of each of these two different kinds of literature (luckily written by the same author!) would be an excellent critical reading activity. Another novel that might be compared and contrasted with one or both of Gerstein's books is Jane Yolen's *Children of the Wolf* (Viking, 1984).

Jackson, Donna M.

THE BONE DETECTIVES: HOW FORENSIC ANTHROPOLOGISTS   *10–14+ YEARS*
SOLVE CRIMES AND UNCOVER MYSTERIES OF THE DEAD
Illustrated with photographs by Charlie Fellenbaum. Boston:
Little, Brown, 1998.

The author clearly explains the procedures used to study bones and teeth to determine a person's gender, race, age, height, and weight, how the cause of death can be established by "reading" the markings on bones, and how a sculptor uses clay to reconstruct a face from a skull. Jackson also identifies some specific cases in which some or all of these procedures led to the identification of bodies or were used to convict persons of their murder. The photographs of bones and the graphs included in this book exemplify effectively the specific clues the "forensic detectives" use to gather the necessary information. A short description is given in the back matter about how each of the following specialists assists in solving specific kinds of crimes and what kind of clues each specialist uses: computer specialists, forensic pathologists, document examiners, forensic toxicologists/chemists, hair and fiber examiners, and firearm examiners. The glossary of forensic terms is quite extensive and the terms are clearly and precisely defined. The "Bone Biography" on the last page consists of two line drawings (a frontal view and a side view of the adult human skeleton); the major groups of bones a forensic "detective" examines for clues to a person's identify are clearly outlined and labeled. Readers who want more information on this topic might be referred to *Mummy Mysteries: Tales from North America,* written and illustrated by Brenda Z. Guiberson (Henry Holt, 1998). Guiberson's book presents various cases of mummies found throughout North America and describes how and what anthropologists learned about the times in which each of the mummified persons lived and how each died.

Numbers and Arithmetic

COUNTING BOOKS

Jahn-Clough, Lisa

1 2 3 YIPPIE   *1–3 YEARS*

Illustrated by Lisa Jahn-Clough. Boston: Walter Lorraine/Houghton Mifflin, 1998.

> This number concept book is bound to provide young children a cheerful reading experience, and it is one they will ask to have read to them many times over! They are certain to be amused by this cumulative account of what happens when two children and a conglomeration of animals have a party in a house that is all alone and will especially enjoy the surprise ending, even if they have heard it many times before. The action-filled illustrations are brightly colored, and the frisky activities of the two human characters and their animal guests will most surely invite anyone looking at them to count them. See also *A B C Yummy* by Lisa Jahn-Clough (Houghton Mifflin, 1998), which is a cheerful alphabet book.

Provensen, Alice

COUNT ON ME: TEN BOOKS IN A BOX   *2–6 YEARS*

Illustrated by Alice Provensen. San Diego: Browndeer/Harcourt Brace, 1998.

> Ten little board books (4"x 4") make counting fun; each book depicts a particular number of related things, usually in double-page spreads.

For example, *The Book of One: Babies* portrays one lamb, one bear cub, one piglet; *The Book of Two: Traffic* depicts two trucks, two vans, and two sedans; *The Book of Five: Birds* shows five bluejays and five woodpeckers; *The Book of Ten: Berries* ends the series with " . . . and blue blueberries. Count them. Are there 10? 1 2 3 4 5 6 7 8 9 10—good. Let's go to 1 and start again!" Be prepared! Children will indeed want to start again with *The Book of One: Babies* and repeat the series again and again. The line and wash pictures are easy to decipher; they fill the tiny pages and not only depict the number concept being focused on in the book, but do so quite appropriately in terms of the action or situation designated in the text. A delightful little library of counting books!

Saul, Carol P.

BARN CAT: A COUNTING BOOK   *2–6 YEARS*

Illustrated by Mary Azarian. Boston: Little, Brown, 1998.

A single-minded barn cat notices the antics of the various kinds of animals around her, but she pays little or no attention to them, for she is determined to find something very special. Children were delighted with the rhyming text and although they were eager to count each of the creatures cited in the text and depicted in the illustrations, they were more anxious to find out what the determined barn cat was so interested in. (In other words, they were willing to consider the concepts about numbers this book offers, but not until they reached the end of this suspenseful story!) Except for the first and last, which are single-page pictures, all of the illustrations in this are double-page reproductions of stunning four-color, hand-colored woodcut prints. After the children found out what the barn cat was looking for, they were eager to go back and count the animals depicted on each page to see if indeed the number of animals they found in the pictures actually agreed with the numeral that appeared at the left-hand side of the page and the number cited in each of the verses. None of the children were satisfied with one or even two readings of this beautifully unique counting book. It was not at all unusual to see two or three children sitting together, examining and talking about aspects of this book during their "free reading time."

Sturges, Philemon

TEN FLASHING FIREFLIES   *3–6 YEARS*

Illustrated by Anna Vojtech. New York: North-South, 1995.

A delightful multidimensional counting book. A simple narrative verse relates how a brother and sister, joyously and energetically romping about on a summer night, notice ten flashing fireflies, catch them one-by-one in a jar, only to release them and enjoy seeing them flash "good-bye" as they fly away until there are none. The night scenes are striking works of visual art. Most assuredly children will ask (demand!) to have this counting book read many times over and soon they will be "reading" it along with you and even on their own. Two picture books children would enjoy and benefit from having read to them along with this book are *The Very Lonely Firefly,* written and illustrated by Eric Carle (Philomel, 1995) and *Fireflies for Nathan,* written by Shulamith L. Oppenheim and illustrated by John Ward (Tambourine, 1994).

ARITHMETIC

Adler, David A.
EASY MATH PUZZLES   *5–9 YEARS*
Illustrated by Cynthia Fisher. New York: Holiday House, 1997.

> The clever black-and-white, pen-and-ink watercolor-wash cartoon-style illustrations support the nonthreatening approach to mathematical concepts that is so pervasive in this book. They cleverly offer some subtle (and some not-so-subtle) hints to the solutions of this fun-filled collection of challenging, occasionally tricky, yet basically easy mathematical riddles involving people, coins, food, weather, and more. The answers to each of these puzzles are given in the back of the book. A riddle entitled "Lost in the Rain" demonstrates the tone and calibre of the puzzles in this picture book: Two mothers and two daughters are walking in the rain. They are all under the umbrella. If there are only three women under the umbrella, where is the fourth woman? (The answer is implied in the picture that accompanies the riddle: There is no fourth woman. The three women under the umbrella include a woman, her daughter, and her granddaughter. The woman is a mother. Her daughter is a mother, too. So there are two mothers under the umbrella. The granddaughter is a daughter. Her mother is a daughter, too. So there are two daughters under the umbrella. There are two mothers and two daughters under the umbrella, but only three women.)

Adler, David A.
FRACTION FUN   *6–9 YEARS*
Illustrated by Nancy Tobin. New York: Holiday House, 1996.

> Adler defines and explains technical terms and mathematical concepts about fractions pertaining to weights and measures in a manner that makes them concrete and understandable. He uses materials, objects,

and events children are familiar with and connects them with these mathematical terms and concepts. He makes effective use of numerous hands-on, no-fail activities teachers have used for decades to engage students in the mathematical processes inherent in understanding fractions. This does not mean these activities are "dated"; it does mean they transcend time. Adler concludes this instructive book about fractions (especially those relating to weights and measures) by asking the readers to "keep on the lookout for fractions. They are everywhere." The informality of the brightly colored and action-oriented cartoon-style illustrations plus the practical applications of the basic concepts so simply defined and explained make this a nonthreatening book of wide appeal to children.

Adler, David A.

SHAPE UP! FUN WITH TRIANGLES AND OTHER POLYGONS   *5–9 YEARS*

Illustrated by Nancy Tobin. New York: Holiday House, 1998.

> What a delightful action-oriented way to learn the basic geometric concepts about polygons! Some of the concepts about polygons (defined as various flat shapes with varying numbers of straight sides) are simple, others are quite complex. This introduction will serve nicely to stretch and embellish the young readers' mathematical knowledge and understanding. The flat, brightly colored cartoon-style illustrations are zany and humorous, and demonstrate very well how one can use ordinary bits of food and objects found in the home or classroom to help children understand some of the basic geometric concepts about polygons. The glossary at the back of the book provides an excellent summary of the geometric concepts presented throughout the book.

Markle, Sandra

DISCOVERING GRAPH SECRETS: EXPERIMENTS, PUZZLES,   *9–13+ YEARS*
AND GAMES EXPLORING GRAPHS

Illustrated with graphs by Sandra Markle and with photographs.
New York: Atheneum, 1997.

> Children are introduced to four major types of graphs (line graphs, bar graphs, pictographs, and circle graphs). They are encouraged to engage in an array of excellent activities, projects, games, and puzzles that can help them learn how to interpret these graphs and develop graphing skills that will enable them to record information they acquire by engaging in science research and surveys or decoding secret messages. The solutions to the story problems and puzzles the children are asked

to solve are given at the back of the book, as are the explanations of how to arrive at the correct answers. The assortment of examples for each major kind of graph is first-rate, and the explanations of how to use and construct them are straightforward and should help children to understand the mathematical concepts on which they are based.

Pinczes, Elinor J.

A REMAINDER OF ONE   *6–9 YEARS*

Illustrated by Bonnie MacKain. Boston: Houghton Mifflin, 1995.

Written in narrative verse, this clever book is intended to help children understand the mathematical concept and process of division. A subtheme worthy of note is: keep trying, eventually you might identify a divisor that "goes into" a dividend without leaving a remainder. In this (slight) story problem told in rhyme, the queen of the bugs demands that her army divide the twenty-five marchers into an equal number of lines so not one marcher will be left out of the parade. The cartoon-style line and watercolor-wash illustrations, which look like linoleum-block prints, add fun and meaning to the selection. Unfortunately, there is no bibliography of children's books for further reading. The glossary and index are comprehensive.

SIZE AND MEASUREMENT

Adler, David A.

HOW TALL, HOW SHORT, HOW FAR AWAY   *7–10 YEARS*

Illustrated by Nancy Tobin. New York: Holiday House, 1999.

There is little doubt young readers will be fascinated with the array of facts Adler provides about several measuring systems and the ancient origins of the terminology we still associate with them. Adler provides precise, easy-to-follow directions that will enable children to understand and apply meaningfully the basic concepts and modes of measuring in terms of the customary and metric systems. The simple line and bright color wash illustrations are excellent. They not only help to clarify and simplify the meaning and application of each measuring system, but make learning about them great fun. A lot of knowledge can be acquired as one reads and applies the mensuration systems focused on in this excellent, mind-stretching informational picture book. Adler offers some terrific activities, all of which are designed to help children recognize the differences between customary and metric systems for measuring. All of the equipment needed to implement these can be found in most homes and classrooms.

Dotlich, Rebecca Kai

WHAT IS SQUARE? *3–6 YEARS*

Illustrated with photographs by Maria Ferrari. New York: HarperCollins, 1999.

> Simple rhymed verses are combined with full-color photographs of many square things in the environment of preschoolers that would often be clearly visible to them *if* they are alert enough to notice them: a biscuit or cracker, a quilt, a caramel, a waffle, a dishcloth, a pair of dice, buttons, a pillow, and more. This attractive and cheerful concept book ends by encouraging the children to look for other square things in their environment.

Leedy, Loreen

MEASURING PENNY *5–8 YEARS*

Illustrated by Loreen Leedy. New York: Henry Holt, 1997.

> This book functions as a realistic and understandable and meaningful way of introducing children to the mathematics of mensuration (measuring) by actually showing them how the book character followed up on a class assignment to measure various parts of her dog, a Boston Terrier named Penny, by using standard units (pounds and inches) and nonstandard units (dog biscuits, cotton swabs, and paper clips). The illustrations, done in acrylics on watercolor paper, are crisp, bright, and simple, and they demonstrate most aptly how Penny's measurements (length of nose, tail, ear, paw print, height, and weight) compare with those of other dogs (a pug, a cocker spaniel, a Shetland sheep dog, a Basset Hound and a mixed breed). Other units the dog's owner measured were the volume of water and dog food Penny consumed each day and the units of time (seconds, minutes, hours) per day and per week she devoted to taking care of her dog. Children will enjoy reading and rereading this worthwhile, entertaining book and, no doubt, will do some interesting measuring on their own.

Miller, Margaret

BIG AND LITTLE *6 MONTHS–5 YEARS*

Illustrated with photographs by Margaret Miller. New York: Greenwillow, 1998.

> Large, sharply focused full-color photographs reproduced as full-page illustrations introduce nursery and preschool children to the concepts of size and opposites in the context of actions and situations they are

likely to identify with: a child and a doll each wearing a hat, a mother and a baby holding hands, a big dog and a little dog playing with a boy, a boy and his baby brother reading a book.

Wells, Robert E.
WHAT'S FASTER THAN A SPEEDING CHEETAH?   *5–8 YEARS*
Illustrated by Robert E. Wells. Morton Grove, Ill.: Albert Whitman, 1997.

Children are bound to enjoy this exercise in one-upmanship. Wells clearly demonstrates how the fastest things in various categories (e.g., animals, machines, objects, or tools) can outdo the others. The simple cartoon-style illustrations, done in pen and acrylic, dramatically demonstrate that the cheetah outruns the fastest marathon runner, the rocket ship travels faster than the fastest jet, but a meteoroid streaks through the sky faster than the rocket ship, and most scientists believe that a light beam can travel through space faster than anything else. The author's note in a section labeled "Some Additional Thoughts on Very Fast Things" tells his readers that the figures given in this book seem to be the best estimates, but some other books may have numbers that differ. He says that the speed of sound is not constant but is affected by altitude and while it is true that the speed of light is one of the few speeds you can count on to be constant, a real light beam becomes bright and visible only when hitting such things as dust or water particles. He also tells the readers that he took some liberties in some of the illustrations to show speed comparisons. For example, in the real world supersonic jets usually fly much higher than the little propeller plane and meteoroids do not often narrowly miss rocket ships. The double-page-spread table comparing the speed (in miles per hour) and length of time it would take each of the things he mentions to travel from the earth to the moon makes these facts more concrete and easy for young readers to understand.

TIME

Behrman, Carol H.
THE DING DONG CLOCK   *2–6 YEARS*
Illustrated by Hideko Takahashi. New York: Henry Holt, 1999.

Together the large, simple, and playful acrylic pictures and the slight lyrical verse depict perfectly what happens in a house when members of the family (and their charming pets) are at home and away. The faithful Ding Dong Clock never stops to rest; unfailingly, it rings in each hour from 1:00 A.M. to 12:00 noon and then starts anew at 1:00 P.M. (See illustration 5.) The sturdy movable clock hands on the cover are just

ILLUSTRATION 5   From *The Ding Dong Clock,* text by Carol H. Behrman, illustrated by Hideko Takahashi. Text © 1999 by Carol H. Behrman, illustrations © by Hideko Takahashi. Reprinted by permission of Henry Holt & Co., LLC.

right for children to manipulate as they learn to tell time and practice what they learn without getting bored or confused. (I would like to digress momentarily to point out that of all the concept books I read about teaching children to tell [clock] time, not one depicted or made any reference to digital clocks! We should consider the implications of this omission, considering how many digital clocks children see in their homes and even in their classrooms.)

Egan, Lorraine Hopping, *Adapter*

TIME   *6–10 YEARS*

Translated from the French. Illustrated. New York: Scholastic, 1997.

One of several in Scholastic's Discovery Box series, this is an efficiently boxed picture book and activity kit. It provides just enough information about some fundamental aspects of determining and measuring units of time by relating to the positions of the sun, earth, moon and the four seasons, the length of one's shadow, history and uses of the sundial, mechanical time, time travels, universal time and much more. Directions for some easy-to-implement activities applying the principles of measuring time are suggested, and the equipment (a sundial, an hour glass, and latitude cards) needed to engage in these activities is provided in the kit. The full-color drawings, photographs, maps, and diagrams and the captions that accompany them add considerably more information to the text. Although some of these illustrations are small, they are clear and sharp enough that the significant details can be identified. A table of contents and glossary are included, but a bibliography recommending titles for further reading is not. Originally published in France under the title *Secrets de le mesure du temps* by Editions Gallimard Jeunesse in 1996.

Harper, Dan

TELLING TIME WITH BIG MAMA CAT   *2–6 YEARS*

Illustrated by Barry Moser and Cara Moser. San Diego: Harcourt Brace, 1998.

Big Mama Cat describes her activities at various times throughout the day, from early morning (6:00 A.M.) to night (12:00 midnight). The title page folds open, so the readers (or listeners) can move the clock's hands as they follow Big Mama from one hour to the next. At the beginning of the book, Big Mama tells her readers she knows how to tell time, and I doubt any child reading or listening to this book would challenge her. No wonder Big Mama is so conscious of what time she does each of her daily activities; in each room throughout her family's home there is a different kind of clock and each one is prominently placed so that it is very visible to Big Mama and quite likely to the readers, too. (Actually, a serious clock collector might well covet the variety of clocks collected by Big Mama's family. I certainly did!)

Shields, Carol Diggory

MONTH BY MONTH A YEAR GOES ROUND   *3–6 YEARS*

Illustrated by True Kelley. New York: Dutton, 1998.

Fast-paced, loosely structured verses describing wholesome, high-energy action-filled activities and weather elements two months at a time are matched perfectly with cartoon-style pen-and-ink line and watercolor-wash illustrations. The last lines "Now the year is at an end/But January starts it up again," will most assuredly encourage the reader to go back to the beginning for a fun-filled repeat. Shields and Kelley joined forces to create a delightful companion book, *Day by Day a Week Goes Round* (Dutton, 1998).

The Physical World

Swinburne, Stephen R.

GUESS WHOSE SHADOW? 5–8 *YEARS*

Illustrated with photographs by Stephen R. Swinburne. Honesdale, Penn.: Boyds Mills, 1999.

Shadows are depicted in a wide variety of shapes and sizes, each indicating the angle from which the sun or other source of light shone on the animate and inanimate object. Stunning full-color photographs of objects depict a fascinating and constantly moving, shape-changing shadow world that depends on the presence of three elements: an object, a source of light, and a surface. All of the photographs are crisp and precisely focused; most are full page in size. They are arranged in order from dawn to dusk; all of them depict scenes often present and of interest to children, and they clearly are intended to motivate young readers to watch shadows of these and other things change size and shape as the sun comes and goes, seen rising in the east in the morning and setting in the west at dusk. Readers will no doubt be surprised to learn that night is the biggest shadow in the world!

Wicks, Walter

WALTER WICK'S OPTICAL TRICKS   *7–11 YEARS*

Illustrated with photographs by Walter Wick and assisted by Dan Helt.
New York: Scholastic, 1998.

> This is a terrific introduction to the study of visual illusion! Most chil-
> dren are intrigued and more than a little surprised when they experience
> the phenomenon of visual illusions and perhaps even confused when
> they discover that what they "saw" was not a real (correct) image, but
> was a false image or visual illusion. They are equally amazed and baffled
> when they look at an image and "see" a particular image only to have
> that image change as they keep looking at it. They tend to enjoy the
> challenge of trying to figure out how optical "tricks" work and will
> ask: Which image is the correct or real image? What does a painter
> or photographer do to trick our eyes so that we think we are seeing
> something but we are seeing a false image instead? The creators of this
> book have compiled fifteen optical illusions—one each on the front and
> back covers plus thirteen between the covers. The readers are given
> opportunities to explore how each of these optical illusions works. They
> are also given a tip or two to help them figure out on their own how the
> illusions work. Just in case they are unable to figure out how any or all
> of the illusions were done, the author explains in the last four pages
> how each illusion was created.

Young, Jay

BEYOND AMAZING: SIX SPECTACULAR SCIENCE POP-UPS   *9–13 YEARS*

Illustrated with photographs and sketches. Paper engineering
by Jay Young. New York: HarperCollins, 1997.

> Short but scientifically accurate explanations, easy to understand and
> apply in practical, day-to-day situations are provided for six important
> concepts pertaining to time and energy; light and vision; photography
> and virtual reality; sound satellites and electronic organizers; weight
> and gravity and orbiting spacecraft; and numerical systems and cal-
> culating machines and artificial intelligence techniques. The brief text
> traces the development and advance of technology related to each of
> these scientific concepts from ancient to contemporary times. Each of
> the illustrations, be they photographs, sketches, diagrams, or manipula-
> tives, support, clarify, and significantly extend the verbal descriptions.
> The ingenious manipulatives included in this book really work. Some of
> the manipulatives are pop-ups (i.e., sand timers, a scale, abacus), others
> are tagboard mock-ups (i.e., binoculars, a pair of telephone receivers,

and a phenakistoscope or motion projector). They are all made of fairly sturdy tagboard and pieces of plastic and metal; all of them (except for the motion picture projector) should hold up quite well if the children use them carefully. A bibliography of titles for further reading would have added tremendously to this well-planned hands-on science information book.

ASTRONOMY

Fisher, Leonard Everett

GALILEO   *9–12 YEARS*

Illustrated by Leonard Everett Fisher. New York: Macmillan, 1992.

In this partial biography Fisher briefly outlines the major discoveries in mathematics, physics, and astronomy by Galileo Galilei, often referred to as "the father of modern science." In simple prose, Fisher explains how Galileo discovered the law of the pendulum, experimented with floating objects and falling objects, constructed the first thermoscope to measure heat, constructed and used the first microscope, and constructed a telescope through which he viewed earth's moon and observed Jupiter's moons and Saturn's rings. In 1613 Galileo published *Dialogue on the Two Great Systems of the World* in which he reported his observations verifying that the sun is the center of the universe (thereby publicly confirming the theory of the universe the Polish astronomer Copernicus had set forth in 1543). Fisher's large black-and-white acrylic paintings of Galileo and his contemporaries are forceful and elegant. They dramatize most effectively Galileo's staunchness and defiance as well as the seriousness and severity that typified the era in which he lived. Because Galileo's stance on the universe contradicted that of the hierarchy of the Roman Catholic Church he was ordered to Rome to appear before the Holy Office of the Inquisition and in 1633 was forced to retract his findings and confined to his home. By publishing *Discourses and Mathematical Demonstrations Concerning Two New Sciences* in 1638, he in essence recanted his retraction. A "Chronology of Galileo (1564–1642)" includes information about his birth, education, experiments, publications, conflicts with the Catholic Church, and death. In an afterword entitled "More About Galileo," Fisher provides more information about the conflict between Galileo and the Catholic Church over this issue, noting that it was not until more than three hundred years later (July 1984) that he Pontifical Academy of Sciences in Rome finally took steps to clear Galileo, acknowledging that he was not guilty of spreading beliefs that were contrary to Church teachings.

Sis, Peter

STARRY MESSENGER: GALILEO GALILEI   *10–13 YEARS*

Illustrated by Peter Sis. New York: Frances Foster/Farrar, Straus & Giroux, 1996.

At first glance this looks like a very simple account of Galileo's life, but in actual fact it is an amazingly sophisticated book! Galileo's life story is told through the interplay between the main text, the secondary text, and the illustrations, which one might say constitute a third text. A minimal amount of biographical information about Galileo, which appears to be the main text, is presented in primary-sized type and can be read in a very few minutes. The secondary text, which is presented in handwritten script, provides a chronology of facts, dates, and quotations from Galileo's own writing about how his construction of the first complete astronomical telescope enabled him to make observations that led him to verify his heliocentric view, which contradicted the Church's teaching that the earth is the center of the universe. His publications on the subject led ultimately to his trial by the Pope's court and sentence to live the rest of his life under house arrest. The secondary text is very dense and mind-stretching, demanding careful reading and mature thinking. The illustrations (the "third text") support and extend the first and secondary texts immensely, but in order to recognize this the reader must be able to recognize and interpret the numerous sophisticated figurative visuals, which introduce profound metaphorical and psychological images and symbols emphasizing that Galileo's view on this matter was and remains valid and correct.

INVENTIONS AND TECHNOLOGY

Baker, Christopher W.

LET THERE BE LIFE: ANIMATING WITH THE COMPUTER   *10 YEARS–ADULTHOOD*

Illustrated. New York: Walker, 1997.

Children and adults who are computer literate will be delighted with this carefully organized and well-written step-by-step explanation of how the computer is used to create animation for everything from Saturday morning cartoons to smash hit special effects production films like Disney's *Toy Shop, Jurassic Park,* and *Terminator 2.* Baker begins his discussion by describing the "old fashioned" animation process first used in 1920 by Walt Disney, "the father of traditional animation," to make his first animated film *Steamboat Willie,* which introduced Mickey Mouse. Disney's first feature-length animation of the now classic *Snow White and the Seven Dwarfs* followed a number of years later. Baker then moves on to explain the computer graphics process invented in the early 1960s by Ivan Sutherland of MIT. Although this new science of computer graphics launched an entire industry, it proved too costly and time-consuming, and the software proved too complex and error-laden. Finally, in the 1980s came the computer animation process as we know it today, with its three-dimensional qualities realized through a process called "modeling." Baker describes two changes computer animation is likely to bring about. One, it will change the economics of filmmaking, making possible kinds of films that might not otherwise be made. Two, as interactive technologies (e.g., virtual realities and simulation) become more sophisticated, computer animation will allow the audience to play a part in a story and affect the outcome. Most of the illustrations are accompanied by informative captions, expanding on the data provided in the body of the text, and sometimes defining terms used but not defined in the text. Amazingly, no glossary is included—a serious omission for so technical and complicated a subject. Nor is there a table of contents. Fortunately, the topics covered are easily identified by large-sized headings, but readers, especially those who already have considerable knowledge about some aspects of computer animation, still have to flip through the entire book to find topics of special interest to them. An index is appended.

Erlbach, Arlene

THE KIDS' INVENTION BOOK   *7–10 YEARS*

Illustrated with photographs by Nancy Smedstad.
Minneapolis: Lerner, 1997.

The brief introduction tells readers that in past years children have created some inventions that were noteworthy, and that children in today's world and in the future are perfectly capable of creating inventions that will improve substantially something that already exists or will create things that are entirely new. Following this inspirational pep talk is a section containing profiles of thirteen children between the ages of eight and fourteen who invented something. Two pages of text embellished with photographs of the young inventor and a model of his or her invention are devoted to each profile. The next section includes a checklist of the eleven steps one should follow to create an invention and a list of the names and addresses of groups or organizations that sponsor invention contests. The kind of recognition (award) offered and the major focus each sponsor has specified are indicated. This section also includes a list of "Winning Tips" for aspiring contest participants. The next section includes a brief description of the three kinds of patents available: utility patents, design patents, and plant patents. In the last section, the readers are advised about how to meet other children interested in inventing and ways they can share their ideas and invent together. A fine bibliography of books that provide additional information about inventing and inventors is included. *Brainstorm! The Stories of Twenty American Kid Inventions,* written by Tom Tucker and illustrated by Richard Loehle (Starburst/Farrar, Straus & Giroux, 1998) is another invaluable resource that looks at some of the surprising inventions that have come from American young people ranging in age from five to nineteen over more than two hundred years.

Fisher, Leonard Everett

ALEXANDER GRAHAM BELL   *7–10 YEARS*

Illustrated by Leonard Everett Fisher. New York: Atheneum, 1999.

> Fisher's carefully crafted text and strikingly expressive full-page black-and-white acrylic paintings provide younger readers a thoroughly convincing portrayal of Alexander Graham Bell as one of the greatest scientists and humanitarians whose life bridged the last half of the nineteenth century and the first quarter of the twentieth century. The chronology of Bell (1845–1922) that appears in the front of the book on the copyright page will alert the readers to the many and varied accomplishments credited to this well-known and highly respected personality. Fisher's treatment of Bell's incredibly diverse accomplishments is fairly skeletal, but the dramatic manner in which he tells his readers about each of them and the artful manner in which his visuals depict Bell in action, provides the right depth and breadth of information for young readers. This account of Bell's life and varied achievements may serve as an excellent motivator, leading readers to check out other sources that will provide more information about Bell's specific inventions and technological innovations and his efforts to assist the hearing and speech impaired. Unfortunately, a bibliography suggesting books for further reading is not provided.

Marzollo, Jean

THE CAMERA: SNAPSHOTS, MOVIES, VIDEOS, AND CARTOONS   *7–10 YEARS*

Translated from the French by Jennifer Riggs. Illustrated by Pierre-Marie Valat. New York: Scholastic, 1993.

> Like the other books in the First Discovery Book series this is a sturdy little book and can withstand the wear and tear it will certainly be exposed to because it is one that will be read and reread. Children are delighted with the brightly colored transparent pages, for each time they turn one of the "magic" pages, they get to see their subject from a different perspective. For example, when they peel back transparent pages they will see such things as how the insides of a camera works

and the step-by-step process of how a film is developed and printed. Children are intrigued when they learn how animated films are made and are surprised to find out that there are so many different kinds of cameras available today. The text is easy to read and illustrations are simple, attractive, and colorful. Marzollo authored the American edition of this book. It was originally published in France under the title *L'Image*, by Editions Gallimard Jeunesse in 1992.

Sandler, Martin W.

INVENTORS   *8–12+ YEARS*

Introduction by James H. Billington, Librarian of Congress.
Illustrated with photographs from the Library of Congress.
New York: HarperCollins, 1996.

This volume in the Library of Congress Book series presents a wealth of information about how great inventors in America's history came up with discoveries and inventions that changed life as we know it. There is no table of contents; the topic sections, which are designated by large, bold-faced type, are based on general categories, few of which will be meaningful to most children. Once the children actually begin to read each of these sections, there is little or no doubt they will be keenly interested. For example, in the section entitled "Products of Inventions," the discussion of the impact of Samuel F. B. Morse's telegraph pertains to the communication revolution, especially how the telegraph affected the development of a national railroad system, the way the Civil War was fought, and the ability of newspapers throughout the nation to report events in a timely manner. The section entitled "World's Greatest Inventor" is devoted to Thomas Alva Edison's remarkable variety of inventions and some of the accomplishments by people he employed in his "invention factory" at Menlo Park, New Jersey. In the section entitled "Hothouse of Activity" a vast variety of inventions patented by the United States Patent Office between 1860 and 1890 are discussed. Most of these inventions never made it into the marketplace, but ultimately variants of them did. For example, the flying machine with a vertical liftoff led to the distinguishing characteristics of modern helicopters, and a device called a pedespeed is comparable to today's in-line skates. Among the successful innovators who were acknowledged at the Centennial Exposition in Philadelphia (1876) were Cyrus McCormick, inventor of the mechanical reaper; Elisha Otis, inventor of the elevator; George Westinghouse, developer of the air brake; and Alexander Graham Bell, who introduced the telephone. And so it goes throughout the book, up to contemporary times with the American inventive spirit described as being not only very much alive, but "almost commonplace." The inventions discussed at this point include such things as the computer, the fax machine, and instant photography as well as the inventions that enable outer space travel and explorations.

There are over one hundred illustrations, which are reproductions from newspapers, book covers, posters, magazine, etchings, and engravings; none of them are supplemented or even explained by the presence of captions. The index is fairly comprehensive and helps to alleviate the lack of a table of contents and the need for more self-explanatory or meaningful section headings.

TRANSPORTATION

Land Transportation

Barton, Byron

TRUCKS   *6 MONTHS–3 YEARS*

Illustrated by Byron Barton. New York: HarperCollins, 1986, 1998.

> An effective board book both visually and verbally! Modern trucks are described and shown doing their jobs. The text is presented in complete simple sentences, which is a rarity in concept books for infants and toddlers but the best technique one can possibly use to foster early and effective language development. The illustrations are simple drawings in crisp, bright, flat colors and are outlined in heavy black lines. Other board books in this series depicting modes of transportation, created by Byron Barton and published by HarperCollins, are: *Boats* (1986, 1998), *Planes* (1986, 19998), and *Trains* (1986, 1998).

Kay, Verla

IRON HORSES   *7–10 YEARS*

Illustrated by Michael McCurdy. New York: Putnam, 1999.

> Sparse rhyming text embellished with striking double-page and single-page art, done in accomplished scratchboard and watercolor-wash, documents the construction of the transcontinental railroad during the last half of the 1860s. After the passing of the Pacific Railroad Act by Congress in 1862, the Central Pacific Railroad began working eastward from Sacramento, California, on January 8, 1863, and the Union Pacific Railroad began working westward from Omaha, Nebraska, on November 5, 1865. In May 19, 1869, the tracks were joined at Promontory Summit, Utah. The information-filled illustrations depict both highly skilled professionals and laborers involved in the major steps of this notable project. Especially noteworthy are scenes of the men working at

the backbreaking tasks of installing the ties and rails, building trestles and laying the tracks on these overpasses, chipping and blasting away the massive rocky shale cliffs, clearing away snowdrifts and the ice formed by freezing rain, and cutting tunnels through granite mountains. There are also scenes of men and women taking time out to engage in dancing and other pleasures, the ceremony celebrating the joining of the tracks from east to west, and, finally, a woman alighting from the train after having supposedly travelled from Missouri to California, a trip that previously took up to six months but could now be completed in six days. A simple map on the last page shows the route and terrain the railroad tracks followed from Sacramento to Omaha.

Keenan, Sheila, *Adapter*

BIKES, CARS, TRUCKS, AND TRAINS   9–14+ YEARS

Translated from the French by Nicole Valaire. Illustrated. New York: Scholastic, 1997.

> This amazing innovative book in the Scholastic Voyages of Discovery series shows the reader how through history human beings have traveled on land; it is the ultimate in interactive books for children. There is a wealth of information to be learned by reading the text, but additional information can be acquired by carefully examining the amazing art and utilizing the array of interactive elements in the book—lifting the flaps, opening the foldouts, turning transparent pages to see the interiors and exteriors of various vehicles, and even completing illustrations by adding reusable vinyl stickers in the right places. The last thirteen pages contain additional valuable information: a bibliography of books for further reading, names and addresses of a variety of transportation museums, profiles of people who invented significant modes of transportation or considerably improved those already in existence, an extensive glossary, and an elaborate time line on modes of ground transportation from prehistoric times through the twentieth century. Originally published in France under the title *Sur les routes du monde* by Editions Gallimard Jeunesse in 1995.

Rex, Michael

MY FIRE ENGINE   3–5 YEARS

Illustrated by Michael Rex. New York: Henry Holt, 1999.

> As a little boy plays with his toy fire engine he imagines himself on his fire engine racing to put out a house fire, fighting the fire, saving people's lives and (at the very last minute) their pet snake. The text is

brief and easy to read. The large double-page expressionistic, slightly cartoon-style illustrations are done with pencil on paper and with hand-separated bright, rich primary colors and depict simply, but accurately, the firemen's clothes and equipment, the pumper engine and the aerial ladder truck, and the techniques used by the ladder truck crew and the pumper engine crew as they clear out the heat, smoke, and poison gas generated by the raging fire, spray water on the fire, rescue the family and then their pet, and finally gather their hose and other equipment and return to the fire station.

Water Transportation

Ballard, Robert D., and Rick Archbold

GHOST LINERS: EXPLORING THE WORLD'S   *9–13+ YEARS*
GREATEST LOST SHIPS

Illustrated by Ken Marschall. Boston: Madison Press/Little, Brown, 1998.

The ships focused on in this book and the dates they met their demise are the *RMS Titanic* (April 14, 1912); the *Empress of Ireland* (May 29, 1914); the *Lusitania* (May 7, 1915); the *HMS Britannic,* which was the *Titanic's* sister ship (November 21, 1916); and the *Andrea Doria* (July 25, 1956). Robert Ballard, the senior author of this excellent book, actually discovered and explored the ghostly wrecks of each of these five legendary ships to find out how and why they and their passengers met such tragic ends. The major theme of Ballard's dramatic and grim accounts of how each ship met its demise is that one should not put one's faith in machines, one should put one's faith in people. In his Epilogue Ballard writes, "Whenever human beings put too much faith in technology, they regret having done so. Each of the ghost liners chronicled in this book sank, at least in part, because the people who built and sailed them believed they were unsinkable. . . . The *Titanic* and the other ghost liners teach us that those who trust too much in their own creations will sooner or later run into an iceberg. In our own time the iceberg may be a continent-wide power blackout or a nuclear meltdown" (pp. 60–61).

The illustrations include full-color reproductions of photographs and paintings of the interiors and exteriors of the liners before and after they sank, as well as photographs surviving passengers took with them and archival materials (posters, objects and mementos found among the sunken ships, newspaper clippings, etc.). The back matter includes a short glossary, excellent but separate bibliographies of books for further reading recommended for children and adults, and a list citing the credits each of the numerous pictures in the prologue, the five chapters, and the epilogue. On the endpapers is a monochromatic print showing the departure of the *Titanic* on its maiden voyage from Southampton port on April 10, 1917. This kind of illustration is in keeping with the title of this book—it exudes the aura of doom emphasized in the major theme of the book and Ballard's accounts of his explorations of each of the sunken ships. Compare *Ghost Liners* with David Macaulay's *Ship* (Houghton Mifflin, 1993).

In the summer of 1999 Ballard was planning an expedition to the Black Sea to search for the remains of Noah's Ark. According to an article in *The Detroit News* (March 9, 1999), his interest in this project was spurred by the findings of William Ryan and Walter Pitman, geophysicists at Columbia University and authors of *Noah's Flood: The Scientific Discoveries about the Events That Changed History* (Simon & Schuster, 1999).

Fields, Sadie

SAILING SHIPS: A LIFT-THE-FLAP DISCOVERY   *7–11 YEARS*

Illustrated by Thomas Bayley. Paper Engineering by Nat Johnstone.
New York: Orchard, 1997.

The reader is provided with a wealth of information about significant aspects of seven sailing ships—the *Santa Maria, Mayflower, La Boudeuse, Batavia, Endeavour, Victory,* and *Galveston.* Each ship is pictured in a double-page, full-color, realistic painting and flaps that, when lifted, show fascinating and invaluable cutaway views of the inside of the ships. Some of the text is always visible on the two pages devoted to each ship, and some of it is visible only when the flaps are lifted. Through an excellent combination of text and illustrations the reader learns a great deal of information about each ship's structure, voyages, passengers, crew, cargo, kind of weaponry or armor, living conditions, supplies, and the significant historical events the ship and its crew were involved in or associated with. Undoubtedly, some students will come to this book already having considerable knowledge about some or most of these sailing ships; for others, it will be their first introduction to this information. Regardless of their previous knowledge, the effective approaches the creators of this book used in the text and in the illustrations to present the information are likely to whet readers' curiosity and interest so they will want to learn more about aspects of this subject. Unfortunately, they will have to go to other sources for leads on more information about aspects of interest to them, for neither an index nor a bibliography of books recommended for further reading is included.

Harness, Cheryl

MARK TWAIN AND THE QUEENS OF THE MISSISSIPPI   *8–11 YEARS*

Illustrated by Cheryl Harness. New York: Simon & Schuster, 1998.

> The biographical sketch of Mark Twain (Samuel Clemens), noted American author, humorist, journalist, and lecturer, focuses on his fascination with the Mississippi River and the rise and demise of the steamboats that sailed on it. The illustrations, rendered in watercolor and colored pencil, are varied in size, perspective, and illustrative purpose. Two large impressionistic paintings, which are stunning panoramic scenes of the Mississippi River at night in the light of a full moon, are especially noteworthy: One picture depicts flatboats, broadhorns, skiffs, and rafts full of people and cargo floating on the water-road at night. The other picture shows a modern-day barge pushed by a diesel-powered tugboat moving slowly along a dredged-out channel of the river as a long freight train on the parallel shore speeds past it and an array of lighted office buildings, factories, and apartments rise up in the background and trucks and cars speed along the bridge that spans the river; a thin white trail of a jet can be seen high overhead. Together these two paintings dramatize most effectively one of the themes proclaimed by the author of this picture book: "Same river, but different now." On the last page, one will find a bibliography listing five books about Mark Twain or the Mississippi River that children might find interesting; there is also a list of Twain's many books, indicating the original publication dates. Children can find out more about Samuel Clemens as a young adventurer (before he became known as Mark Twain, the author) by reading *A Brilliant Streak: The Making of Mark Twain,* written by Kathryn Lasky and illustrated by Barry Moser (Harcourt Brace, 1998). His experiences piloting steamboats on the Mississippi River and other youthful adventures that influenced his entire life and are referred to in his writing are described in this well-written and attractively illustrated partial biography.

Kroll, Steven

ROBERT FULTON: FROM SUBMARINE TO STEAMBOAT   *7–10 YEARS*

Illustrated by Bill Farnsworth. New York: Holiday House, 1999.

> A few basic facts are included in this biographical sketch about Robert Fulton's childhood: his recurring battle with tuberculosis, his talents and accomplishments as a painter and civil engineer, and his failed attempts at inventing a submarine with a torpedo delivery system while living in France and England. The major accomplishments focused on in this book pertain to his efforts to build a steamboat. He did manage to build a version of a steamboat in 1803, but that sank in the river Seine.

About two years after he moved back to America, he finally did succeed in building one in 1807. This was named simply "The Steamboat," and on its maiden voyage on August 17, 1807, it traveled 150 miles, from near State's Prison in New York City to Albany, in thirty-two hours, a trip that usually took sloops and schooners four days. It should be noted that Fulton did not invent the steamboat, but he did manage to combine the right features and produce a commercial success. "The Steamboat" was renamed *North River* and when it was rebuilt it was described as a heavier, wider "floating palace"; it had three cabins, fifty-four berths, a kitchen, and a bar. Over the many years he built twenty-one new boats and brought the steamboat (named the *New Orleans*) to the Mississippi. He also built ferries to cross the Hudson and East Rivers and during the War of 1812 he convinced Congress to let him build the first steam-powered warship, named the *Demologos.* The illustrations, somewhat suggestive of Fulton's style of painting, nicely highlight the facts presented in this expository-styled text.

Maass, Robert

TUGBOATS   *5–8 YEARS*

Illustrated with photographs by Robert Maass. New York: Henry Holt, 1997.

The information included in this photo-essay about the workings of tugboats reflect what Maass learned as he traveled on waterways around the United States, from the east coast to the west coast, to experience tugboat life firsthand and to interview tugboat crews. The text is easy to read and sufficiently comprehensive to acquaint children with the roles these "mighty workhorses of the water" play in helping the shipping industry operate efficiently and safely. The full-color photographs, many of which are full page or larger, reveal explicitly what the wheelhouse, the various controls in the engine room, and the equipment look like and the purposes served by each of them. The crew members are shown carrying out their designated tasks.

Marschall, Ken

INSIDE THE TITANIC: A GIANT CUTAWAY BOOK   *7–14+ YEARS*

Illustrated with paintings by Ken Marschall and photographs. Boston:
Little, Brown, 1997.

Revealing and choice paintings of cutaway views of the *Titanic* include a spectacular four-page spread illustration (measuring 42½"x 14½") that depicts a cutaway view of the entire span of the *Titanic* and small paintings showing close-up views, including the ship's first- and second-

91

class staterooms and third-class cabins, first- and third-class dining saloons, a double-page spread of the rescue of the passengers in the lifeboats by the crew of the RMS *Carpathia,* and a one-and-one-third-page spread of the ship's bow flooding shortly after hitting the iceberg. A number of fine photographs are also included: some of the first- and third-class passengers who are focused on in this account of the ill-fated voyage, some of the crew members, and parts of the ship such as the first-class promenade, the Grand Staircase, the boiler room, the swimming pool and gymnasium, and the kitchens. The book is divided into four sections: Sailing Day (Wednesday, April 10, 1912), A Quiet Sunday (April 14, 1912), Sunday Evening (April 14, 1912, 1:40 P.M.), and The Rescue (Monday, April 15, 1912, 4:30 A.M.).

Actually, the amount of print is quite minimal, but a vast amount of additional information is offered in the content of many of the paintings and photographs provided. The book ends with brief summary statements on two topics that might be of special interest to young readers: One, what happened to the members of the families focused on in this account who survived the disaster, and two, the discovery of the remains of the wrecked *Titanic* by the explorer Dr. Robert Ballard in 1986, its bow and stern in sections lying 1,970 feet apart, more than two miles beneath the sea. The back matter includes a glossary of nautical terms, a bibliography of titles recommended for further reading, a list of credits for the photographs, and acknowledgments.

McCurdy, Michael

THE SAILOR'S ALPHABET   *7–9 YEARS*

Illustrated by Michael McCurdy. Boston: Houghton Mifflin, 1998.

An excellent multidimensional informational picture book in every respect; each aspect of sailing is cleverly, logically, and artfully connected! Furthermore, across the top of each page a nautical term associated with a frigate is named in a line from a variation of an alphabet forecastle chantey (song/ditty), created by an unknown sailor sometime in the 1800s. This term is defined at the bottom of the page. Details of an encounter between a United States frigate and a pirate vessel that took place around 1837 are depicted in the middle of each page, and the nautical term defined on that page is depicted in the illustration. At the end of the book is a drawing of a United States Navy frigate; each part of the ship that is defined earlier in the book is identified by its initial letter and a descriptive key is provided. The illustrations, done in scratchboard and hand-tinted with watercolor, depict the details of the encounter between the crews of the frigate and the pirate ship. They are action filled and wonderfully expressive; they embody all of the necessary qualities of visual storytelling. The Illustrator's Note at the end of the book provides some historical information about the United States Navy frigate illustrated in this book and about frigates in general. McCurdy notes that the twenty-six stars on the American flag flying on the frigate shown in this book establish that the action depicted in his visual interpretation of the chantey takes place during or shortly after 1837. He said at the time there were sixteen active frigates in the United States, and pirates were still a hazard in the Caribbean and even off the shores of New London, Connecticut.

Rockwell, Anne

FERRYBOAT RIDE   *4–7* YEARS

Illustrated by Maggie Smith. New York: Crown, 1999.

> Expressionistic and cartoon-style line and watercolor-wash illustrations are combined with an easy-to-read text to depict details of what proves to be an exhilarating experience for an alert and active little girl when she and her family take a ferryboat ride to their island summer home. Like the protagonist of this book, the reader will be impressed with the great variety of smells and sounds one can experience even during a short ferryboat ride. The design and format vary considerably from page to page: the illustrator uses full pages and double-page spreads to show close-ups and panoramic views; she encloses the pictures in circular and rectangular shapes varying widely in size. The endpapers display a variety of things one might see on the ferryboat, in the water, or on the shore of the lake.

Weitzman, David

OLD IRONSIDE: AMERICANS BUILD A FIGHTING SHIP   *9–12* YEARS

Illustrated by David Weitzman. Boston: Houghton Mifflin, 1997.

> The year was 1793; the nation was young, impoverished and exhausted by the Revolutionary War, and eleven merchant ships had been seized by Algerian pirates. When the twelfth merchant ship, *Polly,* out of Newburyport, Massachusetts, bound for Cadiz, Spain, was seized by pirates, its crew was imprisoned, and the pirates were demanding an incredibly high ransom, President George Washington and most members of Congress realized they needed a fleet to protect American merchant ships and their crews. So Washington commissioned the building of six naval warships, the first of which was the *Constitution.* Weitzman describes the ship's construction in considerable detail, some of which is quite technical, starting with the model making, design transfer, wood selection, use of copper sheeting, forging of cannon, rigging and arming the ship. Weitzman names many people in this account, some

of whom were historical figures actually involved in planning, designing, and overseeing the frigate's construction (e.g., the ship's designer, John Humphreys) and others whom he made up (e.g., the construction chief and his son). There is no fictionalizing in the content of any of the many authentic and detailed draftsmanlike line drawings. In fact, Weitzman explains clearly and precisely in the acknowledgments his sources for fine points of the *Constitution*'s construction. Compare with David Macaulay's *Ship* (Houghton Mifflin, 1993).

Air Transportation

Joseph, Lynn

FLY, BESSIE, FLY   *7–10 YEARS*

Illustrated by Yvonne Buchanan. New York: Simon & Schuster, 1998.

> This picture-book biography about Bessie Coleman, the first black woman in the world and the first black American to earn a pilot's license, is bound to inspire many young readers of all races regardless of gender. This life story highlights Coleman's exuberance and her unrestrained determination, fearless ambition, and above all, her conviction that "We are all born the same under God's eyes." The dramatic content of the oversized crisp, clean watercolor illustrations dramatize most effectively these important traits of this remarkable African-American heroine. (See illustration 6.) The author's note on the last page contains more specific facts about her career as a daredevil stunt flyer and a short bibliography of books about Coleman and other women aviators.

Seymour, Tres

OUR NEIGHBOR IS A STRANGE, STRANGE MAN   *5–9 YEARS*

Illustrated by Walter Lyon Krudop. New York: Orchard, 1999.

> Whimsical, expressionist paintings rendered in gouache are a perfect match for this very skeletal biography of purportedly eccentric Melville Murrell, who invented the first human-powered airplane to take flight. He built it in 1876, and called it "The Great American Flying Machine." With the help of a farmhand and friend, John Cown, the plane flew several yards! Murrell received a patent for it on August 14, 1877—when Wilbur Wright was ten years old and Orville Wright was six years old. Children (and adults) will be surprised to learn that the Wright Brothers were not the first to invent the airplane. Those who are so inclined can probably see the model Murrell built of his plane, which is on display at Rose Center in Morristown, Tennessee. The actual plane is in storage at the Smithsonian Institution in Washington, D. C.

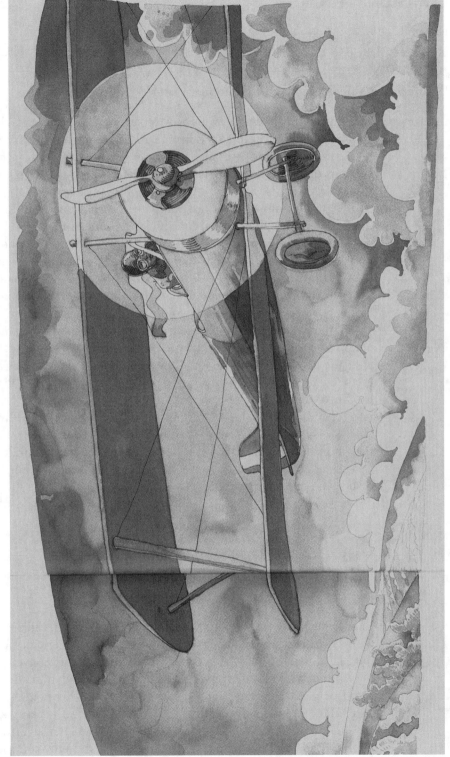

ILLUSTRATION 6 Reprinted with the permission of Simon & Schuster Books for Young Readers, an imprint of Simon & Schuster Children's Publishing Division from *Fly, Bessie, Fly* by Lynn Joseph, illustrated by Yvonne Buchanan. Illustrations copyright © 1998 Yvonne Buchanan.

COMMUNICATIONS

Kraus, Ronnie

TAKE A LOOK. IT'S IN A BOOK: HOW TELEVISION IS MADE   *7–10 YEARS*
AT "READING RAINBOW"

Illustrated with photographs by Christopher Hornsby. New York: Walker, 1997.

Viewers of the *Reading Rainbow* TV series will be intrigued by the step-by-step description of how the major segments of this popular television program are made. Decisions are made about each of the sections of the show through the cooperative and creative efforts of at least thirty people. Preparation of each program involves selecting the book(s) to be featured on a program; researching aspects of the book's theme; preparing the script; identifying the procedures to be followed by the crew, director, sound engineer, and make-up artist, and setting up videotapes of the "wraps" (wraparound segments during which the host of the program, Le Var Burton, will talk about the theme of the show, introduce the book, and lead into the segments taped on location); taping the on-site events related to the book's theme and the segment in which the book is discussed; and the selection, preparation, and taping of children giving reviews of books viewers might like to read. Finally, after the film editor has selected the best shots and close-ups and put them together, the sound effects and musical background are added and the thirty-minute program is ready for audience viewing. There is no table of contents, nor are the various topics discussed clearly divided or labeled. There are no captions accompanying the illustrations; however, they appear adjacent to the relevant portion of the text. A limited index is appended, which may prove helpful to readers searching for the discussion of a specific topic.

Morrison, Taylor

CIVIL WAR ARTIST   *8–11 YEARS*

Illustrated by Taylor Morrison. Boston: Walter Lorraine/Houghton Mifflin, 1999.

This is an intriguing account of how teams of artists and newspaper workers of the late 1800s, especially during the American Civil War, devised a way of delivering images of significant news events to the public and inadvertently provided us with a clear and dramatic glimpse into the past. Morrison's lucid text and accomplished expressive line and full-color wash illustrations document how an artist's sketch of an American Civil War battle or other significant newsworthy event is processed from the time it leaves his hands and moves through the wood engravings and printing processes to its final publication in a newspaper. Today's young readers, so used to on-the-spot, live reporting of breaking news events, will find it surprising and hard to imagine that it took four weeks for readers to see the pictures of the latest events pertaining to this war or other major events. The comprehensive glossary appended at the back of the book should function as a helpful tool for meanings and descriptions of technical terms relating to the processes of duplicating the illustrations that appeared in newspapers.

Tunnell, Michael O.

MAILING MAY   *5–9 YEARS*

Illustrated by Ted Rand. New York: Greenwillow, 1997.

The true-life journey of a little girl mailed via parcel post in 1914 is described in this picture book. The illustration on the cover of the book gives much authentic historical information about the story. On February 19, 1914, five-year-old Charlotte May Pierstorff was mailed via parcel post from her home in the small town of Grangeville, Idaho, to Lewiston, Idaho, seventy-five miles away, for a visit with her grandmother because the family could not afford a train ticket ($1.55). The then-new parcel post service provided an inexpensive means of transportation and, at the time, there was no restriction against mailing humans. To meet qualifications, she was classified as a baby chick and weighed; the 53 cents in parcel post stamps was affixed to the back of her coat. (Leonard Mochel, the railway clerk on the Grangeville to Lewiston mail run, was a cousin of the girl's mother, so the child was not treated in a heartless, inhumane way.) Ted Rand's realistic, sepia-hued watercolor paintings reveal many details about the people who lived in this part of the United States at this time in history: clothing, hair styles, exterior designs of homes, home furnishings, the general store and railway station, and the "spidery" railway trestles, referred to as "steel on stilts," that spanned the mountain valleys, facsimiles of postage stamps issued at that time, even a departure and arrival schedule for the mail train, plus so many more other details. Rand's illustrations not only support and marvelously embellish the details of Tunnell's easy-to-read and brief text, but they enhance immeasurably and so proficiently the plausibility of this incredible historical event.

Finding New Worlds

EXPLORING THE EARTH

Johnstone, Michael

THE HISTORY NEWS: EXPLORERS   *8–10 YEARS*

Consultant Shane Einser. Maps prepared by David Atkinson. Illustrated.
Cambridge, Mass.: Candlewick, 1997.

Information is presented via a collection of "newspaper articles" reporting the explorations of men and women who, from 1500 B.C. through contemporary times, traveled into uncharted lands or sailed into unknown oceans. As with the other books in the History News series, everything about this book (except its hardcover binding) is suggestive of a newspaper: the style and tone in which the news items are reported, the off-white paper that resembles newsprint, and the formatting of the articles. Thus, the title of each article is in headline-style type, followed by a subheading consisting of a brief statement indicating the main thrust of the article and short sentences following the traditional style of who, what, where, when, and how or why, section headings, illustrations, and even advertisements. The content of the articles, illustrations, and advertisements appear to be factually correct. In the middle of the book is an excellent map of the world on which the routes of the major explorations between 1487 and 1895 are accurately identified. Throughout the book are numerous smaller, more detailed maps of the explorers' routes.

The last section, Where to Next?, indicates there are still challenges left on our planet for today's explorers. Nigel Winser of the Royal Geographical Society in Great Britain lists some: several hundred of the highest mountains located in many parts of the world have yet to be climbed; the ice caps that lie at the far north and south of the world have just begun to be explored in detail; the rooftop canopy of the tallest trees in the rain forest is still almost totally unexplored; scientists have found and named less than one in ten of all the species of plants and animals in the world; and we know very little about what the ocean floor is like and what lives there.

The time line in the back matter highlights the accomplishments of each of the explorations discussed in the book and serves as an excellent summary. The index appended should prove helpful. There is a list of sources used by the creators of this book, but there is no bibliography of children's books suggested for further reading, which is unfortunate because many of the students who read the unique "newspaper articles" about the explorers' experiences and accomplishments would certainly want to find out more about them and probably would appreciate some specific titles to look for the next time they visit their school or public library.

Markle, Sandra

PIONEERING FROZEN WORLDS   *8–11 YEARS*

Illustrated with photographs. New York: Atheneum, 1998.

> The latest in Markle's series on pioneering, this book promotes the development of scientific inquiry in general and, more specifically, of procedures for gathering information about the Earth's frozen polar regions, Antarctica and the Arctic, through numerous easy-to-implement scientifically sound activities. There does not seem to be any logic to the sequence of the topics, but readers who have specific rather than general questions or interests about the frozen polar regions may find the index helpful. The full-color photographs aptly depict conditions related to the polar regions and to the questions and problems the activities in the book demonstrate and explain.

Steger, Will, and Jon Bowermaster

OVER THE TOP OF THE WORLD: *9–14 YEARS*
EXPLORER WILL STEGER'S TREK ACROSS THE ARCTIC

Sidebars by Barbara Horbeck. Illustrated with photographs.
New York: Scholastic, 1997.

> Steger and his team's dogsled and canoe-sled journey from Siberia, over the North Pole, and into Canada is an engrossing and tension-filled

account related in journal entries dated March 9, 1995, through July 3, 1995. The team started their journey with six persons (four men and two women) and thirty-three dogs on the edge of the Arctic Ocean at the Siberian coast of Russia. The beginning of the expedition proved to be a false start. The very first day they met with adversities: the ice was unstable, the visibility was at zero, a vicious storm came up, and one of the men on the team almost lost his life when his lead dog dragged him and the other ten dogs in his sled-team over the shaky ice into the deep cold ocean. The explorers decided to go back to land and set up camp near Cape Artichesky where they waited for the gap between the open water and the main pack ice to freeze. The team member who had the brush with death decided to quit the expedition and to take his eleven dogs with him.

In March 21, nine days after they arrived at Cape Artichesky, a Russian helicopter ferried them back to their Russian base camp where they reorganized, repacked, and replanned their expedition. On April 2, five teammates, twenty-two dogs, three sleds, and their gear were taken by Russian helicopter over the three hundred miles of open water and unstable ice between Siberia and the hard pack of the Arctic Ocean. The next day they were on their way again on the ice of the Arctic headed toward Canada. They reached the North Pole exactly as they planned originally—on Earth Day, April 22, 1995. This portion of their trip was challenging, but definitely not as catastrophic as the beginning nor as difficult as the next part of the expedition, which began April 27, 1995. This next portion was during the spring and summer and it was an almost constant battle between the explorers and the water and ice and the deep, sticky snow, the scorching hot sun and the cold temperatures (especially at night). The final resupply plane arrived June 16 on a great iceberg surrounded on all sides by water seventy-five miles from the peaks of Northern Ellesmore Island. After two trips, the dogs were taken out and three canoe-sleds were unloaded as were food and a new team member who was to help with the canoe-hauling. The going was arduous and strenuous: the canoes were heavy, traveling over the deep snow drifts and through blowing snowstorms was slow and hazardous. On July 3, they landed on Ward Hunt Island—three miles off Ellesmore Island in Canada and were picked up by a plane.

The full-color photographs vary in size and include full-page close-up views as well as striking panoramic scenes; all of them add considerably to the dramatic journalistic account of the expedition. The table of contents lists enticing chapter headings indicating each phase of the expedition, a prologue, which describes what motivated Steger to plan and undertake the expedition, and an epilogue in which he addresses the role computers and transmitters played in enabling the team to report daily to the International Arctic Project headquarters in St. Paul,

Minnesota, and communicate with schools throughout the world. Sad to say, one will not find a glossary, index, or recommendations for further reading.

EXPLORING SPACE

Fraser, Mary Ann
ONE GIANT LEAP   *8–10 YEARS*
Illustrated by Mary Ann Fraser. New York. Henry Holt, 1993.

Technical details were carefully selected from air-to-ground transcripts of the NASA Apollo 11 flight and the book *Apollo 11 Moon Landing* by David J. Sayler (London: Ian Allen, 1989) and put together by Fraser to recreate the first space flight to the moon, culminating in Neal Armstrong's first step onto its surface, followed shortly by fellow astronaut Edwin E. "Buzz" Aldrin Jr. The step-by-step actions, described in diary entries, begin on July 16, 1969. They very briefly describe how the families of the astronauts and other spectators waited anxiously, how the astronauts, each in position to carry out his assigned tasks, were strapped in place, clearance was given for takeoff, the towering space vehicle cleared the launchpad, rose above the earth's atmosphere, and sped toward the moon. Exactly 109 hours, 24 minutes and 15 seconds into the mission, with Aldrin guiding him, Armstrong stepped off the Eagle's landing pad, placed the first human footprint on the moon, and uttered his memorable statement, "That's one small step for man, one giant leap for mankind." The author mentions in the section entitled "Beyond the First Steps," which appears in the back matter, that while on the lunar surface Armstrong and Aldrin completed some important experiments designed to answer specific questions about our moon and the solar system. Having accomplished their mission, they blasted off in the top half of their lunar module "Eagle," rejoined Collins in the *Columbia,* and on Thursday, July 24, 1969, safely splashed down in the Pacific Ocean.

Through skill, courage, and teamwork astronauts Neil Armstrong, "Buzz" Aldrin, and Michael Collins helped bring to fruition the contributions of numerous physicists and other scientists to realize the dreams of people worldwide for untold centuries to not only visit the moon, but to accomplish a first step in the exploration of other planets and other solar systems. Fraser states that landing on the moon is considered by many to be humanity's greatest scientific achievement, but she also reminds her readers that, since the moon landing, scientists and world leaders have come to realize that no single nation can explore the unknown; international teamwork for space explorations is our only option. Excellent realistic paintings in full color and accomplished diagrams of particular parts of the Apollo 11/Saturn V rocket and the Apollo 11 spacecraft, which consisted of the Columbia command module (CM) and Eagle lunar module (LM), a pictorial graph and time line showing the various space shuttles launched from 1957 to 1967 by Russia, the United States, and France, all prove immensely helpful in making this sophisticated scientific achievement more understandable and more fully appreciated by children. A useful glossary is appended. Compare with *Man on the Moon,* written by Anastasia Suen and illustrated by Benrei Huang (Viking, 1997).

Ride, Sally, with Susan Okie

TO SPACE AND BACK   *9–13* YEARS

Illustrated with photographs. New York: Lothrop, Lee & Shepard, 1986, 1989.

Superb full-page and half-page illustrations reproduced in rich full color extend and supplement United States Astronaut Sally Ride's exciting and free-flowing personal account of her space flight that started with the launch of the shuttle in June 1983 and circled the earth for several days. The photographs, most of which were taken by Ride and the other four astronauts on board the shuttle, reveal very well how their activities were affected by weightlessness and how they anchored themselves and their food and equipment to keep them from floating around or over in a slow motion somersault in the space ship. For example, she describes how the astronauts prepared meals for each other and how they managed to eat their food before it floated off of their spoon or out of the carton in which it was stored and prepared; how they disposed of the trash that accumulated each day; where and how they slept, since there were no beds in the space shuttle; how they washed themselves, brushed their teeth, combed their hair, and used the toilet, since they did not have a sink, bathtub, or shower; why they did not wear boots or shoes while in orbit; how they did the necessary housekeeping chores each day to keep the computer terminals and the air in the shuttle clean; what each astronaut's position was on the shuttle and the kind of scientific experiments they conducted in space during their flight; and finally, how they prepared for and carried out a space walk. All this information and more is presented in a child-oriented manner that is not the least bit patronizing or demeaning. The author notes in the foreword that the space shuttle *Challenger* exploded on January 28, 1986, just as this book was to go to press, and she dedicated it in the crew's memory. A comprehensive glossary and index are appended.

Children and Families

HUMAN GROWTH AND DEVELOPMENT

Beeler, Selby B.

THROW YOUR TOOTH ON THE ROOF:
TOOTH TRADITIONS FROM AROUND THE WORLD

5–9 YEARS

Illustrated by B. Brian Karas. Boston: Houghton Mifflin, 1998.

> Children in the kindergarten and early primary grades will be thoroughly fascinated and amused by the vast array of traditions that children from around the world "celebrate" when their milk (baby or primary) teeth fall out. In the last four pages the readers will find important facts about their teeth: the differences between their twenty baby teeth and thirty-two adult teeth, the parts of a tooth, the kinds of teeth and the function of each kind, and the position of each kind of tooth in the upper and lower jaws. Of interest to them, too, is the author's note at the end of the book in which she describes how she collected the traditions practiced by people from around the globe to represent both the variety and similarity of tooth customs everywhere. Cartoon-style illustrations created with gouache, acrylic, and pencil are perfect for this topic.

Hubbell, Patricia

POTS AND PANS   *6 MONTHS–2 YEARS*

Illustrated by Diane de Groat. New York: HarperCollins, 1998.

> Infants and toddlers can easily interpret and identify with the large, clean, attractive pictures and the simple verses in this concept book. They will surely be amused and will delight in using the pots and pans, their covers, and wooden spoons as noise makers in exactly the ways the verses and pictures in this book encourage them to! Be prepared, very young children will want this book read many, many times over, and I am certain they (and their parents) will quickly memorize it word-for-word!

Pragoff, Fiona

WHERE IS ALICE'S BEAR?   *1–3 YEARS*

Illustrated with photographs by Fiona Pragoff. Paper engineering by
Iain Smyth and Glynn Davies. New York: Doubleday, 1999.

> This is an upbeat pop-up book! There is a bright, full-color photograph of a child's toy on each page, and each time a page is turned the reader is presented with a surprise, for something pops up out of that toy. The toys shown include such things as a brightly colored paddle car big enough for a child to "drive," a baby buggy, a playhouse, and a baby's crib. Alice and the reader search for a missing teddy bear, which finally pops up in the most logical place. (Logical, that is, from an adult's perspective!) Even though children will most assuredly remember what pops up out of each toy after the first reading of this book, they will want to see the action occur over and over.

SELF AND FAMILY

Adoption

D'Antonio, Nancy

OUR BABY FROM CHINA: AN ADOPTION STORY   *5–10 YEARS*

Illustrated with photographs by Nancy D'Antonio and others.
Morton Grove, Ill.: Albert Whitman, 1997.

> This is a well-written personal account of the international and trans-racial adoption of Ariela Xiangwei, an orphaned baby girl born in a village near East China, by an American couple. The legal details are easy for children to understand, and the emotions experienced by tiny Ariela Xiangwei as well as her adoptive mother and father and grandparents are presented in a manner that children can conceptualize and

appreciate and perhaps even identify with. The text is supplemented and enriched considerably by the fine full-color snapshots.

Molnar-Fenton, Stephan

AN MEI'S STRANGE AND WONDROUS JOURNEY   *4–8 YEARS*

Illustrated by Vivienne Flesher. New York: Melanie Kroupa/DK Publishing, 1998.

> This is a true story of how a girl (An Mei) was born in China, left on the doorstep of an orphanage, brought to America, and adopted by the author and his wife. Although the story of how An Mei came to live with her adoptive parents is told from the perspective of six-year-old An Mei, the author actually began writing this book one year to the day after he returned from China to his home in Northampton, Massachusetts, with his infant daughter Angelica-Tao An Mei. The illustrations, rendered in pastels and wash, exude the theme and mood reflected in the name *An Mei,* which in Chinese means "beautiful peace," and love. In the note to the readers in the back matter, the author emphasizes that although this is An Mei's story, it is, in many ways, "the story of thousands of other babies of every country who have made the strange and wondrous journey to an adoptive family" (p. 28). He also tells some of the reasons parents put their children up for adoption, but he assures the readers that "usually their reasons involve wanting a better life for their child than they could provide." He discusses the "special circumstances" in China that lead many parents to give their children up for adoption. In keeping with his emphasis on the biological parents' love for them is his explanation of why An Mei's mother put a red dot on Mei's forehead just before she placed her on the doorstep of the orphanage. This red dot, he said, is a national symbol of love in China, and it was obviously her mother's prayer that An Mei's journey would lead her to a life of beauty and joy, which An Mei actually finds in her journey to her adoptive family in America.

Self-Concept

Cuyler, Margery

FROM HERE TO THERE   *4–8 YEARS*

Illustrated by Yu Cha Pak. New York: Henry Holt, 1999.

> This first-person, easy to read narrative, printed in heavy, black primary-sized type, is blended with double-page, childlike expressionistic illustrations rendered in rich, clean full-color watercolor and pastels. The matter-of-fact tone of the text leaves little room to doubt that this little Hispanic girl named Maria Mendoza (depicted as around eight or

nine years old) is self-sufficient and very secure in "her world," which includes her own home with her family, the street, town, county, state, country, continent, hemisphere, planet, solar system, galaxy, and the universe. Admittedly, the children who seem to be the targeted audience of this concept book tend to see themselves as the center of their world just as the young narrator seems to, so they would probably be quite comfortable with her perspective of self. It would be nice if the author would soon provide her readers with another book in which Maria is depicted in relationships with members of her family, special friends, other age-mates, and people of various ages she comes in contact with as she explores her place in her world. Both Maria and the readers of this book have to realize that no one exists as "an island, entire of itself," if they are to develop a valid, positive, and adequate concept of self!

English, Karen

NADIA'S HANDS   *6–10 YEARS*

Illustrated by Jonathan Weiner. Honesdale, Penn.: Boyds Mills, 1999.

This account details what happens when Nadia, a young Pakistani-American girl, finds that she will be in a position that will dramatize that once again she has to straddle two cultures. She recognizes that she has mixed feelings about having to live with her Pakistani culture, some aspects of which she understands and enjoys and respects, but she feels self-conscious about some of the practices her immigrant relatives follow that differ from those of her classmates' families. She is pleased that she is to be a flower girl in her aunt's wedding, but she knows that doing so will make her look—and thus feel—different from her classmates. It is a Pakistani custom for the bride and the flower girl to have a design called a *mendhi* applied to their hands with a henna paste and the henna gets darker the longer the paste is left on the skin. Nadia knows that the mendhi will still be on her hands when she goes back to school the Monday after the weekend wedding ceremony. She is right, for on Monday the mendhi on her hands is very obvious. The author's narrative skill combined with the illustrator's full-page expressionistic paintings done in bright, full-color oil pastels, document convincingly the roles played by the members of this loving extended family in preparing for the wedding celebration, the wedding itself, and Nadia's ambivalence about the mendhi. The manner in which Nadia's concerns about her classmates' response to this cultural practice are resolved will prove as satisfying to the readers of this credible story as it was to Nadia.

Kandel, Bethany

TREVOR'S STORY: GROWING UP BIRACIAL   *8–10 YEARS*

Illustrated with photographs by Carol Halebian and sketches
by John Erste. Minneapolis: Lerner, 1997.

>Ten-year-old Trevor Mark Sage-El begins his story by saying, "Once in
>a while someone asks me, 'What are you?' I usually answer, 'Human.'"
>As he continues his story, Trevor says, "...I am biracial. My mom,
>Margot, is white. My dad, Barry, is black. I am kind of a light tan
>color." (Interestingly, he does not use the terms *Caucasian* and *African
>American* to describe his parentage). In this first person narrative Trevor
>elaborates matter-of-factly about the joys and problems of being biracial,
>especially in terms of how that seems to affect his schoolmates, and how
>strangers react to him, his two sisters, and his parents when they are all
>together in public as well as when he is with just his mother or his
>father. Throughout the book light lavender pages alternate with darker
>lavender pages. The numerous full-color photographs of the family aptly
>support the tone and the content of Trevor's personal narrative. Several
>photographs show Trevor wearing in-line skates and skating alone or
>with other children. There is little doubt that at this point in his life
>his favorite sport activity is in-line skating! Soft gray ink sketches of
>Trevor's skates are superimposed on some of the darker lavender pages
>throughout the text; they never appear on the lighter-colored paper. (I
>am certain most children are bound to notice this eventually, but if
>there is a particular message or purpose for this element of the book
>design, I have missed it!) The tone of the book is a bit preachy, even a
>bit defensive at times, but it is nonetheless an honest, from-the-heart
>testimony of one biracial child's experiences and should be valued
>for that. The extensive back matter includes a glossary and a list of
>resources (with the names, mailing addresses, and e-mail addresses
>of support organizations, publishers of books about biracial children,
>exhibit materials, and promoters working to expand the use of the
>"multiracial" classification on official forms); bibliographies of books
>for further reading for children and adults are also included.

Senisi, Ellen B.

FOR MY FAMILY, LOVE, ALLIE   *4–7 YEARS*

Illustrated with photographs by Ellen B. Senisi. Morton Grove, Ill.:
Albert Whitman, 1998.

>Allie, the main character, is biracial—her mother is white and her father
>is Jamaican black. Every picture in this book clearly shows this is a
>biracial family. Allie's story focuses on a concern that will be familiar to

all young readers regardless of their racial or ethnic heritage: what can Allie (who is about age six or seven) make by herself as a present for each of her relatives when they come to her home for a big family party? After Allie's mother tells her that homemade food is always a special gift and does not need to be gift-wrapped, they look through a children's cookbook and her plight is solved. Allie, with her mom's approval, chooses a dessert recipe called "Peanut-Butter Treats." Allie's "present" to all her guests proves to be a smashing success. The numerous full-color photographs (both candid and posed) show Allie distributing her dessert treats to the guests, but they also depict, so very well, the supportive and pleasant relationships and interactions between Allie and the members of her immediate family (mom, dad, and siblings), as well as those between the many relatives from both sides of this biracial extended family. The recipe for Allie's Peanut-Butter Treats is included at the back of the book along with several other things adults and children (alone or together) can make to give to others.

Tarpley, Natasha Anastasia

I LOVE MY HAIR   *5–9 YEARS*

Illustrated by E. B. Lewis. Boston: Little, Brown, 1992.

A thoroughly credible delineation of up-and-down feelings the author recalls experiencing during her childhood when her mother combed and oiled her hair in the evening before she went to bed. The double-page spreads of the realistic watercolor paintings depict so very well the range of these emotions. (See illustration 7.) At the end of the book the narrator says with great pride, "I love my hair because it is thick as a forest, soft as cotton candy, and curly as a vine winding upward, reaching the sky and climbing toward outer space" (p. 22). Compare with *Nappy Hair,* written by Carolivia Herron and illustrated by Joe Cepeda (New York: Knopf, 1997).

Sibling Relationships

Aldape, Virginia Totorica

DAVID, DONNY, AND DARREN: A BOOK   *7–10 YEARS*
ABOUT IDENTICAL TRIPLETS

Illustrated with photographs by Lillian S. Kossacoff.
Minneapolis: Lerner, 1997.

Eight-year-old triplets from Escondido, California, share their experiences and insights about how they are similar to and yet dissimilar from

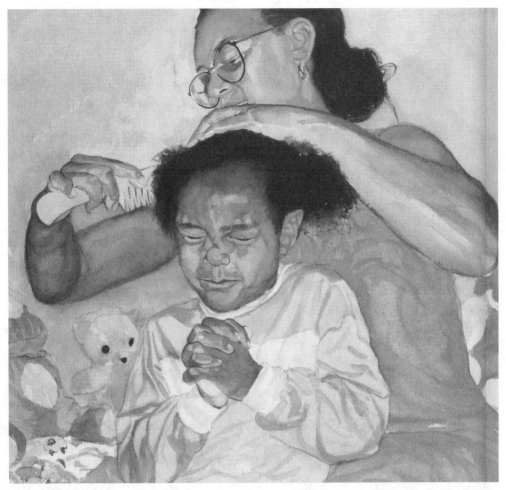

ILLUSTRATION 7   From *I Love My Hair* by Natasha Tarpley and E. B. Lewis. Copyright © 1997 by Natasha Tarpley (text); copyright © 1997 by E. B. Lewis (illustrations). By permission of Little, Brown and Company.

one another. They describe what their parents do in many different ways to assure them they are "individuals," even though they are "identical" triplets. The full-color photographs reveal most aptly the closeness of the triplets and aspects of their relationships with one another, with each of their parents, their younger brother Pauly, their grandmother, and their age-mates. The table of contents, glossary, and photo key should prove helpful to young readers, and the bibliography of resources for parents of triplets and twins should prove a useful ready reference, to parents.

Hiatt, Fred
BABY TALK   *5–8 YEARS*
Illustrated by Mark Graham. New York: Margaret McElderry, 1999.

> Carefully executed, yet free-flowing action-filled oil paintings in clear
> rich colors are done in a realistic, albeit romanticized style. Together
> with an easy-to-read dialogue they convincingly depict how Joey, ap-
> proximately age four, responds to the arrival of a new baby brother.
> Children will enjoy how Joey gradually learns to "translate" Baby's spe-
> cial language and develops a fondness for his baby brother. Eventually
> the two carry on a "conversation" that only the two of them seem to
> understand. The endpapers are attractively decorated with the same
> toys that appear in the illustrations throughout the book.

Schindel, John
FROG FACE: MY LITTLE SISTER AND ME   *3–8 YEARS*
Illustrated with photographs by Janet Delaney. New York: Henry Holt, 1998.

> Told from the perspective of the older sister, this is a straightforward
> statement of the joys and frustrations of having a younger sister. The
> photographs, some in full color and some in black-and-white, dovetail
> nicely with the verbal comments describing the gradual (very gradual!)
> development of interaction, trust, and mutual love between the two
> girls. The closing remarks by the older girl are the most telling about
> their relationship: "Jillian's lucky that I'm her sister. And even though
> we don't get along all the time and sometimes I want to sit on her, I'm
> lucky she's mine" (p. 29).

MEDICINE AND DISEASE

Gates, Phil
THE HISTORY NEWS: MEDICINE   *7–10 YEARS*
Illustrated. Cambridge, Mass.: Candlewick, 1997.

> Information is presented to simulate a newspaper that consists of a col-
> lection of "articles" reporting facts about major medical practices, dis-
> coveries, and inventions. This "news," which reflects on humankind's
> endless battle against disease, is arranged chronologically, from pre-
> historic times (8000 B.C.) through contemporary times (the late 1990s).
> Except for the fact that the "newspaper articles" are bound in hardcover,
> everything about the format and the style and tone of the writing is sug-
> gestive of a newspaper. The content of the articles, the illustrations, and
> even the things and services that are advertised in the ads are factually

authentic. The last section is a time line of the medical breakthroughs discussed throughout the book and serves as a fine summary. The table of contents is excellent; it is detailed and illustrated, so the readers should have no trouble figuring out the thrust of the topics listed in each section and approximately when in the history of humankind they took place. The illustrations should prove most helpful; in fact, I suspect most readers will find them quite intriguing. Some are reproductions of famous paintings and etchings, posters, old photographs, and copies of sketches that appeared in old medical texts. The variety and the content of the many illustrations and the accompanying captions add to the depth and breadth of the information about the field of medicine touched upon in this book. There is no bibliography of children's books recommended for further reading. That is unfortunate, because the content of this book and the manner in which it is presented is bound to whet the appetite of the readers enough to motivate them to head for their school or public library to seek out more information on one or more of the topics the author refers to. A helpful index is appended, as is a list of sources used in creating this unique overview of medicine.

Schulman, Arlene

CARMINE'S STORY: A BOOK ABOUT A BOY LIVING WITH AIDS   *7–10 YEARS*

Illustrated with photographs by Arlene Schulman. Minneapolis: Lerner, 1997.

The narrator of this touching story is ten-year-old Carmine. Born with AIDS, he describes in a straightforward manner how he got it and how the disease has shaped his day-to-day lifestyle. He speaks glowingly about the few years he was able to attend school and enjoy the companionship of age-mates, but seems accepting of the fact that he can still continue his education as he meets regularly with his home-school teacher, now that he is too weak and too ill to leave his home. His comments about his devotion to his grandmother (and her obvious devotion to him) and his dependence upon her as his primary caregiver and companion are wrenching to say the least. The black-and-white photographs help to make Carmine's story very real. That is as it should be perhaps, for all too often children and adults tend to think of this disease as one that primarily affects adults. Carmine's story, told as only Carmine could tell it, will certainly help to correct that misconception! The Epilogue informs the readers that Carmine died on July 13, 1996, an ending that will be hard for children (and adults) to take, but it is in keeping with the tell-it-like-it-is style of this first-person narrative. The back matter contains excellent bibliographies for further reading for children and for teachers and parents, a list of names and addresses one might contact for information about HIV and AIDS, and a biographical sketch of Arlene Schulman, the award-winning author and photographer of this book.

Wolf, Bernard

HIV POSITIVE   *9–12 YEARS*

Illustrated with photographs by Bernard Wolf. New York: Dutton, 1997.

Although the basic medical information about HIV and AIDS is provided, the major focus of this moving photo-essay is on how individuals in a closely knit, loving family are intensely personally affected when someone in their family suffers from this disease. In this situation, a twenty-nine-year-old woman, a single parent of two school-age children, has AIDS. The author describes some of the health problems associated with AIDS that the woman has to deal with, her fears about what will happen to her children when she dies, and her attempts to help them deal with their worry and fears and general feeling of stress about the ups and downs of her ongoing illness. The feelings and concerns and the relationships that the patient's mother and three sisters express in words and behavior are dealt with by the author forthrightly and sensitively. The full-color photographs capture amazingly well the range of emotions the children and adults in the family are experiencing as they try to deal with the ravaging effects the disease has on the patient they all love so very much. This book serves as an effective introduction about the physical and psychological effects that HIV and AIDS have on people with the disease and on the members of their family. The author presents as much information as children can deal with about the disease in general and how this AIDS patient, her children, and her close relatives are dealing with the realities of the disease. There is no doubt children will ultimately need and should have more detailed information about HIV and AIDS, but this book serves well as an honest and perceptive introduction to the subject.

Peoples and Cultures

THE PEOPLES OF AMERICA

Historic Voices

Burleigh, Robert

WHO SAID THAT? FAMOUS AMERICANS SPEAK   *7–12 YEARS*

Illustrated by David Catrow. New York: Henry Holt, 1997.

Children will no doubt enjoy flipping through this collection of thirty-two quotations, some of which are informative, humorous, or mind-stretching. Each quotation is highlighted in large, bold-faced type and is followed by comments that reveal tidbits about the people who expressed them and what prompted the remarks in the first place. The quotations are arranged according to themes or ideas or for the humor Burleigh found in pairing two disparate personalities. The cartoon-style illustrations, done in pen-and-ink line and crosshatching, provide a satirical, almost farcical tone to the quotations, which in-and-of themselves are a mixture of the profound, the witty, the contentious, and the vacuous.

Guthrie, Woody (words and music)

THIS LAND IS YOUR LAND   *6–14+ YEARS*

Illustrated by Kathy Jacobsen. Tribute by Pete Seeger. Scrapbook text
by Janell Yates. Boston: Little, Brown, 1998.

> This is a multidimensional and multilevel book in every way! Most ob-
> viously, it is a visual and graphic presentation of the lyrics and musical
> notation of a well-known classic country folk song, first recorded in
> 1949, that is part of almost everyone's musical repertoire to this day.
> In very tiny print in sidebars at the top and bottom corners of almost
> every page are quotations of sage comments Guthrie made about such
> things as life in general and, more particularly, the richness, poverty, and
> evils of people in America. Some of the illustrations show the beauty
> and the richness of extremes in the wide range of diversity that prevail
> in the climate and terrain throughout the United States. Some depict
> memorable social and political events and economic conditions, major
> technological inventions and accomplishments that quickly changed,
> for good and bad, the lifestyles of people, all of which are alluded to
> in this famous song. Other illustrations amount to a visual biography,
> depicting the major events of Guthrie's life story and the people he
> encountered and came to know and love during his involvement in
> various social causes. The illustrations are reproductions of naive-styled
> paintings that were done in oil on canvas. The painted borders were
> inspired by notch carvings found in traditional "tramp art"—boxes,
> picture frames, and mirror frames crafted by tramps, hoboes, miners,
> and lumberjacks in the early and mid 1900s. The endpapers show a
> map of the different states Guthrie traveled through on the well-known
> Highway 66, starting with his birthplace in Ohemah, Oklahoma, and on
> through Texas, New Mexico, Arizona, and finally California.

King, Martin Luther Jr.

I HAVE A DREAM   *8 YEARS–ADULTHOOD*

Foreword by Coretta Scott King. Illustrated by fifteen Coretta Scott
King Book Artist Award and Honor Book Artist Award recipients.
New York: Scholastic, 1997.

> The words of the moving and inspiring speech presented in this special
> illustrated edition are every bit as relevant in today's world as they
> were when it was delivered on August 28, 1963—and most surely will
> continue to be so well into the twenty-first century. This seminal speech
> is included in its entirety, aptly divided into thirteen parts. Each of these
> parts, as well as the jacket and frontispiece, is illustrated with a full-color
> painting by a recipient of the Coretta Scott King Book Artist Award or

Honor Book Artist Award. At the back of the book each artist explains the significance he or she found in the subject, theme, or metaphor of that particular part of King's speech and how the illustration depicts that. In the foreword Coretta Scott King speaks of Dr. King's legacy of courage, determination, and nonviolence, but asks "May God give us vision and strength to carry forward his unfinished work" (p. 5). A biographical sketch and a full-page photograph of Dr. Martin Luther King, Jr. are included in the back of the book. This special illustrated edition of the "I Have a Dream . . ." speech is an inspiring and thought-provoking picture book that belongs in every elementary and secondary school library and family library. It will most certainly inspire readers of all ages to appreciate King's legacy, to recognize the historic importance of the speech, and to strive for a racially harmonious America.

Kunhardt, Edith

HONEST ABE   *4–8 YEARS*

Illustrated by Malah Zeldis. New York: Lothrop, Lee & Shepard, 1993.

This *very* brief, easy-to-read biographical sketch tells about the life of Abraham Lincoln from his birth in a log cabin to his presidency, his assassination, and the long journey of his funeral train from Washington, D. C., to Springfield, Illinois. It is illustrated in naive-style paintings rendered in bright, flat gouache paints on paper and reproduced as large illustrations. Together, the simple text and the unsophisticated artwork reflect the theme of courage, dedication, and pioneer justice that so often accompanies children's biographies and essays about Lincoln. The complete text of the Gettysburg Address and a time line of events important in the life of Lincoln are included.

Sandler, Martin W.

PRESIDENTS   *8–12+ YEARS*

Introduction by James H. Billington, Librarian of Congress. Illustrated. New York: HarperCollins, 1995.

Something about the achievements, however great or small, of each of the forty-two presidents of the United States is included in this Library of Congress Book. The major thrust of this book is that the presidency is one office, but that office has been held by people who differed in many human ways—personalities and lifestyles, shapes and sizes, age, education, mental acuity, talents, and notable accomplishments. Separate chapters are devoted to such topics as the presidents' favorite forms of recreation, the way various presidents related to their children, the roles of the First Ladies, and even the pets that lived in the White House. The are no captions for the plethora of photographs, reproduction of etchings, magazine covers, posters, and newspaper articles. The president shown in each picture is identified by name; any other relevant information about the contents of that picture must be gleaned by reading the body of the text. There is no table of contents, but the chapter titles are self-explanatory. The index is detailed and comprehensive so readers who want to focus on a specific president should be able to identify the references to that individual scattered throughout the book.

Younger, Barbara
PURPLE MOUNTAIN MAJESTIES: THE STORY   *5–9 YEARS*
OF KATHARINE BATES AND "AMERICA THE BEAUTIFUL"
Illustrations by Stacey Schuett. New York: Dutton, 1998.

Only a few facts about Katharine Lee Bates's life story are covered in this book. We learn that, from early childhood on through her adult years, she kept diaries in which she recorded poems she composed and described the sights she saw during her many travels with her parents, during her years as a student at Wellesley College for Women, and later when she was a professor of English literature there. At age thirty-four, while she was a visiting lecturer at a college in Colorado Springs for three weeks in July 1895, she toured Pike's Peak and recorded in her diary how awed and inspired she was by the beautiful mountain scenes. Two summers later she wrote several verses describing the sights she saw on her trip to Colorado. She sent the poem to *The Congregationalist* magazine and it was printed in the July Fourth issue. It soon became very popular, was set to various tunes, and was even translated into different languages so that immigrants could sing it in their own language. Bates revised what she called her "hymn" several times. The version most commonly sung today is printed on the back cover and on the back of the book jacket. Unfortunately, the score Samuel Ward wrote for this version is not included. The jewel-toned expressionistic illustrations, which are alternately full-page and double-page spreads, capture the idealism and awe so evident in Bates's descriptions of the physical beauty and splendor throughout America's vast and varied terrain.

Community Life

Geisert, Bonnie
PRAIRIE TOWN   *6–10 YEARS*
Illustrated by Arthur Geisert. Boston: Walter Lorraine/Houghton Mifflin, 1998.

Geisert's meticulous panoramic etchings, tinted with watercolor washes, go far beyond what the text offers. In fact, they demand very careful examination if one is to notice the many dramas that happen on the farms and in town to the adults and children, their animals, their homes and machines, at the grocery store, grain elevator, church, post office, and elsewhere in this Midwestern prairie town from season to season over a span of one year. A house burns and is rebuilt, a country house is moved to town, a litter of puppies is born, a wedding takes place, a circus comes to town, more playground equipment is added to the schoolyard. Compare the perspectives on the lifestyles of people living in prairie towns depicted in the Geiserts' book with those depicted by William Kurelick in his classic picture books *A Prairie Boy's Summer* (Houghton Mifflin, 1975) and *A Prairie Boy's Winter* (Houghton Mifflin, 1973).

Geisert, Bonnie
RIVER TOWN   *7–10 YEARS*
Illustrated by Arthur Geisert. Boston: Walter Lorraine/Houghton
Mifflin, 1999.

The minutely detailed etchings and watercolor-wash illustrations depict the activities and events that affect the lives of the people living in a small town located along an unnamed American river. The double-page spreads and full-page pictures show how life in this generic river town is lived throughout a span of one year—how people cope with the challenges that each season offers, celebrate traditional holidays and other pleasant and happy events, and handle disasters caused by nature and by human error as best they can. In each case the life of this town tends to be shaped, or at least influenced in some way, by its relation to the river. The illustrator very cleverly shows the terrain and the activities from different perspectives: an aerial view, some close-up views, and many panoramic views, of which some highlight the river and others minimize its presence. Together they reflect the pace and rhythms of life in a river town, a place where it seems children and adults alike live life to the fullest. The sparse, simply written text provides an intriguing, yet pleasant and comfortable contrast to the intensely busy and embellished quality of the illustrations. Compare and contrast the Geiserts' depiction of life in this small town located along the banks of a river with their portrayals of life in other small towns in *Haystack* (Houghton Mifflin, 1995) and *Prairie Town* (Houghton Mifflin, 1998).

Lourie, Peter

RIO GRANDE: FROM THE ROCKY MOUNTAINS 7–11 YEARS
TO THE GULF OF MEXICO

Illustrated with photographs by Peter Lourie and with archival pictures.
Honesdale, Penn.: Boyds Mills, 1999.

The award-winning author-illustrator of this impressive photo-essay
recounts the sights he saw, the people he met, and what he learned as he
followed the shores of the Rio Grande, almost 2,000 miles from its source
to its mouth, from its headwaters in the Rio Grande National Forest in
the Colorado Rockies to the Gulf of Mexico. Lourie includes in this profusely illustrated book a fascinating array of full-color photographs and
black-and-white archival pictures that substantiate and expand upon his
very readable verbal account of his journey: the ever changing terrain
he encountered, the vast conglomeration of lifestyles he observed, the
vast diversity of flora and fauna he saw, the variety of ethnic food he
ate. He became aware of how the encounter of three cultures—Native
American (Anasazi, Pueblo, Comanche, and Apache), Spanish (later
Mexican) coming up from the south, and European Americans from
the east—brought about cultural change and affected the environment.
He describes the impact of miners, farmers, and missionaries he met as
well as the woman who is the sole resident of an eighteenth-century
ghost town in Guerro Viejo, near the southern tip of Mexico. And so
much more! Be certain to make Lourie's other award-winning River
series books accessible to the children. All are published by Boyds Mills;
they include *Erie Canal: America's Great Waterway* (1997), *Everglades:
Buffalo Tiger and the River Grass* (1994), *Amazon: A Young Reader's
Look at the Last Frontier* (1991), *Hudson River: An Adventure from the
Mountains to the Sea* (1992), and *Yukon River: An Adventure to the
Gold Fields of the Klondike* (1992).

Peterson, Cris

CENTURY FARM: ONE HUNDRED YEARS ON A FAMILY FARM 7–10 YEARS

Illustrated with photographs by Alvis Upitis. Honesdale, Penn.:
Boyds Mills, 1999.

This well-established award-winning author-photographer team tells
the story of a hundred years of growth, technical progress, family dedication, and loyalty to farming. It provides a glimpse of how five generations
of a family were affected by the timeless and sameness and unexpected-
ness of the weather, the seasons, planting, harvesting, the birth of new
generations, and the demise of the older generation. The illustrations

in-and-of themselves are worthy of note. Their presentation constantly compares and contrasts aspects of farming in the past and present: sepia-toned pictures depict the Petersons who founded the farm in the 1890s at work on the farm consisting of a barn and house and granary on boggy, stump-strewn land in Wisconsin. These are contrasted with full-color photographs of the contemporary Petersons (the author, her husband, and their three children). They depict how this family lived in the same house and worked the same farm for the past twenty-five years so that now, with the help of the new mechanized and computerized farm equipment, it is a thriving dairy farm and Cris and her husband can do the work that used to take many hands.

Pringle, Laurence

ONE ROOM SCHOOL   *5–10 YEARS*

Illustrated by Barbara Garrison. Honesdale, Penn.: Boyds Mills, 1998.

This memoir of what it was like to attend a one-room school reflects the author's actual experiences when he was a child living in rural New York in the early 1940s. The school, which was surrounded on three sides by cow pasture, had no name, just a number—14. The eighteen students enrolled in the school were taught by one teacher. Although some of the older students rode their bicycles to school until the winter snows came, most of the students walked miles to and from school each day. The book is filled with picturesque scenes of the teacher reading stories to the whole class or bringing several grades together for a common lesson, instructing small groups of students according to age or grade level while the others worked quietly at their desks, and older students teaching arithmetic and spelling to the younger ones. The teacher is shown taking the whole class on nature walks on warm spring days or walking along the roadsides to collect milkweed seedpods and stuffing them into empty onion bags, for the fluffy parts of the seeds could be used in life preservers to keep sailors afloat when their ship sank in battles at sea. Of interest will be the author's description of the bookmobile from the city library pulling into the school yard and the children stepping into the dark caravan of the bus to be greeted by a librarian who helped them find treasures they could take home for a while. Garrison's detailed description of how she prepared the accomplished collagraphs (collage-graphics) that were reproduced to illustrate Pringle's memoir is included in the back matter.

The Native-American Experience

Ancona, George

POWWOW   *7–12 YEARS*

Illustrated with photographs by George Ancona.
San Diego: Harcourt Brace, 1990.

> George Ancona's carefully prepared text and glorious full-color pho-
> tographs offer the readers of *Powwow* an enlightening and exciting kalei-
> doscope of images of the largest powwow held in the United States by
> Native Americans from throughout North America, which is celebrated
> each summer at the Crow Fair on the Crow Reservation in Montana.
> Each photograph contains a trove of information and together they
> provide a stunning and memorable record of how members of the Crow,
> Lakota, Cheyenne, Blackfoot, Fox, Cree, Ojibwa and many other tribal
> organizations and societies set aside their differences and, in the spirit
> of friendship, celebrate and reaffirm their shared heritage and traditions.

Begay, Shonto

NAVAJO: VISIONS AND VOICES ACROSS THE MESA   *9–14 YEARS*

Illustrated by Shonto Begay. New York: Scholastic, 1995.

> Twenty full-color paintings (some of which are done with acrylics on
> canvas and others with mixed media, such as watercolor, colored pen-
> cil, and ink on paper) are singled out from Begay's body of work and
> combined with his original poems and with traditional chants and
> stories to depict a glimpse of Navajo life today. Begay's poems depict
> moments of his childhood and candid memories of his family and
> members of his community, and reveal the struggle to create a balance
> and harmony between two cultures, namely that of the natural world
> (the ancient world of the Navajo people) and that of the technolog-
> ical world that now surrounds them. The two themes he seems to
> emphasize throughout this unique book are that we are all guardians
> of our mother, the earth, and that Navajo life is encompassed with
> the spirit of love and hope. While *listening* to each of the ancient
> tribal chants, stories, and poems read aloud and, at the same time
> really *looking* at the painting that accompanies each of specific se-
> lection, one is immediately struck with how the two art forms inter-
> act with each other, each making the other so much more expressive,
> each making Begay's comment about his two cultures so much more
> credible and profound. He makes use of solid turquoise endpapers
> and sprinkles splashes and dashes of turquoise throughout many of
> his pictures and emphasizes the ever present reddish-brown soil. The

striking depictions of the far-reaching landscape and the arid mesas, the incredibly expressive features of his family, and the many people of all ages who represent the conflicting cultures serve to dramatize the moods and the themes that permeate this book. Thoughtful, critical readers will most likely return to the selections and the illustrations many times over. The table of contents should prove especially helpful when a reader wants to reread a particular selection or examine a specific illustration. The index of paintings is informative and comprehensive.

Dewey, Jennifer Owings

STORIES ON STONE; ROCK ART: IMAGES FROM THE   *8–11 YEARS*
ANCIENT ONES

Illustrated by Jennifer Owings Dewey. New York: Little, Brown, 1999.

Rock art is ancient visual images on stone pecked out by nomadic people who once lived in that area; these images provide a readable record of their history before the emergence of written language. The author-illustrator describes some of the trips in search of rock art she and her family took when she was a child. They went to a rock site in the Mimbres Valley (in southern New Mexico) where the surfaces of the black boulders of volcanic stone were pecked with hundreds of images depicting birds, snakes, deer, mountain sheep, and suns. They also visited Nine Mile Canyon, a remote site in southern Utah, consisting of sandstone on which they found kachina figures. These figures had boxy bodies, were portrayed with shields, and their faces were covered by decorated masks. They noticed handprints, many of which were the size of a child's, age ten or so. Dewey also describes some Anasazi sites along the edge of the Rio Grande she and a family friend visited. Here, too, they found the images (petroglyphs) pecked out of the boulders of black volcanic rock that lined the river. Some of these images depicted animals they recognized, but others were mysterious and unfamiliar. This very readable introduction to rock art helps young children understand that even though we do not fully comprehend the full meaning of these images we can indeed learn something about these ancient people's experiences, their fears and hopes, their religious beliefs and their fantasies. The illustrations seem to be grease-pencil rubbings on stone or another grainy textured object that suggest the images pecked out of rock art. They serve aptly to give the young readers an accurate idea of what the original rock art looks like.

121

Fisher, Leonard Everett

ANASAZI   *9–12* YEARS

Illustrated by Leonard Everett Fisher. New York: Atheneum, 1997.

> This book is a perfect example of how one can develop a theoretical
> base of knowledge about a civilization that has long disappeared. Fisher
> based most of his theory about the lifestyle of the Anasazi Indians, who
> lived in our nation's Southwest two thousand years ago, on information
> he gathered from a wide variety of archeological sources. The informa-
> tion he gleaned from these "silent witnesses" is reflected in his scholarly
> but accessible text and his accomplished stylized expressionistic acrylic
> paintings reproduced in sepia. (See illustration 8.) Together the text and
> illustrations that comprise a unique informational picture book depict
> to great advantage the little that is currently known about the Anasazi.
> The time line, entitled "The World at the Time of the Anasazi: A.D. 500–
> 1300" and included on the copyright page at the front of this book,
> enables young readers to put the 2,000 years the Anasazi civilization
> flourished into a fairly concrete perspective. The map on the frontispiece
> facing the copyright page makes very clear the exact location of the
> "Four Corners" region in the American Southwest (where the present-
> day states of Utah, Colorado, New Mexico, and Arizona meet). It was
> from this region the Anasazi subsequently emigrated (probably during
> and after a long and severe drought there between 1276 and 1299), then
> joined and ultimately became absorbed into the cultures of the Hopi,
> Zuni, Rio Grande Pueblo, and Acoma communities.

Hoyt-Goldsmith, Diane

BUFFALO DAYS   *9–13* YEARS

Illustrated with photographs by Lawrence Migdale.
New York: Holiday House, 1997.

> The child featured in this photo-essay is ten-year-old Clarence Three
> Iron Jr., a member of the Crow Indian tribe. His nickname is "Indian"
> and his Crow name is Iilappaah Ahoo, which means "has many friends."
> He lives on a forty-acre ranch on the Crow reservation near Lodge Grass,
> Montana, with his father, who works for the Crow tribe as a buffalo
> manager and also raises cattle and horses on the family's ranch, his two
> older brothers, and his mother. The full-color photographs contribute
> significantly to this carefully thought through book; there are excellent
> explanatory comments in the captions that accompany each of the many
> photographs.
>   Maps are also provided to show where the Crow reservation is
> located in relation to the rest of the state in general, and Billings in

ILLUSTRATION 8   Reprinted with the permission of Atheneum Books for Young Readers, an imprint of Simon & Schuster Children's Publishing Division from *Anasazi* by Leonard Everett Fisher. Copyright © 1997 Leonard Everett Fisher.

particular; another map shows where the buffalo roamed in 1500 and 1800. There is a fine glossary at the back of the book; an index is appended, but it is not very comprehensive or detailed. There is no table of contents, but each topic focused on is identified with large, bold-faced type, so the reader is well aware when the author moves on to another topic.

Four major topics are focused on in this photo-essay; together they offer an in-depth look into the lives and heritage of the Crow Indians, most of whom have lived in the valley of Little Big Horn Mountain since the 1700s. The first topic is what the Crow call "The Buffalo Days," which began around the 1730s and ended by the early 1880s. During these years the buffalo was the basis for the tribe's livelihood. In this section Hoyt-Goldsmith explains what caused the buffalo to become almost extinct by the early 1880s, forcing the Crow and other Plains Indians to become dependent on the federal government and eventually to live on reservations. The second focus is designated as "The Buffalo

Return." The Crow tribe's wild buffalo herd started in the 1930s when they brought in several hundred buffalo from Yellowstone Park, the National Bison Range in Montana, and a few from private individuals. By 1995 the Crow's herd had grown to 1,200. There are now more than 10,000 buffalo on reservations throughout the United States. The buffalo on the Crow reservation serve as a link to the past; their skulls are used and their meat eaten on important ceremonial occasions. The buffalo also provide a source of income for the Crow. The third focus is "The Buffalo Roundup," which takes place annually at the end of the summer. People on horseback or in all-terrain vehicles round them up and herd them into large pens. The buffalo are counted and the new calves are examined and vaccinated. The fourth focus is "Celebrating the Buffalo Days." A special gathering of the Crow nation called the Crow Fair and Rodeo takes place on the Crow reservation in August of every year. It began in 1904 as a way to encourage ranching and farming, but over the years it has become a celebration of Native American traditions. People come from all over the United States to experience the way of life that existed during "Buffalo Days." They stay in tepees, hold a powwow that lasts for many days, and hold contests, rodeo competitions, horse races, and parades. For another portrayal of the modern Buffalo Nation (specifically the Nambe Pueblo people of northern New Mexico) see *Thunder Bear and Ko: The Buffalo Nation and Nambe Pueblo,* written and illustrated with numerous photographs in resplendent full color by Susan Hazen-Hammond (Dutton, 1999).

McMillan, Bruce

SALMON SUMMER   *7–10 YEARS*

Illustrated with photographs by Bruce McMillan. Boston: Walter Lorraine/Houghton Mifflin, 1998.

Readers of this informative photo-essay get to see nine-year-old Alex B. Shugak Jr., a Native Aleut, help his father catch salmon in the streams of Kodiak Island, Alaska, as his ancestors did. This is the first time Alex has taken a responsible role in helping his father trap enough salmon to last the family through the year. Each summer season the Aleut men, as did their ancestors, engage in subsistence fishing rather than commercial fishing. At the end of each fishing season the family returns to the village of Old Harbor on Kodiak Island and remains there until the salmon begin running the next summer and it is time to set up camp near the stream once again. Clear photographs in rich full colors capture the inherent beauty of this area of Alaska during the summer and help the readers appreciate the skill and knowledge fishing for salmon requires. The text and photographs depict the procedures followed by the salmon fishermen. The readers are also shown a shallow water trap that is set to catch Dungeness crabs; slices of salmon are used as bait. For recreation Alex goes line fishing. Again salmon is used to bait a line for catching the biggest fish of all—a halibut. Alex is shown catching a halibut almost as big as he is (and the author informs the readers that is not even considered a very big one)! With help from his father Alex pulls the halibut aboard. They take it back to the camp where Alex's grandmother slices it in strips and hangs them up to dry; ten days later it is ready to be eaten as a snack called *tamuug*. The three back pages offer more information: Alex's heritage, an excellent glossary (focusing on terms associated with fishing and ethnic terms pertaining to the Alaskan natives), and a bibliography of books about related topics such as geography; customs, ethnographics, and language of the Aleuts; fisheries; and wildlife, fish, birds, and plants in Alaska.

Sneve, Virginia Driving Horse

THE APACHES   *7–11 YEARS*

Illustrated by Ronald Himler. New York: Holiday House, 1997.

As in the other picture books in her First Americans series, Sneve provides in *The Apaches* a brief overview of the history and heritage of the six tribes that make up the Apache nation: Chiricahua, Jicarilla, Mescalero, Kiowa-Apache, Lipan, and Western Apache. She begins her account of the Apaches' legacy with a combined retelling of the creation myth of each tribe, then provides information on the similarities and differences inherent in each tribe's government, family life, traditional ceremonies, and warfare. Attention is given to how their contacts with white people over the years permanently changed the lives of the Apaches and what their lifestyles and accomplishments are like today. Himler's full-page paintings and numerous small paintings particularize the Apaches' traditional clothing, weaponry, utensils, children's toys, ceremonial garb, and so on; they effectively augment the content and atmosphere of the text. Helpful bibliographical references, an index, and maps are included.

The African-American Experience

Bial, Raymond

THE UNDERGROUND RAILROAD   *9–12+ YEARS*

Illustrated with photographs by Raymond Bial.
Boston: Houghton Mifflin, 1995.

The many black-and-white photographs of the places, buildings, articles of clothing, and toys included in this informative book reflect the atmosphere and the spirit of the incredible courage and conviction of the fugitive slaves and those who aided them. In the foreword, Bial mentions that many of the photographs were taken late at night. Knowing this should add to readers' understanding and appreciation of the aura of hope, tension, and no doubt fear most certainly felt by those involved in the underground railroad. The captions under each illustration are extremely informative; they clearly support and extend the details about the formation of the underground railroad and how it was implemented. There are stories about fugitive slaves who succeeded, with the help of workers, in reaching a free state in the United States or Canada—and those who failed. Some were returned to the plantations because they were caught by their masters or professional bounty hunters ("slave catchers") or went back on their own accord; others died from exposure to the elements, illness, or accidents. The extensive back matter consists of a chronology of the antislavery movement in America and a bibliography of primary sources (for teachers and librarians) and a list of very fine books for children about the underground railroad.

Duncan, Alice Faye

THE NATIONAL CIVIL RIGHTS MUSEUM CELEBRATES EVERYDAY PEOPLE   *9–13+ YEARS*

Illustrated with photographs by Gerard Smith. Mawah, N.J.: BridgeWater/Troll, 1995.

The Lorraine Motel in Memphis, Tennessee, was the site where Dr. Martin Luther King Jr. was murdered in 1968. It now houses the National Civil Rights Museum, featuring state-of-the-art interactive displays and historical artifacts documenting the major events of the Civil Rights Movement from 1954 through 1968. Through words and pictures Duncan and Smith take the readers on a tour through the museum, providing them with an understanding of the injustices of segregation and a glimpse of how ordinary people brought about enormous change. The full-color photographs show how children touring the museum respond to the opportunity to interact with the lifelike displays and to actually "see" these painful events in America's past. The black-and-white photographs are genuine images of the locations behind these actual events. The book (like the museum!) does an excellent job of recapturing the major events of the Civil Rights Movement. The back matter consists of a chronology of the Movement from 1954 to 1968, a bibliography of children's and young adult books for further reading, a bibliography of sources for adults, and an extensive index.

Hansen, Joyce

WOMEN OF HOPE: AFRICAN AMERICANS
WHO MADE A DIFFERENCE

8–12+ YEARS

Foreword by Mae Foner. Illustrated with photographs.
New York: Scholastic, 1998.

Thirteen African-American women whose involvements and achievements in journalism, politics, education, medicine, law, science, and the
arts paved the way for a better future for others are the subjects of the
informative biographical sketches and stunning black-and-white photographic portraits that appear in this book. The portraits were selected
from the poster series included in the "Women of Hope" program, a
major focus of the Bread and Roses project of the National Health and
Human Services Employees union (AFL-CIO). The poster series was
intended to provide the members of the union, who are mostly women
of color, with "images of women, strong and courageous, inspired to
fight against injustice in ways they knew how" (p. v)—to serve as
role models and to inspire young people today to live productive and
meaningful lives. The thirteen women featured in the book are arranged
chronologically in order of their birth. They are: Ida B. Wells-Barnett, the
Delaney sisters, Septima Poinsett Clark, Ella Josephine Baker, Fannie
Lou Hamer, Ruby Dee, Maya Angelou, Toni Morrison, Marian Wright
Edelman, Alice Walker, Alexa Canady, and Mae C. Jemison. In the back
matter the author lists other extraordinary African-American women,
some of whom are famous and others who are little known, but all
of whose lives and accomplishments are worthy of note. The names
of these women are grouped according to their professional roles: an
aviator, artists, writers, musicians, caregivers, educators, activists, and
athletes. An annotated bibliography of books about accomplished and
influential women is appended.

Lester, Julius

FROM SLAVE SHIP TO FREEDOM ROAD

8–14+ YEARS

Illustrated by Rod Brown. New York: Dial, 1998.

Julius Lester has written impassioned meditations that challenge African Americans and everyone else regardless of their race to imagine
themselves in the terrifying and humiliating situations depicted in Rod
Brown's dramatic illustrations. Africans are shown on their voyage on
the slave ships of the Middle Passage, in the decades during which they
were enslaved and their descendants were subjugated and oppressed,
up to the time of their hard won freedom. In the introduction, Lester says
he and Rod Brown ask of the reader what they asked of themselves as

127

they "sought to come to terms with a historical experience whose legacy continues to affect us all." Lester urges readers of this intensely dramatic verbal and pictorial testimony "not to be passive but to invest soul and imagine yourself into the images" (p. 111), to step out of their skins and put on the skins of others. I would strongly recommend that the readers of this book also read *The Middle Passage: White Ships/Black Cargo,* written and illustrated by Tom Feelings (Dial, 1995).

McKissack, Patricia C., and Frederick L. McKissack
CHRISTMAS IN THE BIG HOUSE, CHRISTMAS IN THE QUARTERS   *9–14 YEARS*
Illustrated by John Thompson. New York: Scholastic, 1994.

Meticulous research, sensitive insight, extensive knowledge, and great talent are the obvious and rare qualities of the authors and illustrator who created this very special, profusely illustrated, informational book. Thompson's accomplished full-color acrylic paintings are perfect for the McKissacks' informative carefully written text. Together they provide perceptive glimpses into the lives of the people, both black and white, who lived on a majestic plantation along the James River in Virginia around 1859, a tension-ridden era just before the Civil War. This book is filled with memorable images of the social life, customs, and personal relations of those who lived in "the Big House" and those who lived in the cramped slave "Quarters." The, many songs, games, and recipes that are included in this book provide additional understanding of these images. As the authors indicate, although this re-creation of the Christmas celebrations in the "Big House" and in the "Quarters" is based on real people, events, and places, it is a story that is "more than a season account." It is a reconstruction of the slaves' inner strengths, their rewards and satisfactions contrasted with their persistent hopes and need for freedom. This book is indeed a treasure—one that every school and public library should have multiple copies of and one that teachers and librarians should arrange for students to study in depth. The bibliography includes very fine reading fare students might read along with or after reading *Christmas in the Big House, Christmas in the Quarters.*

Myers, Walter Dean
TOUSSAINT L'OUVERTURE: THE FIGHT FOR HAITI'S FREEDOM   *9–14+ YEARS*
Introduction by Jacob Lawrence. Afterword by Dr. Frederick J. Stielow
of the Amistad Research Center. Illustrated by Jacob Lawrence.
New York: Simon & Schuster, 1996.

Myers briefly, but effectively, presents a biography of Francois Dominique Toussaint (1743?–1803), who changed his name to Toussaint L'Ouverture shortly after helping lead the blacks' successful rebellion (in 1791) against the wealthy owners of the plantations on Saint Dominique, a section of the Hispaniola islands ruled by the French. There were no schools for blacks so Toussaint's father, an African educated by the Jesuits, taught him how to read. Inspired by reading about the American Revolution, which began in 1776, and the overthrow of the French monarchy in 1789, the former coachman gained control of most of Saint Dominique and abolished slavery there. He then turned his attention to Santo Domingo, the other section of the Hispaniola islands (ruled by the Spanish) and quickly abolished slavery there, too. However Napoleon Bonaparte sent troops and a fleet of ships under the leadership of General Charles Leclerc to regain control of Saint Dominique, bring back slavery, and thus strengthen France's economy. L'Ouverture soon realized he could not fight the endless supply of French relief troops, so he agreed to a negotiated peace—only to find that Napoleon and Leclerc had no intention of honoring it. L'Ouverture was taken prisoner on June 7, 1802, and died in a French dungeon in April 1803. Meanwhile the black men, women, and children of Saint Dominique continued their struggle to maintain their freedom, and in November 1803 the French withdrew. The new leaders of this small island signed a declaration of independence on January 1, 1804, and called their country Haiti. To familiarize students with slavery in Haiti and in other parts of the West Indies, be certain to share Lawrence's introductory comments and Dr. Stielow's afterword. In his introductory statement Jacob Lawrence says that the role played by Toussaint L'Ouverture in the slaves' rebellion against the French plantation owners motivated the series of paintings that launched Lawrence's career as an artist in the late 1930s. His commentaries should help readers understand and appreciate more deeply Lawrence's highly sophisticated expressionistic paintings. Many of the students with whom I shared this book had difficulty responding positively to the illustrations. It is not necessary for children to like the illustrations, but they at least should have some understanding of and appreciation for them so they can recognize the contribution they are making to the telling of the author's story.

Two children's books written and illustrated by Lawrence that I have shared with elementary students are *Harriet and the Promised Land* (Windmill, 1968 and Simon & Schuster, 1994) and *The Great Migration: An American Story* (HarperCollins/Museum of Modern Art/the Phillips Collection, 1993). A third book, *Jacob Lawrence: American Painter,* written by Ellen H. Wheat, is profusely illustrated with reproductions of Lawrence's paintings (University of Washington Press/Seattle Art Museum, 1986). It is addressed to adults, but I shared parts of it with students in grades four and five. Finally, since Lawrence's original paintings were considerably larger than the reproductions in this book, you may wish to project them on a screen using an opaque projector.

The Immigrant Experience

Bierman, Carol, with Barbara Hehner

JOURNEY TO ELLIS ISLAND: HOW MY FATHER CAME TO AMERICA   *8–12 YEARS*

Illustrated by Laurie McGaw and with old photographs, period postcards, and sepia prints. New York: Hyperion/Madison Press, 1998.

This book recounts the actual experiences eleven-year-old Yehuda Weinstein and his mother and sister had as they as they fled war-torn Russia, trekked across much of Europe to Holland where they boarded a steamship, the *Rotterdam,* and sailed into New York Harbor in September 1922. Because Yehuda's right arm was weakened by a previous injury, the immigration inspectors questioned his eligibility to enter the country. After some delay, the family was allowed to proceed to the Registry Room of the Board of Inquiry where they were reunited with Abel, the boy's older brother who had immigrated to the United States several years before. Although Abel admitted he was not able to post the required five hundred dollars, he persuaded the board members that he could and would see to it that his family would not become a burden on society and the inspectors allowed the Weinstein family to enter the United States. Yehuda's name was changed to Julius by a teacher when he first enrolled in school in New York City and Julius it remained. This moving immigration story ends with information about the family's enculturation into American society as successful, happy, healthy United States citizens. Readers are told that Julius is now in his late eighties and lives in Florida. On the seventy-fifth anniversary of his entry into the United States he visited Ellis Island with the author of this book (his daughter!) and also visited the museum there. The watercolor and casein paintings reflect most effectively the traumas and emotional hardships as well as the happiness the family experienced during the course of their immigration to this country. The numerous old photographs, period postcards, and sepia prints scattered throughout the book plus the pictures showing the immigrants in the dining room at Ellis Island serve to establish the exact time and place of the Weinstein family's immigration experiences and thus make this story more real and memorable for today's youth. The comments that accompany each illustration are most thorough and informative. Compare the Weinstein family's experiences at Ellis Island with those of award-winning illustrator Beverly Brodsky's mother, whose arrival at Ellis Island is depicted in *Gooseberries to Oranges,* written by Barbara Cohen and illustrated by

Beverly Brodsky (Lothrop, Lee & Shepard, 1982) and with author Edith Tarbescu's mother's immigrant experience as she traveled across the sea to America, which is recounted in *Annushka's Voyage,* written by Edith Tarbescu and illustrated by Lydia Dabcovich (Clarion, 1998).

Cha, Dia

DIA'S STORY CLOTH: THE HMONG PEOPLE'S JOURNEY   *7–11+ YEARS*
TO FREEDOM

Illustrated; stitched by Chue and Nhia Cha. New York:
Lee & Low/Denver Museum of Natural History, 1996.

The text and the illustrations of the pa'ndau (story cloth) pictured on the cover and throughout the book document the cultural history of Hmong people in general, but also, more specifically, the personal history of Dia Cha and her family, their life, their war experiences, their escape, and finally, their arrival in America. Although this book can be read independently by children without being introduced by an adult, it might have greater impact if an adult (teacher, librarian, or parent) first shares the information in "This Is My Story" by the author, provided in the front of the book, as well as the section entitled "Hmong Means Free People," by Joyce Herold, Curator of Ethnology, Denver Museum of Natural History that appears in the back matter. Ask the students to examine the double-page spread reproduction of the pa'ndau that appears in the middle of the book; then ask them to read this book or read it aloud to them. They will soon notice that the full-page illustrations on each page of the text are actually portions of the big story cloth. They might be intrigued with the fact that the pa'ndau pictured on that double-page spread actually measures 66 inches high and 103 inches wide. It is a double-bed-sized piece of gray cotton cloth on which Dia's uncle Nhia Thao Cha drew figures and scenes; his wife, Chue, used chain, feather, satin, and cross stitches to render the hundreds of animals, planes, people, houses, and events that together fill the cloth and document the Cha family's story. Compare the documentation of this family's story with that depicted in *The Whispering Cloth: A Refugee's Story,* written by Pegi Deitz Shea, illustrated by Anita Riggio, and stitched by You Yang (Boyds Mills, 1995).

FESTIVALS AND HOLIDAYS

Luenn, Nancy

CELEBRATIONS OF LIGHT: A YEAR OF HOLIDAYS   *7–10 YEARS*
AROUND THE WORLD

Illustrated by Mark Bender. New York: Atheneum, 1998.

> Twelve festivals are highlighted to show the varied ways in which people around the world use light in worship and celebrations to mark and brighten special days, to light a way for a god or goddess, to celebrate birth and to honor the dead. The highly stylized modern expressionistic airbrush paintings are as joyous and specific as the special days of worship or celebration they designate.

Hispanic/Mexican

Ancona, George

BARRIO: JOSÉ'S NEIGHBORHOOD   *7–10 YEARS*

Illustrated with photographs by George Ancona. San Diego:
Harcourt Brace, 1998.

> This photo-essay portrays the many and varied cultural activities engaged in by the residents of el Barrio (the Mission District of San Francisco). It reflects the extensive diversity evident in the social and cultural milieu of the area's schools, recreation, holidays, family life and churches. The illustrations, which vary in size and shape, are formatted and arranged differently from page to page. There are no captions to explain the numerous full-color photographs, but because they are always placed near the relevant portion of the text, the reader can readily see that each one enriches and extends Ancona's already and enlightening and carefully written text. As in so many of his other photo-essays, Ancona focuses in this book on the life of one child and members of his extended family, friends, and neighbors to depict their social life, local customs and traditions, and ethnic cultural practices and beliefs. To gather the information for this photo-essay, Ancona lived with eight-year-old José's family, staying in their home in the barrio of San Francisco for several weeks, observing them and joining them in the workplace and in their various social activities.

Ancona, George

FIESTA FIREWORKS   *8–12 YEARS*

Illustrated with photographs by George Ancona. New York:
Lothrop, Lee & Shepard, 1998.

The focus of this book is on the preparation of fireworks and the festival honoring San Juan de Dios, protector of the *pirotechnios* and the patron saint of Tultepec, Mexico, a town famous for its master fireworks makers. Ancona identifies the roles the adults play in carrying out their trade and those the spouses and children play in the home and festivities of the celebration. The full-color photographs throughout this photo-essay capture the pride and dedication of the members of this family and their neighbors and friends from the surrounding barrios as they display their fireworks—whooshing rockets, puppets and sculptures of *toros* and *toritos* (heads of large and small bulls), sparklers, and floral designs. A glossary consisting of the Spanish terms used throughout the text is provided, as is a pronunciation guide for these terms. A brief history of fireworks is provided in the Author's Note, informing the readers of the origin of fireworks in China and the role they have played in Mexican festivities since the Spanish brought them to Mexico. A simple and helpful map of Mexico shows clearly where Tultepec is in relation to other major cities of Mexico and countries like Guatamela and Belize.

Ancona, George

FIESTA U.S.A.   *6–11 YEARS*

Illustrated with photographs by George Ancona and decorated with cut paper designs by Rosa Maria Galles. New York: Lodestar/Penguin, 1995.

> Four major holiday festivals traditionally celebrated by Mexicans and Mexican Americans are focused on in this upbeat picture book: All Souls Day or the Day of the Dead (*el Dia de los Muertos*) takes place November 2 and celebrates life and honors friends and relatives who have died by remembering them; *Los Posadas,* a procession reenacting Mary and Joseph's search for lodging in Bethlehem may take place for the entire nine days before Christmas or on just one night before Christmas; *Los Matachines,* the celebration of the arrival of Christianity in the New World occurs on New Year's Day; the Three Kings' Day (*la Fiesta de los Reyes Magos*), a commemoration of the journey three wise kings made to bring gifts to the newborn Christ, is celebrated on the twelfth day of Christmas (January 6) with a parade and the presentation of gifts to children after considerable music, singing, and dancing. Action-filled photographs in vibrant full color, many of them full page, depict festive scenes of costumed dancers, and of family and community gatherings at home, in the streets, in cemeteries, or in church showing Mexicans and Mexican Americans in all their humor, vitality, and solemnity. The book is also decorated with colorful *papel picado* (cut paper). *Fiesta U.S.A.* is available in English and Spanish editions.

133

A fine glossary of the Spanish words that appear throughout the book is included at the end of the book, but most of these terms are also explained in context so their meanings are easily understood as they are used. Compare with *Celebrate! In Central America,* written by Joe Viesti and Diane Hall and illustrated with full-color photographs by Joe Viesti (Lothrop, Lee & Shepard, 1997).

Ancona, George

THE PIÑATA MAKER/EL PIÑATERO   *7–10 YEARS*

Illustrated with photographs by George Ancona. San Diego:
Harcourt Brace, 1994.

> This attractive and useful photo-essay, set in Mexico, tells the story of how Don Picardo makes the piñatas he is so famous for. It begins with a small boy named Beto collecting newspapers and paper bags and bringing them to the piñata maker for pocket money. Picardo takes the steps necessary to make the paste and shape the paper into the form he wants, which in this case is a swan-shaped piñata. Ancona introduces Daniela, a child who has come to choose a piñata for her birthday party. Daniela chooses a less ornate, brightly colored traditional star-shaped piñata instead of the elaborate swan-shaped one because it will "hold more sweets." Ancona then enables the reader to observe how Daniela's blindfolded guests break the piñata open. His clear, bright, full-color photographs complement the detailed text, giving the reader much additional information. This story of how a piñata is made is told in English and Spanish, with both languages on each page. The pages may appear rather dense, with text appearing in two languages plus photographs on each page, but I found in using this book with elementary school children that the content provided in both the visuals and the words is made so interesting children do not seem to be troubled by this design flaw. *The Piñata Maker/El Piñatero* is an excellent example of an authentic, detailed account of one aspect of Mexican traditions. It has wide appeal to children because of Ancona's storytelling talents, and it captures both the individual and universal elements of a child's birthday celebration.

King, Elizabeth

QUINCEAÑERA: CELEBRATING FIFTEEN   *9–15 YEARS*

Illustrated with photographs by Elizabeth King. New York: Dutton, 1998.

> The *quinceañera* is the celebration of a Latina's fifteenth birthday. It is a coming-of-age ritual that begins with a special Mass during which the

young woman reaffirms her faith and dedication to God throughout her adult life. The Mass is followed by a feast and dancing. The author shows how two young women and their parish priest, parents and other family members, godparents, and friends prepare for this once-in-a-lifetime event and follows each of them through the actual celebration. The family of one of the girls (Cindy) is originally from El Salvador; the family of the other girl (Suzana) is originally from Mexico. Although each young woman makes a commitment of her faith during this important event, the details of each are quite different. Cindy's quinceañera is more traditional and has more overt religious overtones; Suzi's quinceañera tends to be more sophisticated and religion is not as central, although she does start the day with a church service. It is more a reflection of her personal style than a traditional service: the focus on the role she plays in her community, her interest in the welfare of the people around her, and her plans for the future. Many of the pictures are self-explanatory to those who know all that is involved in celebrating the quinceañera, but there are no captions to explain exactly what is going on in the pictures for readers who are unfamiliar with this celebration. There are many Spanish words used throughout this photo-essay; they are defined within the body of the text. Unfortunately, a glossary is not provided, so a reader who has forgotten the meaning of a Spanish term when it appears again has to page back through the text to find its meaning. At the back of the book the author explains the origin of the quinceañera and describes how it gradually melded traditions of the Aztecs in pre-Columbian Central America, the native people of Mexico, the Spanish, and the Catholic Church.

Lasky, Kathryn

DAYS OF THE DEAD   *8–11 YEARS*

Illustrated with photographs by Christopher G. Knight.
New York: Hyperion, 1994.

> *Los Dias de los Muertos* (The Days of the Dead) is a traditional holiday period in Mexico and other South and Central American countries. The rites span the evenings of October 31 through November 2; they are a mix of Christian and pagan rituals that honor departed ancestors and friends and observe the passing of summer and return of the animals from the pastures. It is a fun-filled holiday with flowers, fruits, and candy. The superb full-color photographs and carefully written text enlighten the readers about how Mexicans remember, rejoice, and even mock death, but also look for signs of rebirth. For example, butterflies return to winter in the protection of the forests, and some inhabitants of Mexico believe these butterflies bear the spirits of the departed. The

creators of this excellent book focus on how one family celebrates the holiday and honors their departed grandmother. The descendants of the grandmother gather together throughout the night. They place a photograph of the grandmother on a table filled with fruit, flowers, lighted candles, and a glass of tequila, and each person recalls something about their loved one. In the morning they go to the cemetery where they take bouquets of flowers to the grave of the grandmother and the graves of their other relatives, weeds are pulled, the soil is raked and smoothed. They spend the entire night at the grave sites and prayers are said for their beloved deceased.

Jewish

Nerlove, Miriam

SHABBAT   *4–7 YEARS*

Illustrated by Miriam Nerlove. Morton Grove, Ill.: Albert Whitman, 1998.

> Step-by-step procedures show how a nonorthodox Jewish family celebrates the Jewish Sabbath (known in Hebrew as *Shabbat* and in Yiddish as *Shabbos*), one of the earliest of the Jewish traditions. By way of the easy-to-read text accompanied by simple, realistic paintings done in rich, clean watercolors as well as from the information in the author's afterword at the back of the book, the reader is given a considerable amount of information about this Jewish religious custom: the word *Shabbat* means "rest" and reflects the Jews' belief that God created the world in six days and rested on the seventh. By resting on the seventh day too, the Jewish people are honoring God. The Jewish Sabbath begins at sundown every Friday when the family gathers together at home for dinner. At this time the Shabbat candles are lighted as a reminder of the creation of light at the beginning of the world, blessings are said over wine as a reminder of the holiness of Shabbat and over two loaves of bread, pieces of which are passed around to those present to represent the abundance God provides. On Shabbat, this family and other Jewish people go to the synagogue to pray; Saturday evening, "when three stars appear in the sky," the end of the Shabbat and the beginning of a new workweek are marked with a prayer. A long braided candle is lighted to celebrate the beginning of the new workweek just as God began Creation with light, and a small wooden container or silver box filled with sweet-smelling spices is passed to replenish the vitality and force "diminshed by the departure of Shabbat" (p. 22).

Oberman, Sheldon

BY THE HANUKKAH LIGHT   *5–10 YEARS*

Illustrated by Neil Waldman. Honesdale, Penn.: Boyds Mills, 1997.

The grandfather in this slight fiction relates how, during World War II, the Jews living in Europe under Hitler's regime could not share the joy of Hanukkah, but were forced to observe this holiday behind locked doors and drawn curtains. The Nazi persecution of the Jews is likened to what happened to the Jews centuries earlier (in 165 B.C.) when King Antiochus of Syria forced the Greek culture and the Greek religion on the Jews in Jerusalem, persecuting, imprisoning, and killing many Jews. The grandfather tells of the brave soldiers who fought during World War II and made it possible for Jews of today to celebrate together Hanukkah openly, calling them "modern Maccabees." He explains that this term refers to Judah Maccabee and his followers, who rebelled against King Antiochus and his army. He also explains the meaning and symbolism of the term *Hanukkah* and the menorah and their relationship to the rededication of the Great Temple in Jerusalem by the Maccabees. The illustrations, rendered freely in acrylic, are somewhat expressionistic in style and create a warm mood that is quite consistent with the aura of the story. The backgrounds are painted with a sponge dipped in acrylic paint and then pressed on the paper, creating a textured background that nicely complements the figures enclosed by heavy lines. Thoughtful reading and careful examination of the text and illustrations of *The Golden City: Jerusalem's 3,000 Years,* written and illustrated by Neil Waldman (Atheneum, 1995), will add even greater depth and appreciation to the insightful information so artfully presented by the creators of *By the Hanukkah Light.* See also *The Story of Hanukkah,* written by Norma Simon and illustrated by Leonid Gore (HarperCollins, 1997). This last-named title, written by Simon, was originally illustrated by Symeon Shimin (Simon & Schuster, 1966). Both of these editions of Simon's book are worth comparing with Oberman and Waldman's *By the Hanukkah Light.*

Zalben, Jane Breskin

PEARL'S EIGHT DAYS OF CHANUKAH   *4–10 YEARS*

Illustrated by Jane Breskin Zalben. New York: Simon & Schuster, 1998.

By far the most comprehensive and child-oriented introduction to Chanukah is provided by Zalben's description of the practices and activities a family engages in to prepare and celebrate this holiday. Her descriptions of recipes, crafts, songs, and games should prove most helpful and enticing to children and adults alike. The blessings that Pearl and her cousins say before they light the first candle at sundown on the first night of Chanukah are provided in English in the Hebrew alphabet, and in the Hebrew language transliterated into the Roman alphabet. The illustrations are charming and intricately detailed and are in clean jewel-like colors. (See illustration 9.) They were done in gold leaf, colored

ILLUSTRATION 9 Reprinted with the permission of Simon & Schuster Books for Young Readers, an imprint of Simon & Schuster Children's Publishing Division from *Pearl's Eight Days of Chanukah* written and illustrated by Jane Breskin Zalben. Copyright © 1998 Jane Breskin Zalben.

pencil, and watercolor with a triple zero brush on Opaline Parchment. A helpful glossary, with a pronunciation guide and definitions of the Yiddish terms and names of foods, pastries, and religious terms associated with this holiday, is included in the back matter.

Chinese

Hoyt-Goldsmith, Diane

CELEBRATING CHINESE NEW YEAR   *8–12 YEARS*

Illustrated with photographs by Lawrence Migdale.
New York: Holiday House, 1998

This publication provides an impressive explanation of the blend of traditional and modern ceremonies and practices employed by the Leong family (living in San Francisco's Chinatown) when they celebrate the

Chinese New Year (also called the Lunar New Year). The carefully written and comprehensive text and the many full-color photographs, each of which is accompanied by meaningful comments, reveal the thoughtfulness that went into the preparation of this book. Also worthy of note are the excellent sidebars scattered throughout the book. They list the names and symbolic meanings of such things as fruits, vegetables, poultry, and fish for the traditional meals *prepared before* the New Year celebrations begin, but *eaten during* the Chinese New Year's Day meal or over the course of the fifteen-day New Year celebration. On the last two pages of the book are an extensive glossary and index and a list of the twelve animals and traits of each included in the Chinese zodiac calendar. Compare with *Happy New Year! Kung-Hsi Fa-Ts'ai!* written and illustrated by Demi (Crown, 1997).

SPORTS AND GAMES

Baseball

Dingle, Derek T.
FIRST IN THE FIELD: BASEBALL HERO JACKIE ROBINSON   *7–10 YEARS*
Introduction by Hank Aaron. Illustrated with photographs.
New York: Hyperion, 1998.

This picture-book biography of Jackie Robinson is well written and is organized around large blocks of time. The first block of time (1919–1940) covers his early childhood through his early adult years, growing up in poverty and racism. He excelled in sports, especially in baseball, football, track, and basketball while in high school and junior college in Pasadena, California. During the two years he attended UCLA, he made collegiate history as their first four-letter man, and in 1984 he was inducted into the UCLA Sports Hall of Fame.

The next block of time spans 1941–1944. He played with the Honolulu Bears for one year (1941) and then was inducted into the U.S. Army where he was again the victim of overt racism. With the intercession of Joe Louis, the heavyweight boxing champion of the world, he was admitted to Officers Candidate School and achieved the rank of second lieutenant, but left the military when his refusal to sit in the back of the bus led to a court-martial, of which he was eventually cleared and given an honorable discharge.

He played with the Kansas City Monarchs, a Negro professional baseball league in 1945. In August of that same year, he signed with the Brooklyn Dodgers "farm team" to become the first African American to play in major-league baseball in this century and, with the help of Brooklyn Dodgers' president Branch Rickey, paved the way for integration in professional sports. Although he had to prove himself by playing with the minor-league Montreal Royals for two years, he became a member of the Brooklyn Dodgers team on April 9, 1947, to mixed reactions by his team and the public at large. He was named most valuable player in 1949, helped his team win pennants in 1952 and 1953, played in the World Series in 1955, and retired in 1957. In 1962 he was named to the National Baseball Hall of Fame in Cooperstown, New York. He joined the Civil Rights Movement and pushed for the participation of blacks in the corporate world until his death October 24, 1972, from diabetes. Robinson wore number 42 on his uniform, a number that was retired on April 15, 1997, the fiftieth anniversary of his first major-league game, at a ceremony attended by his wife Rachel Robinson and President Bill Clinton.

There are numerous excellent black-and-white photographs throughout the book; the captions under each are elaborate, informative, and supplement the text significantly. The three pages of "Milestones in Black Sports" cover the years from 1845 through 1997; they help readers see how Robinson's and other talented black persons' participation in sports contributed to the image of sports and African Americans throughout the United States and internationally. The selected bibliography of books, films, newsreels, and articles should prove even more helpful to increasing readers' understanding and appreciation of Robinson's contributions to the world of sports.

Horenstein, Henry

BASEBALL IN THE BARRIOS   *7–10 YEARS*

Illustrated by Henry Horenstein. San Diego: Harcourt Brace, 1997.

Nine-year-old Hubaldo Antonio Romero Paez aspires to be a professional baseball player for one of the eight teams in Venezuela's Winter League and with a major-league team in the United States. It is from Hubaldo's perspective that the readers of this book meet his family and his fellow baseball enthusiasts. A variety of full-color photographs in various sizes are strategically placed throughout the text. Many of the photographs are full-page panoramic views of the government-run baseball playing areas for children's teams. Children as young as age four play on teams affiliated with a league called the *Semillitus* (which means little seeds); those who are age ten and eleven play with teams affiliated with the league called the *Infantils*. Children between the ages of four and ten belong to teams affiliated with the *Preparatories* and the *Preinfantils* leagues. Informal or pickup games (called *caimanera*) are played just about any place in the barrios: on basketball courts; on the pavements; when the leagues are not playing on the regulation fields run by the government, the children sneak into these area to play their informal games. In the back matter there is a two-page glossary of baseball-related vocabulary in Spanish and English. There is also a double-page spread with maps showing Venezuela and its proximity to other South American countries.

Thomson, Peggy

TAKE ME OUT TO THE BAT AND BALL FACTORY   *7–10 YEARS*

Illustrated by Gloria Kamen. Morton Grove, Ill.: Albert Whitman, 1998.

> Basic information about making wooden bats, aluminum bats, and the soft and hard balls used by players in the youth leagues and major leagues is provided. The step-by-step manufacturing procedures for this equipment are demonstrated by the experienced and highly skilled employees of Worth, Inc., a well-known manufacturer of baseball equipment in Tullahoma, Tennessee. Bits of information about how, where, and with what kind of equipment famous batters and pitchers learned and practiced when they were children are included. There is a three-page "History of Baseball," beginning with the 1700s and concluding with the accomplishments of Orioles player Cal Ripken, who broke Lou Gehrig's record of playing 2,030 consecutive games. This book went to press before the record-breaking home-run achievements of Mark McGwire and Sammy Sosa late in the 1998 baseball season; no doubt those will be included if and when another edition of this interesting book is issued. As it now stands, there is little doubt it has the potential of being one of the most popular books in both elementary school and public libraries.

Other Sports

Antle, Nancy

STAYING COOL   *6–10 YEARS*

Illustrated by E. B. Lewis. New York: Dial, 1997.

> A little boy relates what he does to train for the local Golden Gloves boxing tournament. To qualify for participation in this amateur tournament or for any of the others which might well follow, he has to learn how to do sit-ups and push-ups, punch the speed bag, heavy bag, and double-end bag, jump rope, shadow-box, and lift weights. Most important, however, he must learn to "stay cool" and not lose control when his sparring partner hits him too hard; instead he must think about throwing good punches and blocking his sparring partner's punches. The full-color illustrations, done in watercolor, help readers "feel" the dedication and

effort of all the young men and boys who work out in this gym and are being trained by the owner of the gym, a man who is not only the little boy's idol and mentor but his loving and very supportive grandfather. Lewis's technique of painting the backgrounds in monochromatic shades so they appear as silhouettes and painting the main characters in vibrant rich hues dramatizes the attire and movements and the great dedication and effort of the boxers. *Staying Cool* received the 1997 Parents' Book Award from *Parents' Magazine.*

Blackstone, Margaret

THIS IS SOCCER   *4–9 YEARS*

Illustrated by John O'Brien. New York: Henry Holt, 1999.

Action-filled, zany cartoon-style expressionistic illustrations rendered in line and watercolor match perfectly the brief, easy-to-read text printed in heavy primary-sized type. Children are certain to enjoy this introduction to soccer and will no doubt appreciate the precise manner in which the author has identified the equipment, players, and basic plays essential to the game as well as the opportunity to see a game "in progress."

Hoyt-Goldsmith, Diane

LACROSSE: THE NATIONAL GAME OF THE IROQUOIS   *8–13 YEARS*

Illustrated with photographs by Lawrence Migdale. New York: Holiday House, 1998.

The author and illustrator of this fine photo-essay make very clear how lacrosse links the heritage of the six nations of the Iroquois Confederacy to their culture, identity, and past. Details are provided about how the game of lacrosse has changed since the Native American ball games of the last century. A wealth of information about the game in contemporary times is offered in this book: the size of the playing field, the number of players on a team, the role and the positions of each team player, special skills required of lacrosse players, and details about the equipment they use. The glossary at the back of the book is comprehensive and includes a pronunciation guide. The full-color photographs are superb. Many of them are action-filled candid shots; none of the subjects seem self-conscious or posed. All of the pictures are crisp and clear and are aptly reproduced in varied sized and shapes throughout the book. (See illustration 10.) Each picture is accompanied by worthwhile and informative captions. Worthy of note is the double-page reproduction of American artist George Catlin's painting (circa 1830s) of a North American Choctaw playing a variation of lacrosse.

ILLUSTRATION 10   Photo copyright © 1998 by Lawrence Migdale. Reprinted in black and white from *Lacrosse: The National Game of the Iroquois* by permission of Holiday House, Inc.

Members of the Lyons family, Native American citizens of the Onondaga Nation Territory in New York have been leading lacrosse players for several generations; they are used as a literary vehicle to relate the fascinating history of the sport and the importance it holds

143

for the Iroquois people, especially the people of the Onondaga Nation. The information is carefully written and logically organized around such topics as the history and membership of the six nations of the Iroquois Confederacy. Lacrosse (known as *Guh-chee-gwah-ai* by the Haudenosaunee or Iroquois) is a ball game that served many purposes, all of which reflected the Iroquois' religion and a way to communicate with the spirit world. It was often used as a form of conflict resolution as well as a medicine game played for the well-being of players, other individuals, and nations, or to lift the hearts of the people.

Krull, Kathleen

WILMA UNLIMITED: *7–10* YEARS
HOW WILMA RUDOLPH BECAME THE WORLD'S FASTEST WOMAN
Illustrated by David Diaz. San Diego: Harcourt Brace, 1994.

This picture-book biography tells a brief and inspiring story of how Wilma Rudolph, who in her early childhood years was frail and sickly and was crippled by polio just before she turned five, overcame gargantuan odds by perseverance and heroic courage to become, at age twenty, the winner of three gold medals at the World Olympics in Rome in 1960. Diaz's illustrations, which are reproductions of dramatic and action-filled expressionistic paintings done in acrylic, watercolor, and gouache, extend and enrich perfectly Krull's straightforward and rather restrained telling of this phenomenal story. In the Author's Note the reader is informed about Wilma Rudolph's other accomplishments after she retired from her career as a runner in 1962. She died in 1994 at the age of fifty-four. This book might be read when students are reading about the Olympic Games or the physically handicapped.

McFarlane, Brian

HOCKEY FOR KIDS: HEROES, TIPS AND FACTS   *7–10* YEARS
Illustrated with drawings by Bill Slavin and with photographs.
New York: Morrow, 1996.

A wealth of information about hockey is introduced in this excellent photo-essay. The aim of the game, the hockey arena or "rink," the length of a game, and the positions of the team's players are briefly described and defined. Also presented are other facts, including a brief history of how and where the game originated and the equipment, rules and penalties, hockey jargon, practice and warm-up activities, special skills and talents, attitudes, women's hockey, and the Stanley cup, trophies for individual players, and so much more! Despite the many facts about the game, much of the text is anecdotal and all of it is interesting and easy to read. In the main, all of the full-color photographs and cartoon-style line and watercolor-wash sketches demonstrate specific skills and game plays. The table of contents is very detailed and an index is appended. Captions under the numerous photographs and drawings support and supplement the text most effectively. Excellent books that most readers would probably enjoy after reading this book by McFarlane include all of those in the Hockey Superstars series written by James Duplacey and illustrated with a fine array of photographs: *Amazing NHL Forwards, Great NHL Goalies,* and *Top NHL Rookies.* All of these books were published originally in Canada in 1994 by the Kids Can Press and in the United States in 1996 by Morrow.

Games

Lankford, Mary D.
DOMINOES AROUND THE WORLD   *5–8* YEARS
Illustrated by Karen Dugan. New York: Morrow, 1998.

> Typical of Lankford's popular formulaic Games Around the World series book, *Dominoes Around the World* provides a brief and precise history and easy-to-follow directions for playing versions of basic dominoes games from Cuba, France, Malta, the Netherlands, Spain, the Ukraine, Vietnam, and several regions in the United States. In addition, there are directions for variations of dominoes for one player and a recipe for "Delectable Disappearing (edible!) Dominoes." There are an excellent "Domino Dictionary" (i.e., glossary) and a fairly comprehensive bibliography of books readers might well take a look at to expand their fun with dominoes. Lankford also suggests her readers make use of other resources to find more information about dominoes and related topics: microfiche, e-mail, Web sites, personal interviews via telephone or face-to-face, and of course their public library facilities and interlibrary loan. Full-page reproductions of full-color paintings done in watercolor, gouache, and colored pencils illustrate and enrich this easy-to-read text.

CAREERS AND OCCUPATIONS

Anderson, Joan
COWBOYS: ROUNDUP ON AN AMERICAN RANCH   *7–14* YEARS
Illustrated with photographs by George Ancona.
New York: Scholastic, 1996.

> Splendid close-up and panoramic photographs in full color embellish the polished text describing the exciting personal experiences two boys (ages thirteen and eleven) have over a span of two weeks as they help

their parents and a crew of seasoned cowboys carry out the annual spring roundup. They gather eight hundred cattle from the barren mesas of Faywood, New Mexico, brand the calves, and weigh the yearlings, which are then ushered into shipping trucks and sent off to be sold. Their experiences teach the boys (and, no doubt, the readers of this fine picture book) that "No jobs on a ranch are one-man jobs," and although a cowboy's day is long and the work is grueling, being a cowboy "is a good clean life."

Carlson, Laurie

BOSS OF THE PLAINS: THE HAT THAT WON THE WEST   *8–11 YEARS*

Illustrated by Holly Meade. New York: DK INK/DK Publishing, 1998.

This is the true story of how the hat created by John Batterson Stetson became identified with America's West. Stetson was forced to move to a drier climate because the dampness and steam of his family's hatmaker shop in Orange, New Jersey, weakened his lungs and he developed tuberculosis. He moved to the West, first to St. Joseph, Missouri, then to Colorado where he tried his luck digging for gold. His face scorched by the blistering sun and eyes stung by the whipping wind,, he decided to make himself a hat with a wide brim and a tall crown from the thick fur pelt of a rabbit. A horseman who rode into the camp liked the distinctive hat and bought it right off John's head, paying far more for it than even the finest hat sold in his father's hat shop. Because the pickings in the Colorado gold fields were so slim, he moved to Philadelphia and resumed his trade as a hatmaker. At first he created hats that looked like those all the other hatters made, but he soon decided to make the high-crowned, wide-brimmed hat that had impressed the horseman out west. He named his hat John Stetson's Boss of the Plains. Even though it was expensive, the Boss of the Plains hat soon became popular with the wranglers and cowboys of the West and with others west of the Mississippi. Bullwhackers who drove oxen, mule skinners who led mule teams, and drovers who herded cattle and sheep wore the Boss of the Plains hat because it protected them from the burning sunshine, drenching rain, whipping wind, or swirling snow. Action-filled, cartoon-styled pictures done in collage befittingly illustrate this well-told, informative text. An excellent, albeit brief bibliography describing the role the Stetson hats played over the years appears on the last page.

Halperin, Wendy Anderson

ONCE UPON A COMPANY: A TRUE STORY   *5–10 YEARS*

Illustrated by Wendy Anderson Halperin. New York: Orchard, 1998.

Told from the perspective of the author's children, this story describes how the children started a College Fund Company, first by making and selling Christmas wreaths and then by making peanut-butter-and-jelly sandwiches and cold lemonade that they sold at the art fair in town. With the help of their parents, grandparents, neighborhood friends and acquaintances—and some good (and lucky) marketing tips—both businesses grew larger and larger. By the end of the sixth year their businesses involved marketing, wholesaling, and investing and netted more than $16,000. The detailed illustrations, done in pencil and watercolor, are reproduced in full color and reflect the exuberance and wholesomeness of the young entrepreneurs whose true story will surely impress and perhaps serve to inspire all who read this delightful informational picture book.

Lester, Julius

BLACK COWBOY, WILD HORSES: A TRUE STORY   *7–10 YEARS*

Illustrated by Jerry Pinkney. New York: Dutton, 1998.

A fictional event that typifies those actually engaged in by Bob Lemmons, a famous former slave turned talented Texas cowboy, is depicted in this narrative about how he and his black stallion Warrior gradually worked their way into a band of mustangs that ran wild in the West, displaced the stallion leader to take over the herd, and led them into the corral. The double-page, full-color art work, done in pencil, gouache, and watercolor, captures the majestic and unrestrained beauty of the mustangs, the wide open spaces of the western plains, and the gradual emergence of Bob Lemmons and Warrior among the herd. Be certain to notice the ethereal presence of the racing mustangs among the puffy clouds moving across the plains; but, if you can resist the temptation to bring them to the children's attention, give them a generous amount of time to notice them on their own. (They will delight in that discovery!) Pinkney's action-filled murals are as elegant a match for Lester's imagery-filled poetic prose as one could get. There are several fine picture books one might use with this fine portrayal of Lemmons' ingenuity and prowess: George Ancona's *Man and Mustang* (Macmillan, 1992); *Bill Pickett: Rodeo-Ridin' Cowboy,* written by Andrea D. Pinkney and illustrated by Brian Pinkney (Gulliver/Harcourt Brace, 1996); *The Story of Nate Love,* written by Robert Henry Miller and illustrated by Michael Bryant (Silver Burdett, 1994); *Reflections of a Black Cowboy* (4 volumes), written by Robert Henry Miller and illustrated by Richard Leonard (Silver Burdett, 1991); *Cowboys of the Wild West,* written by Russell Freedman and profusely illustrated with vintage photographs (Clarion, 1983). Although it is not illustrated, children will enjoy Julius

Lester's short story about the legendary Bob Lemmons, "The Man Who Was a Horse," in *Long Journey Home: Stories from Black History* (Dial, 1972, pp. 89–103).

Lyons, Mary E.

CATCHING THE FIRE: PHILIP SIMMONS, BLACKSMITH   *9–12+ YEARS*

Illustrated with photographs by Mannie Garcia. Boston: Houghton Mifflin, 1999.

This is a profusely illustrated biographical portrait of Philip Simmons, nationally renowned African-American metal sculpture artist, considered by many "a working person's hero and role model" (p. 8). He lived with his grandparents on Daniel Island, a small farming community, until he was eight years old, when he moved to Charleston so he could live with his mother, who worked as a housecleaner, and attend school regularly. At age thirteen he was apprenticed to blacksmith Peter Simmons (no relation), who from that point on served as his mentor and a surrogate father to him. Philip quit school at age fifteen to help support his family and continued his apprenticeship. Since then Philip has become a master blacksmith, forged hundreds of horseshoes, fixed innumerable wagons and trucks, and fashioned more than five hundred pieces of ornamental wrought iron. Most of his gates, fences, and railings decorate the city of Charleston, South Carolina, and several of his works are in major art museums throughout the United States. In recognition of the quality of his ornamental wrought iron sculpture, the Smithsonian Institution bought his "Star and Fish Gate" in 1976 for inclusion in an exhibit that travels around the country. This gate was made as a demonstration piece in August 1976, during the Festival of American Folklife in Washington, D.C. The Historical Charleston Foundation plans to open a Philip Simmons Training Center for Young Blacksmiths, fulfilling his wish to teach children the tradition of blacksmithing. The full-color photographs of Philip and some of the wrought iron sculptured items seen throughout Charleston, plus the black-and-white photographs of Philip as a child, members of his family, and scenes depicting the natural beauty of Daniel Island and the Charleston community that inspired his designs embellish most effectively Lyons' expertly crafted text. The table of contents, the index, and the bibliography listing books on related aspects of blacksmithing and Philip Simmons in particular, the author's note, and the bibliography of the many sources she used to prepare this artist's life story should all prove helpful and of special interest to the readers of this fine biography.

Page, Debra

ORCAS AROUND ME: MY ALASKAN SUMMER   *8–10 YEARS*

Illustrated by Leslie W. Bowman. Morton Grove, Ill.: Albert Whitman, 1997.

> Told from the perspective of seven-year-old Taiga, this picture book relates actual experiences that took place when he and his parents trolled for salmon during the summer in the Pacific Ocean off Southeast Alaska. This true account is exciting and provides a fascinating glimpse of how a family works and lives together during the salmon season: they troll for salmon, clean the fish, prepare it, and keep it fresh until it can be brought to the small village of Elfin Cove where it is sold to a fish-buying scow crew and then sent to the best markets in the United States and other countries throughout the world. The text is done in an explicit narrative style and the detailed illustrations, most of which are full-page pictures but also include quite a few double-page spreads, are done in clean, bright watercolor. Together the text and the pictures offer the reader an array of insights into salmon fishing, including its challenges, excitement, and anxieties, and beautiful scenes of the ocean as well as the wildlife in the cold waters off the Alaska coast as they are presently experienced by those who earn their livelihood fishing for salmon. The glossary names and most aptly describes the appearance and the habitats of the wildlife encountered by Taiga and his family.

Robbins, Ken

RODEO   *8–11 YEARS*

Illustrated with photography by Ken Robbins. New York: Henry Holt, 1996.

> In this photo-essay Robbins describes the riding and racing skills men, and in one case a woman, need to participate in the competitions and wild events of the rodeo: riding "rough stock," i.e., a bucking bronco with or without a saddle or riding bulls, steer wrestling, calf roping, team roping of a steer, and barrel racing. It should be noted that Robbins gives due honor to the crucial and often dangerous work done by the "clown" during the bull-riding events. The illustrations are black-and-white photo prints, hand colored with special water-based dyes, so typical of those in Robbins's other well-known stunning and informative photo-essays; they demonstrate very well the action-packed events of rodeo life of the traditional cowboy. Compare the traditional events shown by Robbins with those depicted in *Apache Rodeo,* written by Diane Hoyt-Goldsmith and illustrated with photographs by Lawrence Migdale (Holiday House, 1995).

Sandler, Martin W.

COWBOYS: A LIBRARY OF CONGRESS BOOK   *8–11 YEARS*

Illustrated. New York: HarperCollins, 1994.

> A quality selection of reproductions of photographs, lithographs, engravings, paintings, sketches, posters, song lyrics, song sheets and other illustrative materials obtained from the Library of Congress portrays the realities of the lifestyle of cowboys compared with the way they have been depicted on the stage, in the movies, and on television. In the main, this Library of Congress Book offers an excellent overview of the life of cowboys in the past and, to some extent, in today's world. There are no captions under the illustrative material and no table of contents, but the index, source citations, and bibliography for further reading are quite comprehensive and should prove helpful to those who want to learn more about specific aspects of the variety of topics discussed throughout this fine book.

Weitzman, David

POURING IRON: A FOUNDRY GHOST STORY   *10–14 YEARS*

Illustrated by David Weitzman. Boston: Houghton Mifflin, 1998.

> The skilled pencil drawings, which look almost like black-and-white photographs, are certain to help readers better understand the procedures and skilled craftsmanship of the iron workers so carefully described in the well-written text. The setting of this informative story is the historic Knight Foundry, one of America's earliest foundry machine shops; it still stands on Eureka Street in Sutter Creek, California. Using the literary device of a time warp, a fourteen-year-old living in today's world walks through the door of the foundry and takes on the role of an apprentice and, with the help and encouragement of "the ghosts of the men" who worked in the foundry in the 1870s and later, experiences firsthand the process of creating iron products ranging from huge water wheels to delicate machinery parts. In addition, the iron men demonstrate for the boy the numerous skills associated with the craft of creating iron products: making patterns and models, pouring molten iron into various shapes, and so on. Drawings of the many tools and pieces of equipment the men used in their craft appear on the endpapers.

Wellington, Monica, with Andrew Kupper

NIGHT CITY   *4–7 YEARS*

Illustrated by Monica Wellington. New York: Dutton, 1998.

At 7:00 P.M., when the little girl is asleep snug beneath her covers, the city does not rest. The reader follows the night people in their jobs through the nighttime hours: Ballet dancers get ready to twirl with artistry and grace for an eager audience; travelers arrive at their hotel after a long and tiring journey and are welcomed and helped by an eager staff; cleaners vacuum, sweep, wipe, and polish the offices, making them ready for the next day; an artist is busy at work in her studio; fire fighters put out a fire in a high rise and rush inside to rescue anyone who may be inside; a watchman makes his rounds in the art museum; cargo is brought into the city by boats, trucks, and freight trains; newspapers roll off the press and by early morning trucks deliver them to the newsstands; nightclubs are filled with melody and people sing and dance to the music; police officers patrol the avenues watching for robbers or for those who may need help; bakers make fresh buns, bread, and pastries; vendors set up their market stall. Early in the morning, the night workers are tired and hungry and head for the diner before going home and to bed. The little girl arises rested and refreshed, ready to begin her day. The stylized, flat, brightly colored illustrations, done in gouache, are filled with clever little details that will keep children intrigued and ever watchful each time they read this book or have it read aloud to them. Compare *Night City* to Margaret Wise Brown's classic concept book *Goodnight Moon,* illustrated by Clement Hurd (Harper, 1947), available in paperback and in a board book edition and still very much enjoyed by nursery school and preschool aged children.

PEOPLE OF OTHER TIMES

Ancient Egypt

Fisher, Leonard Everett

THE GODS AND GODDESSES OF ANCIENT EGYPT   *9–12 YEARS*

Illustrated by Leonard Everett Fisher. New York: Holiday House, 1997.

The large, unembellished illustrations of the thirteen most important Egyptian gods and goddesses were inspired by the art and hieroglyphics of Ancient Egypt. They are painted in bright, flat colors and the heavy black lines that outline them highlight their bold bulky shapes, almost suggesting they are large sculptures carved out of the sandstone of Egypt rather than paintings. The concise discussion of each deity is short yet comprehensive and includes information about his or her parentage, powers, and identifiable forms and images. As is typical of Fisher's informational books, a number of helpful aids are included. An introduction presents basic facts about the geography of lower and upper Egypt, about the Egyptians' religious beliefs, especially those influenced by the elements of nature, and about their rulers over the years. The back matter contains a "Family Tree" depicting the connections of each of the mythological gods and goddesses, a pronunciation guide, and an excellent bibliography of books for further reading. A simple, large map of the Far East on the endpapers depicts Egypt's location in relation to the Mediterranean Sea, the Sahara Desert, Libya, Ethiopia, and Israel.

People of the Bible

Osborne, Mary Pope

THE LIFE OF JESUS IN THE MASTERPIECES OF ART   *ALL AGES*

Illustrated. New York: Viking, 1998.

In this elegant, straightforward retelling of the life of Jesus, Osborne has selected events from the Gospels of the New Testament: Matthew, Mark, Luke, John. Her sources were the Holy Bible in the King James version and the Revised Standard Version (World, 1962). Her carefully prepared, precise text, combined with masterpieces of art created by some of the world's most accomplished visual artists, has resulted in a treasure in-and-of itself. Some of the illustrations are copies of entire paintings; others are copies of only portions of the original works. At the back of the book one will find miniaturized copies of each complete painting, giving the name by which it is commonly known, the name of the artist who created it, and the approximate or actual years the artist lived. This book is certain to be treasured by families, school and public libraries, and art aficionados. *The Story of the Nativity,* written by Geraldine McCaughrean and illlustrated with exquisite large, full-page stained-glass-like paintings, would be an excellent companion book (Doubleday, 1998).

Sanderson, Ruth, *Reteller*

TAPESTRIES: STORIES OF WOMEN IN THE BIBLE   *5–9 YEARS*

Illustrated by Ruth Sanderson. Boston: Little, Brown, 1998.

Using the Revised Standard Version of the Bible, Sanderson has created a verbal and visual tapestry recounting, very briefly, memorable portraits of twenty-three women of the Old and New Testaments. Stunning oil paintings with the aura of rich and decorative tapestry accurately depict each of the women in her setting or in the role for she is reported to have played in history.

Medieval Europe

Gravett, Christopher

THE KNIGHT'S HANDBOOK: HOW TO BECOME   *9–12 YEARS*
A CHAMPION IN SHINING ARMOR

Illustrated with pictures and sketches by Christopher Gravett and
Anthony Drake and photographs by David Armstrong. New York:
Cobblehill/Dutton, 1997.

> This fact-filled book should provide an intriguing introduction to the
> preparation and lifestyle of medieval knights. The easy-to-follow direc-
> tions for constructing a shield of arms, a helmet, a knightly sword, a
> castle, a siege catapult, and even a checkerboard game and the pieces
> needed to play it would pique the imagination and encourage further
> attention and involvement of the independent albeit reluctant reader
> as would the authentic recipe for a knightly snack (Honey Toast with
> Pine Nuts). The numerous detailed sketches, action drawings, and pho-
> tographs are strategically placed, are of different sizes, are skillfully
> executed in full color, and effectively support and extend the easy-to-
> read factual text. Neither a table of contents nor an index is included,
> but each topic discussed is clearly identified, so readers can pick and
> choose the parts of this book they wish to read; nonetheless, they will
> probably end up reading the entire book, and more than once at that.

Hodges, Margaret

JOAN OF ARC: THE LILY MAID   *8–10 YEARS*

Illustrated by Robert Rayevsky. New York: Holiday House, 1999.

> An elegantly designed picture book, this biographical sketch of a peasant
> girl named Jeanne d'Arc (circa 1412–1431), born and raised in the village
> of Domrémy, France, who not only became famous during her lifetime
> but is still revered by many contemporary Catholics as St. Joan of Arc.
> She claimed that she heard voices from God and saw visions of saints
> (especially of St. Michael, who told her to go to bring Charles VII to be
> crowned in the city of Reims, France). In order to carry out St. Michael's
> directives, she disguised herself as a man and became a solider in the
> French army, carrying a white banner embroidered with golden lilies,
> the ancient symbol of French kings. She became famous for leading
> a French army to victory in the battle of Orléans against the English
> during the Hundred Years War and brought Charles VII to Reims for his
> coronation. In 1430 she was captured and imprisoned by the English.
> She was put on trial for heresy and witchcraft (because she wore men's
> clothing), convicted, and burned at the stake on May 30, 1431. The

153

French called her the Lily Maid and the British called her Joan d'Arc and Joan the witch. In 1920 she was named a saint and is known throughout the world—"even by her old enemies, the English" (p. 28)—as Saint Joan of Arc. The simple, fine leaded type is a perfect match for the illustrations done in delicate drypoint and etching and full color wash. The style and content of the drawings reflect skillfully and artfully the medieval setting of this version of Joan of Arc's life story.

Nicolle, David

MEDIEVAL KNIGHT   *9–13 YEARS*

Illustrated with sketches, maps and photographs by numerous artists plus four see-through scenes by Bill Donohue and Terry Gabbey.
New York: Viking, 1997.

An excellent authentic, broad-based historical glimpse of the rise and demise of the medieval knights in Europe is provided in this book. More specifically some facts are presented about the knights: from their beginning as heavily armed soldiers, through the period of their elite status in the fourteenth century when they rose to prominence and transformed the medieval world, to their subsequent demise in the fifteenth century, when western European civilization changed, making feudalism, the extravagant lifestyle of the knights, and their code of chivalry out of date. At the same time the invention of new weapons (e.g., steel-armed crossbows, gunpowder, and handguns) made the heavily armored knights ineffective. A number of clearly designated aids will help readers find topics they are looking for or lead them to new information about these men whose code and actions (justifiably or not) laid the foundation for some of the most celebrated myths and legends in history. There are a precise table of contents, a detailed index, a list of key dates, and a glossary. Also, the nonthreatening page design is bound to encourage thoughtful and careful examination on the part of the readers. The full-color illustrations are well chosen and constitute a fine balance between realistic drawings, sketches, diagrams, maps, and photographic reproductions of sculptures, religious articles, and murals, all of which serve to support and extend immeasurably the brief but precise boxes of informative text provided for each of the many topics discussed. The four see-through scenes do double duty, making such things as the construction, uses, and details of a knights's armor and weaponry; the defenses of a manor house; a fortress of the crusaders; and the ships of the seafaring knights more "realistic" and more comprehensible and memorable.

PEOPLE OF OTHER COUNTRIES

Africa

Onyefulu, Ifeoma

CHIDI ONLY LIKES BLUE: AN AFRICAN BOOK OF COLORS   *4–8 YEARS*

Illustrated with photographs by Ifeoma Onyefulu. Textile designs for
endpapers by Chinye Onyefulu. New York: Cobblehill, 1997.

> This is a fine example of a multidimensional concept book. However,
> the title is more than a little misleading because it does not actually
> reveal the major focus of the book. While this book may well help
> children learn the names of the colors of the rainbow, it will teach them
> a great deal about the ethnic and cultural traditions of eastern Nigeria.
> In fact, colors serve merely as a vehicle for introducing the eastern
> Nigerian people's traditional foods, religious clothing and practices,
> cooking utensils, board games, chewing sticks, jewelry, and so on. I can
> only conclude the intended focus is on teaching aspects of the eastern
> Nigerian cultural traditions, and the naming of colors is of secondary
> importance at best. Nonetheless, the author has done an excellent job of
> introducing the readers to some interesting and worthwhile information
> about the Nigerian people. The clear and sharp full-color photographs
> highlight the spectrum of vivid hues that abound in this part of Africa.
> Numerous Nigerian words sprinkled throughout the text add to the
> cultural aura of the book. In each case they are effectively and smoothly
> incorporated into the body of the text.

Roberts, Michael

THE JUNGLE ABC   *7–10 YEARS*

Foreword by Iman. Illustrated by Michael Roberts. New York:
Callaway/Hyperion, 1998.

> Accomplished collage pictures made from paper cutouts accompany
> alphabetically arranged words (in English) referring to flora and fauna,
> fruits, vegetables, musical instruments, and masks found in the various
> jungles throughout the African continent. Zulu people and the fabric
> designs used on their traditional and contemporary clothing are also de-
> picted in collage. Collectively the illustrations emphasize the harmony
> of the varied elements of the jungle, which "when left to itself," as Iman
> says in the foreword, "is a perfectly functioning organ, sustaining life
> for the rest of the body of Africa" (p. v).

Belize

Staub, Frank

CHILDREN OF BELIZE   *7–10 YEARS*

Illustrated with photographs by Frank Staub. Minneapolis:
Carolrhoda, 1997.

> This photo-essay serves as a nicely comprehensive introduction to the
> diverse, rich cultural life experienced by some of the children of Belize.
> The geography of this small and beautiful Central American nation
> varies from rain forest to sandy shores to rugged mountains. The full-
> color, clearly focused photographs and the accessible text depict the
> children at play and work revealing, without being didactic, that in
> many ways regardless of where they live children are much alike, yet
> their ethnic heritage and special history tend to make them unique.
> The captions that accompany each photograph reflect and oftentimes
> considerably supplement and expand upon the content of the text.
> The pronunciation guide and the index in the back matter are very
> worthwhile. Two other excellent books included in the World's Children
> series published by Carolrhoda are *Children of Vietnam,* written by
> Marybeth Lorbiecki and illustrated with photographs by Paul P. Rome
> (1997), and *Children of Guatemala,* written and illustrated with pho-
> tographs by Jules Hermes (1997).

China

Zhang, Song Nan

THE CHILDREN OF CHINA: AN ARTIST'S JOURNEY   *10–14+ YEARS*

Illustrated by Song Nan Zhang. Plattsburg, N.Y.: Tundra/McClelland;
Toronto: Stewart, 1998.

> A native of Beijing and, since the protest at Tiananmen Square, a resident
> of Montreal, artist Song Nan Zhang traveled along the "Silk Road"
> to provide this rare and insightful glimpse of family life among nine
> diverse nationalities and ethnic groups of China. The content and the
> very detailed, somewhat innocent and romanticized realistic paintings
> reflect the theme of innocence of the children and family throughout
> China. Particular attention is given to the major religions practiced
> in China and to the Spring Festival, the biggest holiday time in the
> country, in which dozens of minorities take part. Statistical information
> about the nine minorities depicted in this book are presented in a
> listing entitled "About the People in This Book." Ethnographic statistics
> include population numbers, areas of China where they tend to live, and
> their primary religion. A simply sketched map identifies the provinces
> and regions, major mountains, rivers, and deserts mentioned in the text
> and the statistical table.

Ireland

McMahon, Patricia

ONE BELFAST BOY   *8–11 YEARS*

Illustrated with photographs by Alan O'Connor. Boston: Houghton Mifflin, 1999.

> This unusual photo-essay presents a provocative parallel between early adolescent Liam's motivation to win a boxing match in order to get beyond the peace wall in Belfast without risking his life and the current attempt to end the conflict between Protestant and Catholic factions that has preoccupied every facet of life in Ireland for so many years. Liam loses the local boxing match that would have enabled him to go to Dublin, the only way he can think of to get away from the violence of gang-infested Belfast. He vows to keep up his training and try to win the next local championship match that would take him to Dublin, just as so many people have dedicated their efforts to devising a way to keep the peace accord from failing. The full-color photographs display various aspects of Liam's life: his family and friends, his participation and involvement in school routines and special activities, the Holy Trinity Boxing Club where he trains. They also portray scenes depicting the ever-present tensions and conflict around him: the helicopters that hover overhead, soldiers patrolling or fighting in the streets, a hearse driving slowly, followed by the mourners on foot, the teenage gangs hanging out on the street corners, and the teenage boy hired to keep order in the local movie theater every Saturday afternoon. Two large, flat, colorful maps appear in the front of the book. One of the maps provides a good visual perspective of Northern Ireland and the Republic of Ireland and their relationship to the countries of Great Britain. It also contains an enlargement of the six countries of Northern Ireland, pinpointing the location of Belfast where the bulk of the tension and fighting is taking place. The other large map highlights, by color coding, the locations in Belfast of the majority Catholic and Protestant neighborhoods and shows the city boundary and main roads. To say there is much in this photo-essay that one will mull over and speculate about long after its covers are closed and the book is returned to the shelf is an understatement at best.

Tibet

Demi

THE DALAI LAMA: A BIOGRAPHY OF THE TIBETAN   *9–13+ YEARS*
SPIRITUAL AND POLITICAL LEADER

Illustrated by Demi. New York: Henry Holt, 1998.

> In the introduction, Demi tells her readers that in the Tibetan language *Dalai* means "ocean" and *Lama* means "teacher"; thus *Dalai Lama*

157

means "the ocean of wisdom." She said since the 1500s the Buddhist leader in Tibet has been the Dalai Lama, worshiped as the bodily form of the Buddhist saint of compassion, Chenrezzig. Each new Dalai Lama is believed to be the reincarnation of all the previous Dalai Lamas. Demi's carefully scripted text and meticulous paintings, rendered in gouache and ink on vellum and watercolor-washes on paper to create the remarkable illustrations, pay a stunning tribute to the current (the fourteenth) Dalai Lama. (See illustration 11.) She recounts how this Dalai Lama was found by the holiest of the men of Tibet in a small village in eastern Tibet when he was a precocious two-year-old boy named Lhamo Shondup, living in a peasant hut with a loving family. When he saw the search party, the boy was said to have declared, "Now I am going home!" He demonstrated to the monks that he remembered things from a previous life picking out the objects that had belonged to the thirteenth Dalai Lama from among others that had not. The boy was taken to live with the monks and became the fourteenth Dalai Lama at age four (February 22, 1939). He was given the name Getsul Ngawang Lobsang Tenzin Gyatso Sangpo, which means The Holy One, the Gentle Glory, Powerful in Speech, Pure in Mind of Divine Wisdom, Holder of Faith, and Ocean Wide. He began his training in philosophy, calligraphy, and metaphysics at age five. A regent ruled the country until he reached the age of fifteen, at which time he was named the spiritual and political leader of Tibet. Demi discusses the effects of the Chinese Communist rule on Tibet, the Dalai Lama's escape to India (at age twenty-four, in 1959), and his role in forming a government-in-exile in Dharamsala, which to this day serves as a model for a restored Tibet. He continues to live the spiritual life of a monk and remains a model spiritual and political leader of his people, teaching that war is not stopped by war, but by peace and love. He was awarded the Nobel Peace prize in 1989.

Dolphin, Laurie

OUR JOURNEY FROM TIBET   *8–11 YEARS*

With a letter from His Highness the Dalai Lama. Afterword by Rinchen K. Choegyal. Illustrated with photographs by Nancy Jo Johnson. New York: Dutton, 1997.

> The author describes the challenges and hardships that nine-year-old Sonam, her two sisters, Payamg and Dekyi, and a group of other children experienced during their illegal and dangerous journey from their village in Tibet to a safe haven in India. At the Tibetan Reception Center near Nepal they were interviewed, fingerprinted, and sent on to Dharamsala (where they met briefly with His Highness the Dalai

ILLUSTRATION 11   From *The Dalai Lama: The Biography of the Tibetan Spiritual and Political Leader* by Demi, © 1998 by Demi. Reprinted by permission of Henry Holt & Co., LLC.

Lama); they were finally settled at the Tibetan Children's Village and enrolled in a Tibetan "school in exile" where they were privileged to study the Tibetan language, the religion of Buddhism, and the history of their people. For over forty years, under the Communist Chinese colonization, Chinese has been the official language in Tibet, and Tibetan history and culture have not been taught. Teachers in Tibet are

159

often ill-prepared and there are virtually no schools in the nomadic areas; thus one can see why Sonam and the children who escaped with her from Tibet to India were so pleased to be able to attend their "school in exile." The photographic illustrations, reproduced in full color, capture aspects of Sonam's traditional Tibetan family life in the small village of Sog Dzong; the varied landscapes through which the children traveled during their escape to India; the processing procedures at the Tibetan Reception Center; and the Children's Village in Dharamsala where Sonam and the other children lived and attended school together. Compare the perspective set forth in Dolphin's book with that presented by Peter Sis in his 1999 Caldecott Honor Award book *Tibet: Through the Red Box* (Frances Foster/Farrar, Straus & Giroux, 1998), described below.

Sis, Peter

TIBET: THROUGH THE RED BOX   *10 YEARS–ADULTHOOD*

Illustrated by Peter Sis. New York: Frances Foster/Farrar,
Straus & Giroux, 1998.

Named a 1999 Caldecott Honor Award book, this erudite, rather mystical informational book was inspired by and purportedly quoted in large measure from Peter Sis's father's journal recording his experiences in the Himalayas while filming the Chinese military construction of the highway into Tibet. Some of the entries tell how the elder Sis got separated from his film crew, was caught in a snowstorm and became ill while wandering around the mountains, entered the city of Lhasa and met the Dalai Lama, and was finally reunited with his crew. There is an unusual melding of the father's actual adventures before and during his wanderings in the Himalayas and his gradual learning a smattering of the Tibetan language, some of the practices of Buddhist monks and the lamas, and the son's commentaries on the journal entries. Many of the pages look as if they are actually enlarged photocopies of the handwritten journal entries. The illustrations in this oversized book are amazingly intricate and tiny, but are worthy of meticulous and thoughtful examination; those depicting the elder Sis's adventures are filled with traditional Tibetan maze-like designs and Buddhist graphic symbols such as the mandala, a circular pattern divided into multiple projections bearing an image—usually that of a deity. Children (and adults) might enjoy identifying some of these same symbols and motifs in Demi's picture book biography, *The Dalai Lama: A Biography of the Tibetan Spiritual and Political Leader* (Henry Holt, 1998), described above.

PEOPLE AT WAR

Bolshevik Revolution (Russia)

Brewster, Hugh

ANASTASIA'S ALBUM   *9–13 YEARS*

Illustrated with photographs. New York: Hyperion/Madison Press, 1996.

Readers of this brief biography are given glimpses of what life was like for Her Imperial Highness the Grand Duchess Anastasia Nicholaievna Romanov and the other members of the Royal family of Russia when the Tsar Nicholas Romanov II reigned over Russia, up to and including the tragic series of events that happened to them during the Bolshevik Revolution (March 1917 through July 1918). In this account of the Romanovs, carefully selected quotations and facts gleaned from numerous primary sources are melded with numerous black-and-white photographs from Anastasia's personal albums (as well as some that were hand colored by Anastasia herself), many from the State Archive of the Russian Federation in Moscow, plus some full-color photographs of Romanov-related sites as they appear today. Quotations from Anastasia's albums, letters she wrote to and received from members of her family and friends, plus the numerous quotes from the diary of her father, memoirs of the Romanov children's tutor and family friend, etc., are sprinkled throughout this biography and personalize and individualize the people involved. Graphic details are included about the family's imprisonment in Tobolsk, Siberia, where life was described as boring, but not unbearable. They were later moved to Eikaterinburg to a house the Bolshevik officials called the "House of Special Purpose" where the guards took delight in humiliating them and they experienced extreme suffering. The Epilogue tells readers that the family was massacred on the night of July 16, 1918, in the cellar of the house in Eikaterinburg. In January 1919 their charred remains and some of the family's jewelry and articles of clothing were found in a forested area near an abandoned mine shaft outside the town of Eikaterinburg. For sixty years (up to her death in 1984), a woman who called herself Anna Anderson contended that she was Anastasia, but her assertions were later disproved by blood tests. In 1991 when some skeletons were dug up out of the grave in Eikaterinburg, additional scientific tests determined that they were indeed the bones of the imperial family, but the skeletons of Anastasia and her younger brother Alexi were missing. (The book was published before the entombment of the family's remains in Russia occurred in the spring of 1998, so no discussion of that event is included in this first edition.) The design of the endpapers is the same pattern as the one in Anastasia's real album. An excellent glossary is appended, as is a fine bibliography of primary works and sources the author consulted in the preparation of this book.

Civil War (War Between the States)

Lincoln, Abraham

THE GETTYSBURG ADDRESS   *7 YEARS–ADULTHOOD*

Foreword by Gary Wills. Illustrated by Michael McCurdy.
Boston: Houghton Mifflin, 1998.

>Lincoln gave this speech at the consecration of the Soldiers' National Cemetery at Gettysburg, Pennsylvania, in 1863, shortly after thousands of Civil War soldiers of the North and South who killed each other in the fields surrounding the town of Gettysburg were buried. An appropriately somber, yet beautiful collection of black-and-white scratchboard illustrations reflects masterfully the power and intensity of Lincoln's remarks. Each page contains some lines of the speech; the accompanying illustrations serve as witness to the circumstances and events and individuals involved in this battle at Gettysburg. Each page provides readers an opportunity to function as participant observers—to view all that went on during this battle from different perspectives: from a panoramic view, then close up, then face-to-face. McCurdy has done a remarkable job of depicting soldiers, statesmen, and onlookers as individuals, each unique as to features, body structure, and age, and each distinctive in his or her emotional responses to the circumstances of this battle and the commemoration service. Historical details, such as the military weaponry and the clothing worn by the soldiers and civilians, are accurately portrayed.

Revolutionary War (War of Independence)

Kroll, Steven

THE BOSTON TEA PARTY   *6–10 YEARS*

Illustrated by Peter Fiore. New York: Holiday House, 1998.

>Excellent verbal and visual descriptions detail the series of enactments issued by the English Parliament (April 1764 through May 1774) to tax and coerce the colonists—events that ultimately led to the Boston Massacre (March 5, 1770), the Boston Tea Party (December 16, 1773), and the Battle of Lexington and Concord (April 19, 1775), which finally amounted to the beginning of the war of American independence. The enactments of the English Parliament and the resulting actions by the colonists described in the body of the text are listed and briefly summarized at the back of the book in the table entitled "Important Dates."

The watercolor paintings reproduced in large, full-color illustrations vary nicely in perspective—landscapes, seascapes, portraits, and action-filled scenes, making these facets of American history come to life.

Lunn, Janet
CHARLOTTE   *8–10 YEARS*
Illustrated by Brian Deines. Plattsburg, N.Y.: Tundra, 1998.

> The year was 1783; thirteen rebellious American colonies had just won their eight-year war of independence from Great Britain. Ten-year-old Charlotte Haines was disowned by her father, a staunch Patriot, because she defied him to say a last good-bye to her cousins just before they and their parents, who were Loyalists, were sent to Nova Scotia by the Patriots to live in exile. Before her uncle and his family were to embark, he tried unsuccessfully to persuade the girl's father to change his mind, and her mother would not counter her husband's decision. Charlotte traveled to Nova Scotia with her relatives, lived a long and productive life there, and never saw New York or anyone in her family again. The illustrations capture masterfully the aura of these troubled times and the range of emotions that ravaged families torn apart by their conflicting political opinions.

Peacock, Louise
CROSSING THE DELAWARE: A HISTORY OF MANY VOICES   *9–12 YEARS*
Illustrated by Walter Lyon Krudop. New York: Atheneum, 1998.

> The events leading up to the Battle of Trenton, the battle itself and its effect on the enlisted men of the Continental Army, and the morale of Revolutionists after they won this battle are reported through a number of difference voices: narrative statements by the author, who is a present-day historian; excerpts from a series of letters between a fictional soldier and his wife; and excerpts from actual letters and diaries written or oral comments known to have been made by such persons as General George Washington, an officer on Washington's staff, an enlisted man, and General Thomas Gage. These events are illustrated with impressive and informative full-color paintings made by Walter Lyon Krudop especially for this book and copies of familiar engravings of paintings by such well-known artists as Amos Doolittle, J. C. Armytage, and Gilbert Stuart. Be certain to notice the endpapers at the front and at the back of the book. These scenes depict the sequence of the major events beginning with the Boston Massacre (March 5, 1770) that led to the Revolutionary War and ending with Washington's farewell to his officers (December 4, 1783).

World War II

Bunting, Eve

SO FAR FROM THE SEA   *8–11 YEARS*

Illustrated by Chris K. Soentpiet. New York: Clarion, 1998.

The author and the illustrator have told a moving story about a tragic time in America's history when Japanese Americans were relocated shortly after the Japanese bombed Pearl Harbor in Hawaii in 1941. It is a story that should be told to all American children, but be prepared to handle the questions that are bound to arrive about the rationale and justification for the United States government implementing it. In this story, young readers are introduced to a Japanese-American couple; they are now husband and wife, but in 1942 they were children and they, along with their parents, were "relocated" from their home in California. The couple is taking their young son and daughter to visit the Manzanar War Relocation Center in eastern California. This center was one of ten war relocation centers in which approximately ten thousand people of Japanese ancestry were placed in 1942. It was closed in 1945, its buildings were sold at auction, and the area where the camp stood is now a National Historic Site; a small cemetery surrounded by a wire fence remains there. Inside the fenced area is a tall white obelisk and inscribed on it in black Japanese script are the words "Memorial to the Dead."

The setting for this story is 1972. The young couple and their children are planning to move from their home in California to Boston, Massachusetts, and this is to be their last visit to the Manzanar War Relocation Center. The reader learns that in 1942, when the children's father was eight years old, he and his parents were brought to the Center; in 1943 his father (their grandfather) died of pneumonia—but he was also disillusioned and heartbroken. The burial site for each of the deceased was marked with a circle of rocks instead of a headstone, and the person's name and the date of his or her death were painted on the top stone. The family members place meaningful mementos on the father's grave site and leave the Center.

The presence or absence of color effectively designates two different eras alluded to in this story: The parts of the story that occur in the present (1972) when the family makes its farewell visit to the grandfather's grave site are depicted in large realistic paintings rendered in rich, full-color watercolor paintings. The illustrations depicting the scenes from the past (1942–1945) are rendered in large sepia-toned watercolor paintings. All of Soentpiet's paintings, whether in full color or sepia, masterfully enhance and extend Bunting's understated and elegant, yet easy to read, controlled text.

Kaplan, William, with Shelley Tanaka

ONE MORE BORDER: THE TRUE STORY OF ONE FAMILY'S   *8–11 YEARS*
ESCAPE FROM WAR TORN EUROPE

Illustrated by Stephen Taylor and with photographs.
Toronto: Groundwood Books/Vancouver, B.C.: Douglas & McIntyre
(Distributed by Publishers Group West), 1998.

A gripping account of how the Kaplans, a Jewish family (a Russian mother, a Lithuanian father, their son and daughter), in the spring of 1939 fled their family home in Memel, Lithuania, two days before the Germans invaded the city. They stayed in Kaunas, the capital of Lithuania, for a short time and there they sought the help of Sugihara, the Japanese consul, to acquire transit visas to leave Russia, enter Japan, and then move on to their final destination in Ontario, Canada, where they planned to be united with their relatives. Unfortunately, Sugihara could issue a transit visa that allowed only the children to travel on Mr. Kaplan's passport. Mrs. Kaplan could not be included in the visa because she was Russian; she had to get separate visas, one from the Russian consul in Kaunas and then another from the Japanese consul in Moscow. The account of how the family managed to travel together all the way to Canada is an amazing tale in-and-of itself.

The epilogue informs readers that a condition of their immigration to Canada required that the Kaplan family settle on an abandoned farm and work the land for one year. After their year was over, they moved to Windsor, Ontario, where the mother opened a photography studio and the family began a new life. Although the family experienced some difficult times, they prospered and quickly came to love their new country. The boy became a lawyer and the girl became an artist. This grim, anxiety-filled story is effectively illustrated with full-color realistic paintings and with full-color and faded black-and-white photographs. The glossary lists and clearly defines terms pertaining to foreign travel permits, Russian terrain, major Jewish holidays, and aspects of World War II. A map on the endpapers shows the extremely long route the Kaplan family followed from Memel, Lithuania, to Cornwall, Ontario, in eastern Canada where they ultimately settled. Be certain to encourage the students to read *Passage to Freedom: The Sugihara Story,* written by Ken Mochizuki and illustrated by Dom Lee, and the afterword by Hiroki Sugihara (Lee & Low, 1997) to find out more about this heroic man who helped the Kaplan family and so many other Jews reach freedom.

Mochizuki, Ken

PASSAGE TO FREEDOM: THE SUGIHARA STORY   *8–11 YEARS*

Afterword by Hiroki Sugihara. Illustrated by Dom Lee.

New York: Lee & Low, 1997.

In defiance of an order from the Japanese government, but with the support of his family, Chiune Sugihara, who served as Japanese consul to Kaunas, Lithuania, in 1940, issued visas to thousands of Jewish refugees who had escaped from Poland when the Nazis had taken over that country. These visas allowed the refugees to travel through the Soviet Union to Japan, and then on to another country that would accept them. Chiune Sugihara's son Hiroki told the story of his father's courage to noted writer, journalist, and actor Ken Mochizuki, who in turn retold it in this first-person narrative from Hiroki's perspective. Adding to the realism of this inspiring personal story are the large sepia-toned multimedia illustrations that look like old photographs, but were actually made by applying oil paint and colored pencil over images scratched out of encausted melted beeswax and resin. Teachers and librarians who want to learn more about Chiune Sugihara and his family's real-life story in order to share it with their students might read *Visas for Life* by Yukika Sugihara, translated by Hiroki Sugihara (Edu-Comm Plus, 1995).

Language

WRITTEN LANGUAGE

Alphabet Books

Ada, Alma Flor

GATHERING THE SUN: AN ALPHABET IN SPANISH AND ENGLISH   *7–10 YEARS*

English translation by Rosa Zubizarreta. Illustrated by Simon Silva.
New York: Lothrop, Lee & Shepard, 1998.

Twenty-eight short, simple poems, written in Spanish and English, are alphabetically arranged according to the Spanish titles. There seem to be two themes in this collection of poems. One is to celebrate the history and cultural heritage, family and friends, and the bounty of the harvest (especially things grown, cultivated, and produced by Spanish farm-workers from Cuba, the Yucatan, and Mexico); the other is to take pride in and honor one's language and cultural heritage. These themes are dramatically enhanced by the oversized, double-page paintings rendered in gouache on illustration board. The rich, hot colors suggest the bright sun and humid atmosphere and the ever present rich, brightly colored flora and fauna that are so much a part of the Latin and Central American countries colonized by the Spaniards. *Note:* Before sharing this book with children it might be wise to point out that traditionally there have been twenty-eight letters in the Spanish language alphabet instead of the twenty-six letters included the English language alphabet and in most

167

Romance languages that make use of the Roman alphabet. (The letter pairs Ch and Ll are considered separate letters in the Spanish language alphabet.) The author notes at the beginning of the book that by the year 2000, to make it easier for computers to alphabetize, Ch and Ll will no longer be considered separate letters. She says she chose to include them in this book because she considers them "as unripe fruit not yet ready to be taken from the tree, since all of us who love our language and the traditions it keeps alive will need some time to grow accustomed to this change" (p. ii).

Graef, Renee, *Adaptor*

MY LITTLE HOUSE ABC   *3–6 YEARS*

Illustrated by Renee Graef, inspired by the art work of Garth Williams.
New York: HarperCollins, 1997.

> Part of the My First Little House Books series, this alphabet book is a collection of statements that appeared originally in books written by Laura Ingalls Wilder and illustrated by Garth Williams. In each case, the title of the original book from which the statements came is acknowledged. An illustration, created by Renee Graef but inspired by Garth Williams, accompanies each quotation. The books from which the quoted statements were selected are: *Little House in the Big Woods* (Harper, 1932, 1959); *Little House on the Prairie* (Harper, 1933, 1961); and *On the Banks of Plum Creek* (Harper, 1937, 1965). An example of how the alphabet is presented and related to Wilder's statements follows: "F is for fiddle. 'Pa sat for a long time in the doorway and played his fiddle' " (p. 5). From *Little House on the Prairie.*

Testa, Fulvio

A LONG TRIP TO Z   *3–6 YEARS*

Illlustrated by Fulvio Testa. San Diego: Harcourt Brace, 1997.

> A refreshing account of the alphabetically arranged sights a little boy sees as he flies around the world in his little red airplane. Children will delight in finding the clever and humorous details contained in the full-page colorful, simple line and wash paintings depicting the flight that begins when the boy's plane soars about the house from one room to the next, out through the window, across a desert island, over a jungle, past an observatory, among planets, and back home to the his bedroom where he collapses into bed and snuggles into his pillow with its pattern of galloping zebras.

Words

Jones, Charlotte Foltz

EAT YOUR WORDS: A FASCINATING LOOK   *7–11 YEARS*
AT THE LANGUAGE OF FOOD

Illustrated by John O'Brien. New York: Delacorte, 1999.

Cartoon-style pen-and-ink sketches profusely illustrate this interesting book about the history and meanings of the names and phrases, customs and beliefs associated with many kinds of foods. Some of the connections point to specific people (i.e., beef stroganoff, eggs benedict, graham crackers, etc.); cities, states, countries, and islands (i.e., sardines, mayonnaise, buffalo wings, etc.). The full-page sketches add a refreshing element of humor to this unique collection of trivia about food, ranging from spoofs to puns and even satire. Included are an efficiently organized table of contents, an extensive index, and a bibliography of titles listing cookbooks containing recipes for many of the foods mentioned in this book, as well as discussions of some superstitions and practices about certain foods, all of which will help to extend and satisfy the reading interests and needs of the children who read this book.

Yoon, Jung-Huyn, *Designer*

POPPOSITES: A LIFT, PULL, AND POP BOOK OF OPPOSITES   *3–6 YEARS*

Paper engineering by Roger Culbertson and Jung-Huyn Yoon.
Illustrated with photographs by Paul Bricknell and others.
New York: DK Publishing/Boston: Houghton Mifflin, 1996.

When I read this book to a group of pre-kindergarten children, a little boy said with great delight, "That's a magic book!" Indeed it appears to be a book full of "magic" surprises as one pulls at the arrow and a short pencil becomes a long pencil, or a bowl filled with fruit becomes empty, or a little girl jumps up and down. When one lifts the flap of a picture showing a boy leading a few musicians of the marching band, one finds he is leading many musicians in the band; when one flips the picture of a sad baby one finds a happy baby, and so on. The words naming the concepts that result from lifting or pulling or spinning the tabs, flaps, or arrows are printed in bold-faced, primary-sized type. Some of the opposite terms depicted are open-closed, sad-happy, few-many, inside-outside, and up-down. A delightful participation book bound to delight children and extend their conceptual understanding and vocabulary.

Ziefert, Harriet

BABY BUGGY, BUGGY BABY: A WORD PLAY FLAP BOOK   *4–7 YEARS*

Illustrated by Richard Brown. Boston: Walter Lorraine/Houghton Mifflin, 1997.

> Each page has a flap on which there is a simple colorful sketch outlined in heavy black ink. Each sketch depicts an action or situation that is also described in a phrase printed in bold-faced, heavy primary type. Open the flap and you will see a picture that depicts an action or situation described in which the words are reversed and mean something very different from the first scene and statement. Some of the phrases and the new meanings depicted in pictures and words are: "water in the sink, sink in the water; ring in a box, box in a ring." An amusing way to introduce word play!

Ziefert, Harriet

NIGHT-KNIGHT   *5–8 YEARS*

Illustrated by Richard Brown. Boston: Houghton Mifflin, 1997.

> Simple pictures, outlined in heavy black lines and painted in crisp, bright colors, demonstrate clearly the different meanings of pairs of words that sound alike but are spelled differently. This engaging word-flap book introduces young readers to the concept of homonyms in the English language (e.g., bare-bear, flower-flour, and oar-ore). Each homonym is spelled out in bold-faced manuscript type, one word in bold black type and its pair in bold red type, so the difference in their spelling will also become readily apparent to the reader.

Symbols

Samoyault, Tiphaine

GIVE ME A SIGN! WHAT PICTOGRAMS TELL US WITHOUT WORDS   *9–12 YEARS*

Translated from the French by Esther Allen. Icon illustrations by Fabienne Auguin. New York: Viking, 1997.

> The author provides, classifies, and discusses numerous pictograms, drawings, or symbols that usually can be understood by people from all over the world, and thereby has created a valuable resource for students. Once they become aware of these virtually worldwide visual symbols, students will be more likely to notice them when, where, and as they travel—in a car, on a train, in airports or train stations; printed on containers in the kitchen cupboards or medicine cabinets; on labels stitched to clothing or glued on packages; signs designating restricted access

for the handicapped or the location of men's or women's restrooms, fire exits, stairs, escalators, or elevators. The pictograms in this book are shown in the same flat, bright colors one usually sees in everyday life. There is a fine glossary of a limited number of the technical terms used throughout this easy-to-read text, but there is no table of contents; nonetheless, each of the sections and chapters is clearly highlighted. The pictograms are grouped into broad categories, each of which constitutes a chapter (e.g., Going on Vacation, Traveling, In Public Places). The topics included in the introductory sections are: Communicating with the World, What Does "Pictogram" Mean?, A Little History. This book was first published in 1995 in France under the title *Le Monde des Pictogrammes* by Circonflexe.

LANGUAGE FOR THE VISUALLY IMPAIRED: BRAILLE

Adler, David

A PICTURE BOOK OF LOUIS BRAILLE   *6–10 YEARS*

Illustrated by John and Alexandra Wallner.
New York: Holiday House, 1997.

This is a short, well-written biography of Louis Braille, who invented the system of raised letters we now call braille. In this brief, but comprehensive, easy-to-read and interesting account of Braille's life story, readers will find out that Louis Braille, who was born in 1809, spent his early childhood years in Coupvray, France. He was blinded at age three in an accident while playing with a sharp-pointed tool his father used to make saddles. His father attempted to teach his son how to read by feeling the heads of round-tipped upholstery nails hammered into a board to form letters; after Louis learned to "read" the letters of the alphabet his father taught him to read words formed by these letters. At age ten Louis began studies in Paris at the National Institute for Blind Children, where he spent the rest of his life. At age fifteen he invented the method of reading and writing by braille and was appointed assistant teacher at the school; two years later he was appointed a full-time teacher. He died of tuberculosis on January 16, 1852. The full-page, simple and rather sentimentalized four-color illustrations, done in ink line and watercolor wash, aptly support Adler's text and give young readers a good idea of how the people dressed and lived in the small hillside village of Coupvray, in the bustling city of Paris, and in the controlled and sequestered environment of the National Institute for Blind Children itself. The alphabet and numbers are printed in large, bold-faced type and in the raised lettering system that Braille invented. There is also a table of facts and relevant dates important to Braille's life story.

Carter, Alden R.

SEEING THINGS MY WAY   *5–9 YEARS*

Illustrated with photographs by Carol S. Carter.
Morton Grove, Ill.: Albert Whitman, 1998.

> Second grader Amanda describes how she and her fellow visually impaired classmates learn to use a variety of equipment and methods to learn to read, to communicate, and to express themselves verbally with others as well as to simply cope with their impairments: closed circuit television (CCTV), magnifiers, big-print books, a monocular, braille magazines and books, a brailler (a braille typewriter), a computer that "speaks" the words that are typed into it, a cane, and for a child afflicted with blind spots, balance and depth perception therapy. Some of the photographs are blurred in special ways to simulate how things look to a person who has blind spots and/or who needs to use a monocular. Amanda ends her discussion about growing up with blind spots by offering some upbeat messages. She names a number of people she has met as well as some famous people she has heard of who are blind and have achieved as educators, authors, musicians, dancers, or radio disc jockeys. She says forthrightly, "Some kids have asked me if I feel bad about being vision impaired. Well, I don't like it much. I mean, who would. But I don't have time to feel sorry for myself. I am *toooo* busy. . . . I'm thankful for every day I can see. . . . And if someday I lose more of my sight, I'm still going to be the star of my own life" (pp. 22–28).

LANGUAGE FOR THE HEARING IMPAIRED: AMERICAN SIGN LANGUAGE (ASL)

Rankin, Laura

THE HANDMADE COUNTING BOOK   *5–10 YEARS*

Illustrated by Laura Rankin. New York: Dial, 1998.

> Realistic drawings created with colored pencil on charcoal paper show how to count from one to twenty and twenty-five, fifty, seventy-five and one hundred, using American Sign Language (ASL). Images of folk toys, seashells, fish, flowers, origami figures, Russian nesting dolls, butterflies, etc., depict the number demonstrated by the finger "spelling" and the numeral printed in large, bold-faced type on the top right-

hand corner of the page. It should be emphasized to the readers of this book that they will not be able to follow the directions for counting in ASL after one quick reading. Indeed, they will have to follow the directions depicted on each page many times over and will have to practice repeatedly to get the correct shape, movement, position, and placement of the hand (near the face or touching an arm, etc.).

Riggio, Anita

SECRET SIGNS: ALONG THE UNDERGROUND RAILROAD   *5–9 YEARS*

Illustrated by Anita Riggio. Honesdale, Penn.: Boyds Mills, 1997.

This thoroughly informative historical fiction picture book tells the story of Luke Richards, an eight-year-old deaf boy who attended one of the twenty schools for the deaf that existed at the time of the Civil War. Luke used American Sign Language as well as his talent as a painter of miniatures to pass along information about the underground railroad. His mother was supposed to meet a stranger at the general store and give her directions to the next safe haven for runaway slaves. A slave catcher who suspected the mother of helping fugitive slaves locked her in their home, but agreed to take the boy to the general store so he could sell the candied panoramic eggs that his mother had made. Neither Luke nor his mother had ever met the person who was supposed to be given the information; they knew only that she would be wearing an indigo scarf. Readers are bound to be thoroughly intrigued and delighted with the way the boy managed to pass along the needed information unbeknownst to the slave catcher.

The full-page oil paintings are in full color and masterfully detail the crucial aspects of the action, the setting, the range of emotions and feelings as well as the personalities of the characters of this informational story about the underground railroad and the people who risked their lives to help the runaway slaves find their way to freedom.

Wheeler, Cindy

MORE SIMPLE SIGNS   *3–8 YEARS*

Illustrated by Cindy Wheeler. New York: Viking, 1998.

Signs (gestures, movements, pictures) for thirty words and actions are depicted in line drawings. Each word is also depicted in full-color watercolor paintings so young readers will see them in some specific context. Helpful hints for remembering each sign are also offered. The hand sign alphabet is included on the endpapers so children might spell out via American Sign Language (ASL) other words of interest to them that are not included in this book. *More Simple Signs* and its companion volume *Simple Signs* (1997), also created by Wheeler, are fine examples of informational picture books which demonstrate that American Sign Language is a complete, effective means of communication. Also see and use *Handtalk Birthday: A Number Story Book in Sign Language,* written by Remy Charlip and Mary Beth Miller and illustrated with full-color photographs by George Ancona (Macmillan, 1987); *Handtalk Zoo,* written by George Ancona and Mary Beth Miller and illustrated with full color photographs by George Ancona (Macmillan, 1989); *Handtalk School,* written by Mary Beth Miller and George Ancona and illustrated with full-color photographs by George Ancona (Macmillan, 1991).

Arts and Crafts

DANCE

Ganeri, Anita

THE YOUNG PERSON'S GUIDE TO THE BALLET   *7–11 YEARS*

Illustrated. San Diego: Harcourt Brace, 1998.

> This very brief and broad introduction to ballet covers such aspects as how the ballet began, descriptions of some ballet techniques and ballet steps, ballet shoes and costumes, a sampling of some of the great ballet dancers, choreography and some great choreographers, music for the ballet (ranging from the classical to the contemporary), a sampling of some of the great ballet composers, stories from the ballet, and the preparation one needs to become a professional ballet dancer. An audio CD recording (Performance Ltd.) of the ballet scores from Tchaikovsky's "The Nutcracker Suite," "Swan Lake," "The Sleeping Beauty" is enclosed with the book. The illustrations, which are primarily black-and-white photographs, are from the archives of England's National Ballet; they depict members of the company in rehearsal and in actual performances. The sidebars scattered throughout the book offer bits of information that perk up the matter-of-fact style of the body of the text.

LITERATURE

Anderson, William, *Compiler*

LAURA'S ALBUM: A REMEMBRANCE SCRAPBOOK
OF LAURA INGALLS WILDER   *8–12 YEARS*

Illustrated. New York: HarperCollins, 1998.

> This elegantly formatted picture book biography should be considered a
> must-purchase for every elementary school library and public library's
> children's collection. It would also make a fine addition to children's
> personal libraries. It is filled with many, many excellent black-and-
> white, sepia, and colorful photographs and mementos that help im-
> measurably to make the life story and the legacy of Wilder's well-loved
> "Little House" series real and memorable. The illustrations are accompa-
> nied by informative captions. Included is a table of contents indicating
> clearly to the reader what the focus of each chapter is; a thoroughly
> comprehensive Wilder chronology is included in the back matter.

Anderson, William

PIONEER GIRL: THE STORY OF LAURA INGALLS WILDER   *7–10 YEARS*

Illustrated by Dan Anderson. New York: HarperCollins, 1998.

> This is a sanguine account of Laura Ingalls Wilder's life story from her
> early childhood years with her family in the "Big Woods" in Wisconsin,
> through her adult years as a hardworking and devoted farmer's wife and
> mother in Missouri, to her later years as the celebrated author of the
> Little House books. The full-page panoramic landscape paintings and
> rather staid illustrations of Laura, the members of her family, and her
> husband Almanzo Wilder reflect perfectly the ever hopeful tone of this
> picture-book biography. Compare with *Laura Ingalls Wilder,* written and
> illustrated by Alexander Wallner (Holiday House, 1997).

Lester, Helen

AUTHOR: A TRUE STORY   *6–9 YEARS*

Illustrated by Helen Lester. Boston: Walter Lorraine/Houghton
Mifflin, 1997.

> Basically, this account of how Lester became a successful published
> author of children's books is a thoughtful delineation of statements
> alerting children to the idea that writing a book worthy of publication
> takes perseverance, effort in thinking up ideas worthy of writing about,
> choosing the right words, and humility. She cautions that it calls for

rewriting and rewriting again and again, "looking for ways to make it better and making changes here and there" (p. 26), writing on anything you can find to jot down ideas that suddenly come to mind. Lester recommends that aspiring authors keep a "fizzle box" in which they keep "fizzled thoughts and half-finished books," names, funny words, or a wise lesson. She reports that there are times when she cannot come up with a single idea and times when ideas "hatch so fast" she can barely write them down. She acknowledges that she tends to focus on writing stories, working with a professional illustrator. She recalls that when she became a teacher writing was her favorite subject to teach. Finally, after encouragement from her friends and colleagues she decided to write her own stories. The cartoon-style illustrations in this little book exude the joys and frustrations, disappointments, challenges, and ultimate satisfactions she has experienced as a successful author of children's books about a penguin named Tacky. Her popular series includes *Tacky, the Penguin* (1988) and *Three Cheers for Tacky* (1994). All of these books are illustrated by Lynn Munsinger and published by Houghton Mifflin.

Schachner, Judith Byron
MR. EMERSON'S COOK   *8–11* YEARS
Illustrated by Judith Byron Schachner. New York: Dutton, 1998.

Annie Burns, the subject of this book, was hired to serve as Ralph Waldo Emerson's cook shortly after she arrived in the United States from Ireland. Emerson's wife was upset because he often forgot to eat. Apparently he became so involved pondering, philosophizing, and writing about the beauties of nature that he professed to live by imagination alone. So she hired Annie to cook him nourishing meals. Annie was confused and disturbed when Mr. Emerson did not eat her meals, and she certainly did not understand what he meant when she heard him actually say, "We live by our imaginations" (p. 16) and "Imagination is to flow, not to freeze" (p. 18). When Annie's mother sent her a little cookbook in which Annie had recorded recipes she made up when she was a child—recipes for such "desserts" as mud pies and moon cakes—Annie suddenly understood the full meaning of Emerson's saying.

She let her imagination flow and dreamed of making meals that would delight Mr. Emerson and his guests; these meals consisted of "a comet-tail stew so spicy hot, it sent Mr. Emerson's guests into orbit around the moon, a snow pudding that shimmered beneath a cloud of vanilla custard and snow began to fall from the ceiling, but all the while summer hummed like a bee outside the window." Annie woke from her dream convinced that she would cook with imagination. And cook with imagination she did! When Mr. Emerson awoke the next morning to the aroma of Annie's Summer Pie, filled with the colors of the morning sky and sweetened with cinnamon spice, she greeted him and invited him "to a wee taste of the morning sun." Mr. Emerson regained his appetite; Annie was filled with happiness and watched with delight as he and his wife and children enjoyed their breakfast and subsequent meals together.

The ink line and wash cartoon-style expressionistic illustrations highlight the lively and lyrical text that mixes fact and fiction about very real people. Annie Burns was the great-grandmother of the creator of this book; reportedly, the portrayal of how Annie finally got Mr. Emerson to eat her cooking was based on often-told family tales.

Spivak, Dawnine

GRASS SANDALS: THE TRAVELS OF BASHO   *9–13 YEARS*

Illustrated by Demi. New York: Atheneum, 1997.

Basho Matsuo (known as Basho) is recognized and appreciated worldwide as one of the most celebrated poets in the history of Japan. I cannot imagine how any author-illustrator team could create a biographical sketch of this great poet in the picture-book genre and match this one for its genuine understated elegance and unpretentious sophistication. Basho's enjoyment of and sensitivity to the beauty in nature during his wanderings throughout Japan in the last half of the seventeenth century are highlighted in Spivak's sparse descriptions of them.

The aesthetics of Basho's responses to these elements of nature are superbly reflected and enhanced by the inclusion of haiku poems throughout the book by Demi's delicate double-page illustrations done in brush and ink. The presence of the Japanese written character (kanji) that follows the form of nature focused on in each haiku adds substantially to the aura that so strongly pervades this special picture-book biography. Demi's paintings artfully suggest Basho's sensory responses to the visual beauties that moved him during his travels, to their sounds, smells, textures and tastes, and to their movements. All of the poems and illustrations deserve to be examined more than once!

In the back matter, Spivak offers a few brief paragraphs about Basho, telling the readers that Basho kept journals of his travels in a *haibun,* a diary of prose and poems, and that the shrines, mountains, and villages he loved can still be visited. She emphasizes that Basho's "poems remain as fresh as new leaves." The poems included in this elegant picture book do indeed seem to be timeless in their appeal, and they are just a minuscule sampling of the haiku he wrote during his lifetime. All but one of the poems in this book are by Basho. That one poem, which appears on the page with the Japanese character *Tsuki* (moon), was created by another well-loved Japanese poet named Issa, who lived a century after Basho. The endpapers contain a comment written in Japanese characters; they also contain a picture of a man writing in a *haibun,* suggestive of Basho recording his response to something in nature that moved him.

MUSIC

Littlesugar, Amy
SHAKE RAG: FROM THE LIFE OF ELVIS PRESLEY   *7–11 YEARS*
Illustrated by Floyd Cooper. New York: Philomel, 1998.

> This is a moving account of the alienation felt by Elvis Presley growing up in the segregated South near a section of town called Shake Rag, among black people and a few poor white families some people in the other part of town called "white trash." Elvis attempted to escape from the loneliness and the taunts of his white classmates by focusing on learning how to play a secondhand guitar his mother gave him and by daydreaming of becoming a famous entertainer. He strummed his guitar and sang cowboy songs heard on the "Grand Ole Opry" and other radio programs as well as the blues songs he heard coming from the jukehouse joints in his neighborhood, and the "good news music" played and sung at the tent services conducted each summer by a traveling group called the Sanctified Church. In 1954, at age nineteen and sporting sideburns, shy, still very poor, and using the same secondhand guitar his mother had given him when he lived in Shake Rag, Elvis's voice was recorded by Sam Phillips, owner of Sun Records, a small company with a recording studio near downtown Memphis. From that point on Elvis's success became legendary. The content of Floyd Cooper's pictures, his choice of colors and the unique technique he uses in his oil-wash paintings capture the aura of Elvis's poverty, his feelings of loneliness and alienation, the escape and emotional high he experienced by hearing and playing the music he learned to love so much. Worthy of note is the excellent bibliography of titles of books about the blues, black gospel music, the guitar, black consciousness, and about Elvis himself.

Monceaux, Morgan
JAZZ: MY MUSIC, MY PEOPLE   *10–16+ YEARS*
Foreword by Wynton Marsalis. Illustrated by Morgan Monceaux.
New York: Borzoi/Knopf, 1994.

> Like the creator of these biographical sketches, most of the African-American jazz musicians featured in this stunning collection started

out singing or playing an instrument for themselves, their family, and their friends, and then became professional musicians when they were in their teens. In the introduction, Monceaux says he wanted to put his emotional response to music into paintings and to tell the stories of jazz performers who brought their own experiences and emotions as Americans and African Americans to their concerts, jam sessions, and recordings. There is no doubt that Monceaux accomplished his goals. The biographical sketches of these jazz greats are informative and clearly identify the role model(s) of each performer, what kinds of experiences influenced his or her music, and how each musician influenced and enriched the lives of many others. Multimedia (pastels, paints, Pentel markers, and multimedia collage) were used to create the full-color paintings that illustrate the text. The portraits of the musicians are in the expressionistic style and most of them are reproduced as full-page illustrations. Surrounding each portrait are "scribbled" the dates of that person's birth and death and information about his or her schooling, career highlights, and major accomplishments as a jazz performer. (See illustration 12.) Monceaux also created some markedly abstract paintings that depict his personal emotional "visual" interpretation of individual performers' unique style of jazz. The twenty-nine individual musicians and two jazz combos are arranged chronologically into three time periods. First are fourteen musicians who introduced jazz in the United States in the 1890s and early 1900s, shaping it into a distinctive musical form that had never been heard before. In the next major era (beginning in the 1920s), he focuses on twelve individual musicians and the members of one jazz ensemble who firmly established swing music. He then highlights twelve jazz greats and members of one quartet who steered jazz in the direction of Bebop (in the 1930s and 1940s) and modern jazz. A helpful glossary is appended, as is an index.

Orgill, Roxanne

IF I ONLY HAD A HORN: YOUNG LOUIS ARMSTRONG   *6–9 YEARS*

Illustrated by Leonard Jenkins. Boston: Houghton Mifflin, 1997.

This partial biography of Louis Armstrong, the legendary blues jazz horn player, focuses on his middle-childhood years as a poor boy growing up in New Orleans. Because their mother was often away from home, Louis and his little sister Mama Lucy were left to fend for themselves. Louis spent many days and nights on the street enthralled by the dancing, singing, and music that surrounded him. Occasionally he and Mama Lucy could get meals from an uncle and his family who lived nearby; more often Louis would buy food for the two of them with the pennies passersby threw in his cap when he and his gang sang on the corners of

ILLUSTRATION 12   From *Jazz: My Music, My People* by Morgan Monceaux. Copyright ©1994 by Morgan Monceaux and Morgan Rank Gallery. Reprinted by permission of Alfred A. Knopf, Inc.

181

Perdido and Rampart Streets. One New Year's Eve Louis was arrested and taken to jail for shooting a gun in the air six times to frighten a boy who shot at him and his buddies as they were collecting pennies by the capful for their singing on this street corner.

Louis was placed in the Colored Waifs' Home for poor boys who got into trouble with the law. When Louis discovered that the home had a brass band he asked the band teacher if he could join, but the teacher told him he didn't need any new players and "boys from Perdido Street were nothing but trouble anyway." Months later the teacher invited Louis to join the band, giving him first a little tambourine, then a drum and then a bugle; eventually, he gave Louis an old battered cornet. The author retells the well-known legend that next time the Colored Waif's Home band marched down Perdido Street Louis' sister and mother, his uncle's family, his neighborhood friends, and other residents from the area appeared from nowhere, following the band and dancing to its happy beat. When the teacher passed the hat the residents of the Perdido Street area contributed enough money to buy new instruments for everyone in the band.

The full-color paintings, done in acrylic, pastel, and spray paint, capture the decadence and poverty of Louis' home and neighborhood. But the artist's use of contrasting colors and the flow of the shapes and lines that create his figures exude the tone and rhythmic movements blues jazz music typically evokes on the part of the musicians themselves and by those who hear and feel it. Compare and contrast the text and pictures in this version of Armstrong's middle-childhood years with those in *Satchmo's Blues,* written by Alan Schroeder and illustrated by Floyd Cooper (Doubleday, 1997). I would urge teachers and librarians who want to get a more comprehensive scholarly and accurate version of Armstrong's childhood years (in fact, his complete life story) to read and share with their students relevant portions from *Louis Armstrong: An American Success Story,* written by James Collier (Macmillan, 1985, 1991).

Pinkney, Andrea Davis
DUKE ELLINGTON: THE PIANO PRINCE AND HIS ORCHESTRA   *7–10 YEARS*
Illustrated by Brian Pinkney. New York: Hyperion, 1998.

Named a Coretta Scott King Honor Award Book for Illustrations, this biographical sketch of a symphonic master, celebrated classical jazz composer, and pianist Edward Kennedy Ellington, better known as "The Duke," is a special book. The illustrations, which are attractive full-color scratchboard pictures rendered with luma dyes, gouache, and oil paint, will most certainly fascinate and hold the attention of children, for they are filled with insights about the people and the aura of the music that still influences music throughout the United States and all over the world.

Many of Duke Ellington's songs mentioned in the text are well known to adults and even young jazz aficionados, but I suspect few of the children in the age range for which this book appears to be targeted will recognize them. Since all of them (i.e., "Mood Indigo," "Take the 'A' Train," "Black, Brown, and Beige," "Sophisticated Lady," and "I Got It Bad") are easily available on CDs and audiotapes one need only play a few of them or share some tidbits about a few of the titles cited in the bibliography appended to get the younger children interested in reading this book and help them appreciate his greatness. If you have to limit the book(s) to share from among the many fine ones listed in this bibliography, I would especially recommend *Duke Ellington,* written by James Lincoln Collier (Macmillan, 1991) and *Music Is My Mistress,* written by Duke Ellington (Doubleday, 1973).

Duke Ellington's original orchestra was "a musical mix like no other"—then or now. It was made up of men who were great soloists, and eventually accomplished acclaim on his own: drummer Sonny Greet, trombonist Joe "Trucky Sam" Nanton, saxophonist Otto "Toby" Hardwick, trumpet player James "Bubber" Miley, and of course, Ellington's long-time composer and arranger and partner Billy Strayhorn. Of particular interest is the manner in which the author describes the unique talents of each one and his specific contributions to the orchestra and how the illustrator so very cleverly visually interprets each member's unique qualities.

Turner, Barrie Carson

THE LIVING FLUTE   *11–14+ YEARS*

Illustrated. New York: Knopf, 1996.

This sophisticated-looking book provides a comprehensive survey of the background of the flute: its historical and geographical origins, how it is made, how it works, and how it is played; some information about its role in the orchestra is also provided. Short profiles of ten leading composers whose music featured flutes are included in the book, and these works are highlighted on a full-length audio CD (EMI Records, Ltd., United Kingdom, 1996), which is packaged with the book. These ten composers are Antonio Vivaldi, Georg Philipp Telemann, Johann Sebastian Bach, George Frideric Handel, Johann Joachim Quantz, Johann Christian Bach, Carl Stamitz, Wolfgang Amadeus Mozart, Daniel Friedrich Kuhlau, and Claude Achille Debussy. Biographical sketches of twelve great flute players are also included in the book, as is a photograph or portrait of each. The quality of the illustrations in the book varies as do the media from which the illustrations are rendered, but in the main they are quite good. The sidebars are most informative and supplement the body of the text considerably, as do the captions that accompany most of the illustrations. The index appended is extensive and comprehensive. All in all, it is a book that is packaged to inspire and inform current and potential flute players and enthusiasts, and I think it accomplishes that goal quite well.

VISUAL ARTS

Architecture and Structural Design

DuQuette, Keith

THE HOUSE BOOK   *5–7 YEARS*

Illustrated by Keith DuQuette. New York: Putnam, 1999.

The simple rhymed text moves the reader along on this memorable tour through a uniquely designed and exquisitely decorated two-story home. Richly detailed realistic paintings rendered in soft pencil and full-color wash meticulously detail many parts of this large house. As he guides the readers through the house, the illustrator uses a variety of perspectives to show off its special qualities, creating a fascinating and most effective impression of and elegantly structured and furnished, yet unpretentious and comfortable, family home. For example, the front entrance hallway is viewed from above, so one can see at a glance the rich hardwood floors on which an exquisitely designed hooked area rug and small oriental rugs are strategically placed, the patterned brick tile floor in the alcove on the left, and the marble tile floor of the room seen on the right. Another view from above shows all of the rooms on the first-floor level of the house: a sun room, kitchen, dining room, etc. As one moves through the house one sees a beautiful pan-eled wooden door with an antique stained-glass window, a large closet with a wooden folding door, and large windows, some with leaded stained glass, many of which are shaped and positioned to capture the different views of the outside. Another cross-section view of the house directly from the front enables one to look into each room—from the basement level to the attic. Even the details of the rooftop cupola and the dormers on the topmost floor are shown. The tour ends outside, showing the exteriors of three neighboring houses. Each house represents a different style of architectural design; the landscaping of each family's property differs considerably from the others. Thus one gets an idea of the neighborhood in which the house focused on in the book is located. My thought at this point was, wouldn't it be fun to see how the other three houses were designed and decorated. The endpapers depict sixteen different shapes and styles of homes. More specifically, each endpaper is designed to look like an album, showing eight different kinds of homes located in varied geographical and residential areas during different seasons of the year. Pictured are a log cabin in the woods, brownstones, row houses, a high-rise apartment building, an A-frame house in a mountain skiing area, a trailer home parked near a river among the sand dunes, a farm home, and so much more.

Hunter, Ryan Ann
CROSS A BRIDGE   *4–8 YEARS*
Illustrated by Edward Miller. New York: Holiday House, 1998.

This is a creative and enlightening portrayal of different kinds of bridges, noting in each case how these bridges are used. Crisp and accomplished graphics in bold, flat colors depict an array of bridges: log bridge, arch bridge, covered bridge, suspension bridge, trestles, and drawbridge. Some are made of rocks, logs, animals skins, steel, and concrete. There is even a superstition in connection with a covered bridge: Hold your breath and make a wish when you pass through a covered bridge. The text is easy to read and is printed in bold, primary-sized type. It thoroughly fascinated and aroused the curiosity of young readers who examined it over and over! Compare with *Bridges Are to Cross,* written by Philemon Sturges and illustrated by Giles Laroche (Putnam, 1998), described below.

Hunter, Ryan Ann
INTO THE SKY   *5–8 YEARS*
Illustrated by Edward Miller. New York: Holiday House, 1998.

A skyscraper is defined and the basic concepts about how a skyscraper is constructed are simply explained. The flat, stylized illustrations match beautifully the clarity and simplicity of the basic concepts presented, yet amazingly they make them so much more understandable. Be certain to note the endpapers. They include pictures of some of the major skyscrapers throughout the world and each one is clearly labeled: the Chicago Tribune Tower, Home Life Insurance Building, Empire State Building, New York Life Insurance Company Building, Palace of Culture (Warsaw, Poland), One Canada Square (London, England), World Trade Center, and so many more.

Macaulay, David
ROME ANTICS   *9–13 YEARS*
Illustrated by David Macaulay. Boston:
Walter Lorraine/Houghton Mifflin, 1997.

> The story begins on the frontispiece with a young woman releasing a
> homing pigeon, and after a zany flight over the metropolis of Rome,
> the pigeon finally delivers the woman's message, written on a paper
> attached to its leg, to an artist working in a garret. The names of each
> historic landmark the pigeon sees during its flight through Rome appear
> in small type, on the lower left side, below the border of each double-
> page picture. Turn to the back of the book for a pictorial map of the
> pigeon's flight through Rome and a description of each of the historic
> sites it saw during its flight. Macaulay's pen-and-ink line and crosshatch
> sketches depict a pigeon's-eye view of the magnificent structures of
> ancient Rome amidst the hustle and bustle of vehicles and the glitz
> of modern Rome.

Sturges, Philemon
BRIDGES ARE TO CROSS   *6–10 YEARS*
Illustrated by Giles Laroche. New York: Putnam, 1998.

> Fifteen kinds of bridges from all over the world are briefly discussed
> and beautifully portrayed in three-dimensional illustrations created on
> a variety of paper surfaces through a combination of drawing, painting,
> and paper cutting. They reflect people's differing values and lifestyles,
> a variety of symbols, celebrations, and solutions and emphasize that
> crossing is only one of a number of reasons to have a bridge. Some
> examples of the bridges included in this very attractive and upbeat
> book are the Golden Gate Bridge, which is a steel suspension bridge in
> San Francisco, California; the Firth of Forth Bridge, a double-cantilever
> steel bridge in Edinburgh, Scotland; Ponte Sant'Angelo, a stone arch
> bridge in Rome, Italy; Salginatobel Bridge, a three-hinged concrete arch
> bridge in Schiers, Switzerland; Sydney Harbor Bridge, a bowstring arch
> bridge in Sydney, Australia, and Tower Bridge, a drawbridge in London,
> England. Compare the perspective on bridges by Sturges and Laroche
> with that presented in *Cross a Bridge,* written by Ryan Ann Hunter and
> illustrated by Edward Miller (Holiday House, 1998), described above.

Book Illustration and Graphic Arts

Christelow, Eileen
WHAT DO ILLUSTRATORS DO?   *7–10 YEARS*

Illustrated by Eileen Christelow. New York: Clarion, 1999.

A creative approach to inform young readers, visually and verbally, how to go about illustrating a thirty-two page picture book. Two artists demonstrate how they each follow through on a contract to illustrate a picture-book edition of "Jack and the Beanstalk." Christelow most effectively helps the children understand some of the most significant facts about illustrating a picture book. Illustrating a book requires careful thought and planning and is intricate work . For example, the illustrator must pay close attention to details included in the text so they will be interpreted correctly in the visual images. Illustration often involves considerable research on the part of the artist to assure authenticity of such factors as time and place. The artist must keep in mind the size, shape, and construction of the book as he or she designs each page. It is not unusual for the artist to have to redo some or all of the illustrations in order to achieve quality visuals. There are a number of things an illustrator may make creative choices about and there are others about which he or she is given little or no say. In the main, the artist works closely with the editor and designer in light of these choices and restrictions. All of the illustrations in this book are done in the cartoon style, yet Christelow has managed nicely to use two different kinds of cartoon sketches to create the illusion that the two artists did indeed each create a very different picture-book version of "Jack in the Beanstalk." This accomplishment underscores the major theme of this book: "Each illustrator has a different *style* of drawing, just as every person has a different style of handwriting" (p. 27).

Fellows, Miranda

THE LIFE AND WORKS OF ESCHER   *10 YEARS–ADULTHOOD*

Illustrated with photographic reproductions of Escher's prints.
London: Parragon Book Service, 1995.

This is a brief, but critical biographical sketch of Maurits Cornelius Escher. The clear explanations of and comments about the illusionary techniques and set of spatial dimensions and planes in each of the reproductions of his wood etchings and linoleum prints included in this book help readers to enter into and appreciate the unusual surrealistic world he created. This selection of M. C. Escher's prints is informed and is taken from all periods of his life. It constitutes an excellent sampling of the artist's body of work and enables the readers to understand how important it is for the viewer to suspend disbelief in order to appreciate and enjoy Escher's talent and perspective.

Joyce, William

THE WORLD OF WILLIAM JOYCE SCRAPBOOK   *7–12 YEARS*

Illustrated with art by William Joyce and photographs by Philip Gould
and others. New York: Geringer/HarperCollins, 1997.

> William Joyce, author and illustrator of popular zany picture books, tells
> his readers where he gets the ideas for his stories—those he has already
> published and those he is currently working on—and how he goes
> about writing and illustrating them. These choice bits of information
> are certain to fascinate the readers of this book, especially those who
> are already familiar with the many books he wrote and/or illustrated,
> such as *The Leaf Man and the Brave Good Boys* (HarperCollins, 1992),
> *George Shrinks* (HarperCollins, 1985), and *Santa Calls* (HarperCollins,
> 1993). They will also gain valuable insights as to how challenging,
> laborious, and ultimately satisfying Joyce finds his career as an author
> and illustrator of children's books. The excellent variety of pictures
> of Joyce as a child, as an adult with his wife, children, friends, and
> neighbors, plus the reproductions of a great variety of sketches he
> made for books already published and those he would like to publish
> eventually are exactly the kinds of things children like to have an author
> or illustrator share with them.

Painting

Druggleby, John

ARTIST IN OVERALLS: THE LIFE OF GRANT WOOD   *9–14+ YEARS*

Illustrated. San Francisco: Chronicle, 1995.

> This is a very readable, personal and informative biography of Grant
> Wood, the American artist who became famous for his simple paintings
> depicting people and places around him. His paintings were done in
> a style that came to be known as "regionalism." His painting called
> *American Gothic,* which shows a man and his wife standing rigid and se-
> rious in front of a little wooden house with a large bullet-shaped Gothic
> window, catapulted him into fame when it was awarded a prize at the
> Chicago exhibition (1930) and was bought by the Art Institute of Chicago
> for $300. This famous painting and many others done by Wood are re-
> produced in this book in stunning color. Also scattered throughout this
> picture-book biography are realistic, quickly-made sketches he made
> of his subjects—people he knew well, farm animals, pieces of farming
> equipment, buildings and landscapes of the Iowa countryside he was
> so very familiar with and fond of—before attempting to make full-color,
> detailed, lifelike paintings of them. The three-page afterword, written
> and illustrated by Bruce Pritchard, should prove helpful for those who

aspire to learn how to draw and paint as Grant Wood did. A comprehensive index and a listing of the museums and private collections throughout the world where the original paintings that are reproduced in this book can be seen are provided. The date Wood completed each painting and lithograph picture, the number of lithograph prints made of each lithographed picture, and the media he used to make them are provided. A bibliography of sources Druggleby used to write this fine picture book biography is included.

Greenberg, Jan, and Sandra Jordan
CHUCK CLOSE UP CLOSE   *10 YEARS–ADULTHOOD*
Illustrated. New York: DK Publishing, 1998.

In this polished biography Chuck Close, one of the most admired and successful revisionist artists in the world, is presented as a child with learning disabilities who was labeled as difficult and a slow learner; but he loved to draw and was good at it. In fact, this interest and talent in art was the first thing that made him feel special, in the good sense of that word, because he knew he had skills his age-mates did not have. Although the learning disorders had not disappeared, the deliberate and intense discipline he put forth to get through the elementary grades, high school, college, and ultimately the Yale University School of Art became the beginnings of a detailed system to organize his art characterized by breaking the image down into small units. He often "recycles" the same photographs, painting thirty or more different pictures from the original photograph—changing the size or material, applying different techniques and processes to create each painting, i.e., by using a pulp paper, individual dots of color (pointillism), airbrush, his fingerprints, etc. He repeatedly sets obstacles for himself to keep his painting from becoming too "easy"; this approach to his painting reflects his ardent belief that the greatest enemy for an artist is ease, repeating oneself once one gets good at it.

The titles of the chapters listed in the table of contents clearly elucidate the various topics covered in this picture-book biography. In the back matter the authors provide a very comprehensive glossary of art terms used throughout the book to explain Close's techniques and works of art. There is also an essay entitled "What Is a Portrait?" in which they discuss the specific works of some famous portrait painters and photographers. They pose some questions about each of the portrait artists discussed to help the readers recognize the distinct characteristics Chuck Close has in common with them, those the artists share with each other, and those that are unique to each. There is also an excellent bibliography listing books and articles about Close plus catalogs of his exhibitions and shows and some of museums and art galleries in the United States, Australia, Canada, and England where one will find his paintings exhibited. Other superb informational picture books for readers ten and older by Greenberg and Jordan are: *The Painter's Eye: Learning to Look at Contemporary American Art* (Delacorte, 1991) and *The American Eye: Eleven Artists of the Twentieth Century* (Delacorte, 1955).

Lyons, Mary E., *Editor*

TALKING WITH TEBÉ: CLEMENTINE HUNTER, MEMORY ARTIST   *9–14* YEARS

Illustrated with paintings by Tebé and with photographs.
Boston: Houghton Mifflin, 1998.

Clementine Hunter, known to her friends by the name of Tebé, was the first self-taught artist to receive a fellowship from the Julian Rosenwald Fund in 1945 for her "worthy artistic endeavor" and the first self-taught African-American woman artist to receive national media attention. Mary E. Lyons gathered the bulk of information for this book from the artist's own words in magazines, newspaper articles, and taped interviews. The events in Tebé's life were rearranged in order and combined with her thoughts about a particular subject; dates and place names were inserted; and Lyons changed a word or phrase or sentence to ease the transition from speech to written text or when Tebé's words were confusing.

Born in the Cane River region of northwest Louisiana in 1886, Clementine Hunter was not born enslaved, but she was born on a plantation. She went to the Melrose Plantation when she "was not a little girl and not old enough to marry" (p. 14). She lived on or near that plantation for the rest of her life.

Clementine Hunter's art serves as an invaluable record of how the workers and servants lived, their good times and bad times, the conditions under which they lived, worked, and socialized. She created art in different forms. Using flat images and clean, bright colors, her paintings were done in the naive art style, described by some as innocent art, folk art, or outsider art. Her quilt tops, made of scraps of paper or corn sacks, resemble story banners from Benin, West Africa. She made dolls out of empty wine bottles and painted on plastic milk jugs, snuff jars, wine bottles, cast-iron kettles and frying pans, key chains, and gourds. She painted at night after her cooking, cleaning, field work, and child rearing were finished. She continued to paint until she was well in her nineties and lost her sight. Her pictures are on permanent display at twenty-two museums around the United States.

ILLUSTRATION 13 "Fishing on the Cain River," a painting by Clementine Hunter (Tebé), used in *Talking with Tebé: Clementine Hunter, Memory Artist,* written by Mary E. Lyons, Houghton Mifflin, 1998, reprinted with permission of Thomas N. Whitehead on behalf of the Mildred Hart Bailey Collection, Natchitoches, La.

There are numerous reproductions of Tebé's paintings and photographs in this profusely illustrated biography. (See illustration 13.) Each illustration is dated and is accompanied by an informative caption that supplements the text immeasurably. An excellent bibliography of sources is included. This is a fascinating biography!

Micklewait, Lucy, *Selector*

I SPY A FREIGHT TRAIN: TRANSPORTATION IN ART   *6 YEARS–ADULTHOOD*

Illustrated. New York: Greenwillow, 1996.

Some mode of transportation is depicted in each of the well-known paintings compiled in this book. In her foreword the author indicates that one does not need to have any knowledge of art to introduce children to these paintings nor does one need to know or focus on the name of the artists who created them. However, she advises that one should encourage children to look at each picture and engage them in conversations about the content of the pictures, the effect of the colors used in them, if and how they blend and contrast, the shapes, and what the children like and dislike about a painting, the differences they notice about one painting when compared with another, and so on. Art books such as this provide a nonthreatening way for children to learn and appreciate that artists seldom choose to imitate the way other artists paint or draw pictures and that it is perfectly all right for several persons to look at the same picture, and each one respond differently to it—one may like what he or she sees in a painting and another may not like what he or she sees.

Stanley, Diane
LEONARDO DA VINCI   *9–12+ YEARS*
Illustrated by Diane Stanley. New York: Morrow, 1996.

What a stunning and authentic introduction to the life story and art of Renaissance artist Leonardo da Vinci! The text details, but not over-whelmingly for young readers, major aspects of da Vinci's successes and failures, his diverse talents as a well as his human weaknesses, his place in the history of art in general, and how his status and artistic accomplishment compares and contrasts with other noted artists of his time. Stanley's full-color, full-page paintings competently merge with her carefully written and accessible text; they also support and extend and make so much more concrete the specific paintings, frescoes, and sculptures that are discussed in the text. Worthy of note are the repro-ductions of many of da Vinci's study sketches that appeared originally in his notebooks. They are shown in Stanley's colorful full-page paintings and are discussed in the text of this book. This exceptional picture book was named winner of the Boston Globe-Horn Book Award for Nonfiction in 1997.

Throughout this picture-book biography are comments about how the times during which da Vinci lived probably shaped his personality and influenced his accomplishments. Stanley also includes a foreword entitled "An Incredible Age," which provides a definition and excellent discussion of the Renaissance period in art and its influence on some of da Vinci's most widely known and respected works. In an afterword, entitled "Postscript," Stanley tells the readers what happened to da Vinci's remains when the chapel of Saint Florentine in Ambrose, Italy, was demolished and also informs them of the fate of his notebooks, paintings, and frescoes, including *Mona Lisa* and *The Last Supper*. A helpful pronunciation guide is provided at the beginning of the book.

Two excellent bibliographies for further reading are included in the back matter—one bibliography is for adults and the other is for children.

Winter, Jeanette

MY NAME IS GEORGIA   *6–9 YEARS*

Illustrated by Jeanette Winter. San Diego: Silver White/Harcourt Brace, 1998.

> Told in the first-person voice, this biographical sketch of the legendary Georgia O'Keeffe, combined with illustrations depicting some of the most common images and tone associated with O'Keeffe's paintings, emphasizes the artist's singular personality, her oneness with nature, and her compulsion to paint things on canvas as she saw them. O'Keeffe's story is told by Jeanette Winter as Georgia O'Keeffe would tell it, but some statements included the text are actually quotations from O'Keeffe's published writings and are indicated in the text by italics. These titles are listed in the bibliography of sources that appears on the copyright page. To supplement this biographical sketch, teachers and librarians might share with their students some of the illustrations and information contained in the following books: *Inspirations: Stories about Women Artists,* written by Leslie Sills (Albert Whitman, 1989), for children 8–12+ years; *Georgia O'Keeffe,* written by Robyn Montana Turner (Little, Brown, 1992) for children 9–14 years; and *The American Eye: Eleven Artists of the Twentieth Century,* written by Jan Greenberg and Sandra Jordan (Delacorte, 1991) for children 10 years through adult).

Sculpture

Houston, James

FIRE INTO ICE: ADVENTURES IN GLASS MAKING   *9 YEARS–ADULTHOOD*

Illustrated with photographs. Plattsburg, N.Y., and Toronto: Tundra, 1998.

> Exquisite and sophisticated glass sculptures designed by explorer, author, artist James Houston for Steuben Glass are shown in all their glory, in stunning full-color photographs and hand-colored pencil sketches. Each of these amazing pieces of sculpture was inspired by the conditions, ways of life, or specific events Houston experienced during the fourteen years he lived and worked in the Arctic. Houston has provided a brief description of the experiences or circumstances that inspired him to create each piece of art shown in this very special book.

Morrison, Taylor

THE NEPTUNE FOUNTAIN: THE APPRENTICESHIP   *7–11 YEARS*
OF A RENAISSANCE SCULPTOR

Illustrated by Taylor Morrison. New York: Holiday House, 1997.

> This fictionalized account of the varied experiences a fifteen-year-old boy living in seventeenth-century Rome had during the course of his three-year apprenticeship to a famous sculptor will give readers an understanding of the patience, knowledge, skill, talent, and long, long, hours of hard labor it takes to carve a beautiful figure out of marble. Two kinds of illustrations depict the steps of this laborious process: numerous full-page expressionistic paintings in full color show action scenes of the master sculptor and his apprentices at work. Small sepia-toned pen-and-ink line and crosshatch sketches offer close-up views of the sculptor and his apprentices engaging in each of the many steps in the process of making a sculptured figure out of marble. A glossary of technical terms related to the process of sculpture and the instruments and equipment used by the sculptor is included. An excellent picture book to read after reading this fine picture book is *Leonardo da Vinci,* written and illustrated by Diane Stanley (Morrow, 1996). A companion to Morrison's picture book about the apprentice to the sculpture is *Antonio's Apprenticeship: Painting a Fresco in Renaissance Italy,* written and illustrated by Taylor Morrison (Holiday House, 1996). Students will enjoy this book about painting a fresco as much and most certainly will also learn as much from it as they will learn about sculpture from Morrison's *The Neptune Fountain.*

CRAFTS

How-to Books

Ehlert, Lois

HANDS   *3–6 YEARS*

Illustrated by Lois Ehlert. San Diego: Harcourt Brace, 1997.

> Shaped like a canvas work glove, this "participation" concept book informs young readers about the tools and equipment they will need to make a bird house, an undefined garment, and cloth toys. The child narrating the story does many things "by hand"—makes a pot holder, plants seeds with father, helps mother weed the flower garden, and paints a picture of the flowers in bloom. The illustrations are done in collage and throughout the book the colors of the pages, the objects made by hand, and the tools and equipment used are bright and rich and varied in texture.

Zweifel, Frances

THE MAKE-SOMETHING CLUB IS BACK: *3–7 YEARS*
MORE FUN WITH CRAFTS, FOOD, AND GIFTS

Illustrated by Ann Schweninger. New York: Viking, 1997.

> Cartoon-style illustrations in pen-and-ink line and four-color wash detail the procedures Winky, Skipper, and Tag (the members of the Make-Something Club) follow when making something new each month to play with, to look at, or to give away as gifts. For example, in January's dark days they make Light-Catcher Punch: pictures to catch some light and keep it; in March, to celebrate the coming of spring, they grow new plants in the kitchen; in June they collect ants and set up an ant farm; in September, to satisfy their craving for something to eat, they prepare Crunchy Stuffed Dates for their friends; and in December they make pomanders to give to their friends. All of their supplies are inexpensive materials found in most homes or schools. The text is easy to read and is in primary-sized manuscript type.

Traditional Crafts

Bial, Raymond

WITH NEEDLE AND THREAD: A BOOK ABOUT QUILTS *7–10 YEARS*

Illustrated with photographs. Boston: Houghton Mifflin, 1996.

> The processes of marking, piecing, and quilting are described. A historical overview ranges from the Colonial period to the AIDS Memorial Quilt, and the multicultural scope of this art form is highlighted in full-page, full-color photographs of quilts made by such ethnic groups as the Amish, African Americans, Appalachians, and Hmong (mountain people of Southeast Asia). Some of the quilt patterns invented by quilters over the generations shown in these pictures include those named Album Patch (or "autograph" or "friendship" quilts), Bow-tie, Brick Wall, Broken Dishes, Crazy Quilt, Flower Garden, Jacob's Ladder (or The Underground Railroad), Jacob's Tears (or Slave Chain), Log Cabin, Nine Patch, Ocean Wave, Rocky Road to Kansas, Wheel Spoke. Photographs of story and pictorial quilts are included. The bibliography, which lists the books the author consulted in the preparation of this book, provides excellent references for further reading (primarily for adults).

Miller, Cameron

WOODLORE   *7–10+ YEARS*

Illustrated by Dominique Falls and Cameron Miller.
New York: Ticknor & Fields, 1995.

Everything about this book epitomizes excellence! Each picture is a work of art in-and-of itself. Each kind of master woodworker is pictured putting his unique talents, knowledge, and experience to work as he carries out his craft. An object the craftsman has made is shown on the facing page. The illustrations were rendered with aquarelles (water-soluble pencils) on plywood primed with gesso and each was framed with the actual kind of wood described in the verses; a variety of other woods were used for the inlay work and the decorations. The simple but nicely structured verses state why a particular kind of wood is especially suited for a specific kind of musical instrument or piece of furniture, flooring, or toy. At the back of the book the author provides more details as to when, where, and by whom (in terms of ethnicity or nationality or religion) a specific kind of wood was first used, the major qualities or characteristics of a given kind of wood that suit it to a specific purpose, and how or why a master woodworker usually followed specific proce-dures making a wooden item. Grease-pencil sketches on the endpapers serve to summarize everything that was seen in the illustrations or mentioned in the verse: they depict the woodworkers' tools and the assorted items they made from wood as well as the kinds of trees whose timber was used to make each kind of wooden object. Each kind of tree is labeled with both its common and its scientific name.

Index

201

Patricia Jean Cianciolo is Professor Emeritus at Michigan State University in East Lansing, Michigan, where she taught courses in the critical reading and reviewing of literature for children, adolescent literature, and illustrations in children's books. She holds a doctoral degree from The Ohio State University and a master's degree from the University of Wisconsin, Milwaukee. She has done extensive research in children's response to literature and to book illustrations as well as in the study of teaching and learning of literature in the elementary grades. Cianciolo has published numerous professional books and articles on aspects of literature for children and adolescents, has presented papers and led workshops and institutes at the state, national, and international levels, and has served as a visiting professor at universities and as a literacy consultant to school systems nationally and internationally. She has also served on several children's literature award committees. She now records children's and adolescent literature for *Radio Talking Books* for Michigan public radio (WKAR-FM).